The United States and the Far East

(Second Edition)

◆ The American Assembly
Columbia University

A SPECTRUM BOOK

Englewood Cliffs, N. J.
PRENTICE-HALL, INC.

Preface

This is the second edition of *The United States and the Far East,* revised under the supervision of the original editor, Willard L. Thorp of Amherst College. The volume was designed for general readership but was first used as background for the Tenth American Assembly held at Arden House, home of the Assembly in Harriman, New York, in the fall of 1956. It also served as source material for eight subsequent regional Assemblies on this subject. All Assemblies published their own final reports which they arrived at independently. For a summary of the reports, see the *Conclusion* beginning on page 183.

The views expressed in the chapters which follow are those of the authors and not of The American Assembly, which takes no official position, or of the Ford Foundation, which generously supported the Tenth American Assembly program.

Henry M. Wriston
President
The American Assembly

Table of Contents

Introduction.

The significance
of the Far East

◆ WILLARD L. THORP
Editor

The last two wars in which the United States has been involved began for us as Asian wars. In the last twenty years, millions of Americans, most of them in uniform, have crossed the Pacific Ocean. Billions of dollars of goods produced in America and paid for from our national budget have been transported to the Far East. Books about the Far East, both novels and nonfiction, have begun to appear on many publishers' lists. And in recent years, our policies toward northeast Asia have provided some of our bitterest debates at home.

1

◆ Willard L. Thorp, the general editor of this volume, is Director of The Merrill Center for Economics and Professor of Economics at Amherst College. After a number of years in economic research, teaching, and business positions, he entered the U. S. State Department in 1945 and was Assistant Secretary of State for Economic Affairs, 1946-1952. He served as a Special Advisor at the Paris Peace Conference and at several meetings of the Council of Foreign Ministers. He was American Representative on the United Nations Economic and Social Council, 1947-1950, and a member of the U. S. Delegation to the United Nations General Assembly in 1947 and 1948. In 1955, he spent several months in Japan under the auspices of the Japan Committee on Intellectual Interchange. More recently, he has headed special missions to Bolivia and Cyprus.

OUR EXPANDING INTEREST

Before World War II, our interest in the Far East was casual and sporadic. To be sure, Commodore Perry had opened Japan in 1853, and after the turn of the century we tried to keep the door open in China by diplomatic efforts. Our cultural and economic relations were more important than our political activities. We introduced Christianity, Concord grapes, and cash registers to the area. In turn, we decorated our American homes with Japanese prints and Chinese jade, we wore Far Eastern silk, and we drank Formosa tea. Baseball became the Japanese national game and mah jong had its day in American homes.

But the Far East really was far; and it was different. Its languages, spoken and written, were completely unfamiliar. Its religions were concerned with different gods, different forms of worship, and different explanations of the purpose of life. Its organizations—government, school, and family—rested on a different basis of authority. Even its people had different characteristics and capabilities.

Nor did we make any great effort to learn about the Far East. The attention of our educational system and most of our scholars was concentrated upon our immediate society and its origins. This enterprise carried us across the Atlantic, and we studied European history and culture. We pursued our cultural ancestry back to the Greeks, the Romans, and the Hebrews. But the usual college graduate knew more about the moon than he did about Korea, more about the early Romans than he did about contemporary China. Nor were there many who had a closer contact. In the first twenty years of this century, the number of Americans traveling to Japan in any year was between two and five thousand persons; in the next twenty years, the peak of 8,527 was reached in 1929.

Before World War II, American foreign policy toward the Far East was also fragmentary at best. To be sure, we concerned ourselves with such diplomatic actions as were needed to facilitate trade and commerce. On occasion, such as at the time of the Boxer Rebellion, we sent a small military force to rescue and protect our citizens, and we maintained a small detachment of American troops in Peking and Tientsin thereafter. From 1898 on, we assumed responsibility somewhat uneasily for the Philippines. President Theodore Roosevelt had arranged the Japanese-Russian peace in 1905. In 1922, we agreed on a formula for the limitation of navies with Japan as well as with the United Kingdom, France, and Italy. But it was not until the late thirties, when we became concerned over the expansion of a militaristic Japan, that the Far East assumed a position of major importance in American foreign policy.

There may have been those who had hoped that the tremendous efforts of World War II would prove to be merely a temporary expedition across the Pacific, and that at its end, we might again return to our preoccupation with Western civilization. But that was not to be. Modern transportation has destroyed the notion that the Far East is far away. And the new concepts of global diplomacy and global war make it possible to disregard only those areas without economic resources and without strategic importance. Today, Far Eastern affairs rate equally with European affairs in the hierarchy of the United States State Department.

REVOLUTIONARY CHANGE

This book deals with four countries—Japan, Korea, Communist China, and Taiwan (Formosa). They have certain similarities and major differences. In all cases, their basic cultures and social patterns are unfamiliar to us. Each is faced with a problem of an increasing population, even though its present numbers are pressing heavily upon its resources. Each is a country with a background of poverty, landlordism, and corruption. Each has a relatively new form of government with which it has had limited experience. And all but Japan are diverting a large part of their resources to building up their military strength and posture.

Perhaps most important is that each is in a process of change—perhaps one should say, of revolution. Japan's revolution started one hundred years ago and, during the century, she has changed greatly from a feudal pre-industrial society to one characterized by modern steel plants, universal literacy, physicists capable of working in the atomic field, women's suffrage, and industrial labor unions. On the other hand, after a period of increasing confusion and disorder, Communist China started less than a generation ago along the Marxist-Leninist-Stalinist route to political

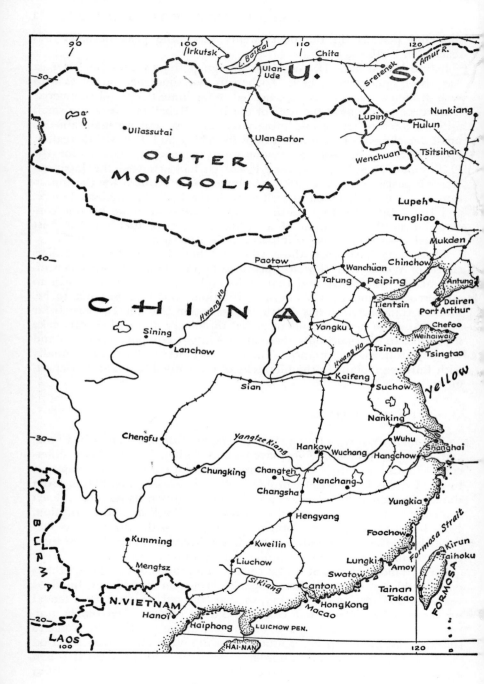

totalitarianism and economic development via forced savings, heavy industry development, and collectivization under the punishing procedures
of the police state. South Korea and Taiwan, both fragments of an
earlier empire, have been wrenched out of the processes of historical
continuity and are seeking to develop new political forms and economic
reconstruction with substantial additions of new elements in the population, with new faces in government, and with large amounts of external
assistance.

The treatment of the four countries in the following chapters reflects
the difference in the character of their revolutionary processes. Japan
has deliberately followed a course of change and adaptation for the
last century. On this evolutionary path was superimposed the tremendous impact of World War II and the subsequent Occupation. The
Japan chapter therefore gives special emphasis to the historical setting
and the shifts in Japanese-American relations over the decades. The
other three countries have been subject to cataclysmic forces within our
time. To be sure, their basic characteristics and social habits persist,
but the new circumstances are dominant today. Discussions of them of
necessity have a much more contemporary emphasis. Communist China,
the Republic of Korea, and the Nationalist Government in Taiwan are
all new figures on the world stage, and the play has only begun.

One fact is clear for all of them, that instead of civilizations famous
for their durability with only imperceptible modifications decade after
decade, each of these countries has now exchanged stability for change.
New political institutions, accelerated economic modernization, and shifting social patterns all have been superimposed upon the old ways with
resulting tensions and strains. American policy vis-a-vis Western Europe
can rely upon fairly predictable behavior because of a substantial degree
of continuity. With the Far East, we are far less familiar with the old
patterns, and even less certain about the sweeping changes which are
recasting their national life. Of one thing we can be sure—these are
countries in transition. This makes our policy decisions more difficult,
and more important. We cannot control their future, but we cannot help
exerting our influence by example, by assistance, and by the intangible
effects of opposition or cooperation.

These four countries are inevitably interrelated and need to be considered together. The course of history for each will be influenced by
the character of the development of the others. The larger countries,
China and Japan, have more scope for independent action, but they
are greatly concerned with each other and, to a lesser degree, with the
smaller countries which are so close to them. Korea and Taiwan, in
turn, will be greatly influenced by the behavior of their large, overshadowing neighbors.

It could be argued that the area should have been extended to include
the Philippine Islands. This is another country whose political character

has been revolutionized in recent years. However, it has much less in common with the other four then they have with each other. It has not grown from the same cultural sources and it has had a long period of development under Western tutelage. While the Philippine Islands are most important in terms of military arrangements in the Pacific, that country's political life has a pattern of its own and it still has preferential economic arrangements with the United States which support its trade and development policy. One might argue further that the countries of Southeast Asia should also be included, but limitations of manuscript space have necessitated a corresponding limitation in geographical coverage. This volume therefore deals with four Far Eastern countries, selected because they are entangled with each other in such a special sense that many of the policy judgments to be made must rest on wider considerations than those relating to any one of the countries alone.

THE UNIVERSALITY OF FOREIGN POLICY PROBLEMS

Foreign policy problems are subject to a kind of centrifugal force which tends to make them global. Even though only four countries are covered in this survey, and they all are in one small sector of the globe, nevertheless nearly all the problems which will be highlighted in the background papers are but special cases of more general questions which perplex American foreign policy today:

How shall we deal with a Communist state? For nearly fifty years, we have lived in a world with the Soviet Union but, in the thinking of most Americans, the threat of Communism to our own future has become clear only within little more than the last decade. Can we co-exist and on what terms? Our present attitudes toward Communism have largely taken form in connection with the rhetoric, cryptography, and behavior of Moscow and its satellites. We have very limited contacts with them, and their impact upon us has been largely in affecting our own behavior (in building up defensive strength, for example) and in emphasizing the importance of our relationships with third countries. Now we are faced with the same set of problems in the Far East because of the emergence of Communist China.

What arrangements are best to give us maximum military security? This problem in its modern form came to the fore in American policy with the failure of the Soviet Union to demobilize after the War, the Czech coup, the Soviet development of the atomic bomb, and its demonstration of willingness to support aggression in Korea and Indo-China. Our answer first developed in Western Europe with the commitments of the North Atlantic Treaty and the program of military assistance. Somewhat similar treaty commitments and relatively larger military assistance programs underlie our relationships today with Korea, Japan, and

Taiwan. But how should military strategy be planned and how should the heavy burden of building adequate defenses be shared?

What trade policy will best serve our foreign policy and our domestic interests? Again, our main trading interests have been with other countries on the American continents and with Western Europe. Our policy of lowering trade barriers has been multilateral and on a most-favored-nation basis. But particular demands for American protection against foreign competition continually jeopardize the broader objective of expanding trade. Today one of the leading trouble spots is in the Far East. In spite of our recognition that Japan must trade to live and our national interest in a healthy Japanese economy, Japanese textiles promise to be as threatening to an open foreign economic policy as Swiss watches. More and more Far Eastern products are entering the American market. Likewise, the general problem of restricting East-West trade is as troublesome in the Far East as it is in Western Europe.

What are the limits which should apply to economic assistance? Our programs of economic assistance began as postwar relief and rehabilitation programs, related primarily to war-devastated areas. The European Recovery Program was a broader effort to put the European economies back on their feet. More recently, the accent has shifted to economic development and aid to the underdeveloped countries. Today, technical assistance, loans, and grants are recognized as part of our continuing international operations, although the present extent and character of the programs is subject to review and challenge. Looking to the Far East, both Korea and Taiwan are among the more important beneficiaries of these programs. Are we doing too much or too little, and how can the requirements for rapid growth be achieved more effectively?

What is the place of the United Nations in the new world? Originally, the United Nations was the symbol of the "one world" concept. It failed of that purpose through no fault of its own. Today, its significance in international affairs is subject to wide fluctuations. It has provided much public debate and some peacemaking, some military achievements, and some economic assistance. The question of the extent of its responsibility and of its effectiveness has been reflected in its various activities in the Far East, to which has been added the troublesome organizational problems of United Nations membership and appropriate representation.

How can we improve our international relations? Any of us who travels in foreign countries is likely to be disturbed by the widely accepted picture of America as a combination of Midas and Mars. To be sure, we are concerned with economic efficiency and whatever military strength seems to be necessary for security, but we do not believe in exploitation, piracy, imperialism, or war-mongering. In fact, we have used our wealth to help other countries and our military strength to defend the independence of small nations. And we do believe firmly in freedom and in economic progress. But Japan views us as being primarily interested in her rearmament and our military bases; and the strong men of Korea and Taiwan feel that we tend to interfere with their sovereignty and are chiefly concerned with our own security. Here again, the world problem is typified in the Far East. How can the image of the United States be made to reflect our quality and qualities more accurately?

Even some of what may seem to be special Far Eastern problems are really not unique. Korea with its division at about the 38th parallel is not unlike divided Germany and divided Indo-China in that it is facing the problem of how to reintegrate or to survive half-Communist and half-free. The Korean-Japanese fishing contretemps is no different from that of American shrimp fishermen off the coast of Mexico or our tuna fishermen in the Pacific off Peru. The Americans still held prisoner in Communist China remind us of our multifarious efforts to free Mr. Oatis. And Chiang's Taiwan seems to have been favored in the legislative halls just as has been Franco's Spain.

The Far East therefore is a microcosm of American foreign problems and American foreign policy. It cannot be completely abstracted from the rest of the world nor from policies relating to other countries. Nevertheless, the same foreign policy objectives may find different means and forms of expression according to the particular nature of the country concerned. Cultural interactions will vary, and much depends upon the popular notions of and attitudes toward each other. The extent and importance of our contact and exposure with other countries also is exceedingly unequal, providing wide variation in possible sources of irritation and opportunities for cooperation. Foreign policy must combine the general objective and the specific application. It must be global, functional, and particularized by country all at the same time. In discussing the problems of the Far East, these overtones must never be forgotten.

THE PROBLEM OF OBJECTIVITY

The assumption underlying the original preparation of the book and the holding of the Tenth American Assembly for which it was prepared was that United States policy toward the Far East is vitally important, and that there had not been sufficient public understanding and discussion of the issues and problems involved. To be sure, even before that time, our Far Eastern policy had twice been the basis of violent debate, once in connection with the effort to attribute responsibility for the defeat of Chiang Kai-shek and the success of the Communists on the mainland, and again over the recall of General MacArthur and the strategy of the Korean War. On both these issues feelings ran high and they still can evoke a highly emotional reaction.

Some years have passed, but the Far East continues to play an active part in the world drama. One incident after another keeps the area in the headlines. Governments change by election or coup d'etat. The President of the United States cancels a visit to Japan. The United States agrees to allow newspapermen to visit Communist China, but China does not admit them. The Chinese and the Russians appear to disagree. Communist China purchases wheat from Canada. Korea experiences a severe inflation. Japan invades the transistor market. And there always is the recurrent question of the relation of Communist China to the United Nations. No longer are these far away events to which we can be indifferent.

The specific incidents are of some importance as they may represent continuity or change in basic conditions and attitudes, but it is more important to be aware of the long-term trends which are taking place in the area. While American policy must have stability in its objectives, it must be flexible in practice as its adjusts to shifting international conditions. It represents action in behalf of the American interests in a world where other nations are seeking what they believe to be their best interest.

Different individuals may reach different conclusions as to what is the American interest and as to what are the intentions of other countries. Our immediate goal must be to keep our inevitable disagreements in the temperate zone—that is, to recognize that these are difficult and complicated problems and that they require objective and careful study rather than emotional reaction. It may be that the result of such an examination will be to support and even strengthen many of our present policy positions. It may be that some modifications will appear to be justified. But conclusions should not come before the history and development of each country is examined. Even then, clear-cut conclusions may not emerge but at least appreciation of the complexities of the problems involved will be achieved. In the world of today and the future, the United States can disregard the problems of the Far East only at its peril.

1.

The United States and Japan

A Century of Contact

◆ ROBERT A. SCALAPINO

Despite their many differences, the United States and Japan have one important thing in common: both are supreme examples of the miracle of the past century—the miracle of basic social change so rapid and so pervasive as to seem unbelievable even in retrospect. When Commodore Perry's small fleet sailed into Tokyo Bay a little over one hundred years ago, Japan was a prime symbol of the forbidding and medieval East, the United States yet a minor power on the periphery of the Western world. And whatever the potentials for change already existent in these two societies, those potentials scarcely seemed to presage the phenomenal explosion of energy, productivity, and power that actually occurred.

It is important to remember that in a certain sense, America and Japan have grown

◆ Robert A. Scalapino is Professor of Political Science at the University of California, Berkeley, and Chairman of its Group on Asian Studies. He has also lectured at Waseda University and Keio University in Japan. His public and professional service includes consulting work with visiting Japanese study groups for the Governmental Affairs Institute, and extension work in the Far East for the Armed Forces Program. Dr. Scalapino has written a number of books and articles on Japan.

up together in the modern world, albeit from very different backgrounds and with somewhat different results. Each of these societies has contained a dynamic quality that had first a regional and then a global influence of major proportions. Each has also represented in some degree a society under pressure, and paid the price of rapid progress with various forms of individual and collective tensions. This one similar feature shared by modern America and Japan should be coupled with their many and important differences when one is exploring the problems and nature of their relationship.

If this is done, it will be easier to understand why American-Japanese relations have been extremely volatile—why as people, we have responded to each other in radically different fashion almost from one decade to the next. In part, the answer lies in the fact that relatively free societies undergoing rapid change frequently experience dramatic shifts in policies and attitudes, reflective sometimes of successive stages of development and sometimes of sudden upsets in the precarious internal balance of power. Thus at the policy levels, the quest for harmony can quickly give way to adamant opposition, and at the emotional levels, admiration can turn into hatred or resentment. Certainly one of the major challenges for both Americans and Japanese is to replace the past fluidity of their relations with a more enduring structure of cooperation and good will.

AMERICA—YOUNG ADVENTURER IN ASIA

In these days of Point Four, TCA, MSA, ICA, and AID, it seems strange that we were first attracted to the Far East because of our weakness, not our strength. We saw in Asian trade some solution to the serious economic dislocations that followed the Revolutionary War. Relations between the British and ourselves were strained, and many of her ports such as those in the West Indies were now closed to us. American shipyards and merchant-traders faced an economic crisis when we turned to the China market. Throughout the nineteenth century, our interest in Asia was much more strongly economic than political, in sharp contrast to the present era.

At first, Japan did not enter our calculations at all. Most trade was conducted on a tramp steamer basis and we used the route around Africa, taking advantage of the many intermediate ports between New England and Canton. Subsequently we discovered that the Pacific held certain products of interest to the Chinese: sea slugs, sandalwood, and above all, seal furs. At this point, an important part of the Canton trade began to move around Cape Horn into the South Pacific. Gradually the trade shifted northward; the seals of the south were being decimated and now whaling in the north became important. In addition, bustling ports on the American west coast, led by San Francisco, opened up American eyes to the entire northern Pacific region. It was at this point that Japan became a topic of interest and concern to the Americans engaged in sailing the new and speedy clipper ships.

We needed a northern fuel station and a place to secure water and other supplies. Moreover, it had become increasingly important to establish some protection for our sailors shipwrecked in this vicinity. All unauthorized foreigners were subjected to seizure and imprisonment under Tokugawa edict. There was also hope of American trade with Japan. It was relatively virgin territory not yet dominated by the powerful European trading companies that operated with government support. Such markets were always interesting to Americans, who could offset to some extent the handicaps of limited capital and meager political protection with greater freedom of action and more flexible operational methods.

Thus after several unsuccessful attempts, an American expedition was finally launched, this time under the command of Matthew C. Perry. One can imagine that the young American sailors watched the approaching coastline of Japan with as much interest and excitement in early July, 1853, as those shipmates of a much different American fleet that once more moved into Tokyo Bay in late August, 1945.

PERRY'S JAPAN—SOCIETY IN FERMENT

The Perry expedition could not be expected to appreciate the complexity of Japanese society, especially since no one was anxious to explain the system to visiting barbarians. Nor could the Americans guess that this expedition would in the long run topple a government and a way of life already under considerable challenge. Japanese feudalism was in its final stages. A vigorous commercialism had developed on the foundations of internal peace and increased agricultural productivity. It was creating tensions throughout the country. The ruling military class saw their traditional status and power threatened as their economic position became more precarious. Within the agrarian class, socio-economic divisions appeared as commercial crops and district enterprise assumed importance; tenant and landlord classes emerged in place of the undifferentiated peasantry of an earlier period. The urban merchants through their guilds acquired a wealth and influence which belied their low social status. All of these trends were well advanced by the early nineteenth century, when once again the problem of Western intrusion was posed for the Japanese officials.

At first, the chief culprits were the Russians and the English. Both were treated to stern refusals when they sought to establish relations. Japanese spokesmen took the position that there was to be no repetition of the sixteenth century when Westerners peddling strange articles of commerce and a new religion had produced serious internal repercussions and threatened political stability within Japan. It had been necessary to use force in ejecting them on that occasion, and even so, they had left behind subversive elements that had had to be stamped out ruthlessly.

Actually, the Western barbarian represented a type of threat that had been faced many times before. Japanese history recorded successful campaigns against the Ainu barbarians to the north. And a glorious page in that history was devoted to the destruction of the Mongol fleet by a *kamikaze* (divine wind) more than five hundred years earlier. These new barbarians looked something like the Ainu, but were rather clever like the Mongols. Indeed, their inventions were quite remarkable and frequently worth using when supplied by the Dutch, who were allowed to come to Nagasaki once a year. But the morals and customs of the Western barbarians were low and vulgar; their religion was false; and if permitted to get a foothold, they could be very dangerous, as news from China illustrated.

When Perry and his men negotiated on the beach with the very reluctant representatives of the Tokugawa government, they did not realize the dilemma they were posing for that government. If the American requests were rejected, it would probably mean force, with which Japan was too backward to cope. But if the demands for entry and ports were met, it would undoubtedly produce grave internal opposition. It is small wonder that the Japanese representatives asked for time to consider the matter, and then as Perry sailed away, hastily summoned the provincial nobility for conference.

The government decided it had no choice but to accept a treaty with the American barbarians, despite strong provincial opposition. And this was merely the opening wedge. We were most unhappy with the limited nature of the first concessions, and almost immediately our representative, Townsend Harris, called for important revisions. Harris used as his major weapon the warning that of all Westerners, we were the most sympathetic to Asian interests and the easiest with whom to deal;

if the Japanese delayed in coming to amiable terms, he suggested, they could court the fate of China at the hands of more arrogant Westerners like the British. Once again, the Japanese government was thrown into confusion. This time it was finally forced to confer with the Imperial Court in Kyoto, something it had not done since the beginning of its era, some two hundred and fifty years before.

Like the fateful Imperial Conference of August, 1945, the issue was acquiescence in American demands and the opening of the country. But whereas the Emperor cast a decisive vote in favor of accepting American terms in 1945, his role and that of the Imperial Court in this earlier period were ones of bitter opposition. Only after the government made the impossible promise to expel the foreigner in a short period was it able to get the Emperor's begrudging acceptance of the new treaties of 1859. Now the revolutionary tides were running strongly; mounting economic disorders stimulated political attacks on the government's "weak-kneed" foreign policy. The rallying cry of the dissidents became "Revere the Emperor—Oust the Barbarians!" The United States, without precisely intending it, had helped to create what became in 1867 the first successful revolution in modern Asia.

AMERICAN CULTURE AND THE JAPANESE RESPONSE

In many respects, the Meiji Restoration of 1867 is an excellent illustration of the ambivalence with which Asia has regarded the modern West. In its origins, this political upheaval was a reaction against the West and primarily a demand for the restoration of an old order; but in its unfolding, the Restoration became an acceptance of certain broad aspects of Westernism and in truth a far more revolutionary change than had first been envisaged. To some Japanese, the West represented an implacable foe; to others, a skillful competitor; to a few, a potential friend and councillor. But to all, it represented in some form both a challenge and a stimulus—and herein lay its revolutionary role. One cannot easily separate the United States from Western Europe in this general respect, but their common impact bears directly upon the historical setting of American-Japanese relations.

Perhaps the most exciting idea that the West carried to Asia was the concept of progress. It would be difficult to overestimate the influence of this new idea upon the Asian mind. Traditional thought in the Far East had been dominated almost completely by the concept of the cycle or the circle. Cyclical theory condemned man and society to a kind of endless repetition; one rose only to fall—moved only to return. It was to relieve the utter dreariness, indeed, pain, of this ceaseless and undeviating process that such a great religious expression as Buddhism found its Nirvana in the final power of the individual through saintliness to climb off the wheel of life, and philosophic Taoism found its ultimate in non-action, non-knowledge—even non-being. Against this background, the West brought to Asia an assuredness that man's destiny was onward and upward, that all life was geared to evolution and growth, and that both the individual and the society were intended to advance toward new goals.

American society of the nineteenth century was in the vanguard of this Western optimism and faith in the future; especially toward the end of that century, our self-confidence in most respects seemed to know no bounds. We had spread rapidly over a continent, conquering one obstacle after another. The West, with its sense of vitality and action, with its unique combination of individualism and communalism, was not the only American frontier. There was the advancing "frontier" of the Eastern immigrant, the moving "frontier" of industry and commerce, and the still different "frontier" of the religious circuit rider. A substantial Protestant evangelical movement during this period left its mark upon many Americans. Its objective was personal salvation, its method to connect the individual intimately with God, producing in that individual a deeply felt emotional experience and a sense of intense joy in the act of conversion. It was the desire to share this great emotional experience that motivated many of the early American missionaries who went to Japan.

This was America, at least in its more obvious aspects. It should not be difficult to understand why such a society symbolized revolution to Japan of the late nineteenth century. Like a magnet, we drew toward us those young Japanese who wanted to think in "modern" and iconoclastic terms. And to the Japanese conservatives of this period, we were often subversive agents too powerful to be taken by frontal assault. In the beginning, it was our missionaries who made the most substantial, personal impact. Christianity in nineteenth century Asia was almost always far more radical in its socio-political implications than in the contemporary West. Inevitably, whether it produced the discontent or fed upon it, Christianity provided a challenge to Asian traditionalism at many levels.

THE IMPACT OF CHRISTIANITY

In the very act of accepting the new faith, the Japanese Christian risked the charge that he was denying traditionalism at precisely those points where it was important to the modern Japanese state. The cosmology of the Bible was certainly at major variance with that of the Shintoist classics. There was not the faintest suggestion in the Bible that the origins of Japan and the Japanese (including the Emperor) indicated superiority or uniqueness. Yet Shintoism asserted this with vigor and in its so-called state form was an essential part of the Japanese nationalist creed. Its rather primitive mythology served to buttress the entire

Emperor system and could be openly questioned only at great peril. While some difference was established between State Shinto and religious Shinto, still the path of the Japanese Christian was precarious.

It is true that many Christians in Japan managed to revere the Emperor and serve the State in approved fashion while retaining their faith. If in so doing, they were forced to live with some contradictions or unresolved dilemmas, at least the eclectic traditions of their society provided support. Even within this group, however, there was a certain stream of dissent which among the band of Christian "radicals" swelled into a mighty river. And though this band was small in numbers, it was highly articulate and influential among all Japanese intellectuals, Christian or not. Against the dominant note of Japanese expansionism and military strength, these Christians called for pacifism and brotherly love. Against the strident nationalist appeals, they matched the concept of full-fledged internationalism. And they read the message of Christian humanism with its broadest socio-political implications. Its emphasis upon the dignity and worth of the individual provided them with daring new concepts of political rights and new theories of social and economic justice. Supported by a growing number of translated Western political treatises, they called for the liberation of the individual from the group, his establishment as a separate entity entitled to personal rights, and the relation of these rights to every aspect of his life. It is no accident that Japanese radical liberalism and democratic socialism were both closely connected in their beginnings with the Christian movement in Japan. The first Japanese Socialist Party was born in an American-sponsored Christian church in Tokyo, and the majority of its members were Christians with intimate American connections.

It would be highly inaccurate to imply that all American missionaries were deliberately fomenting political discontent. To the great majority of missionaries, the essential task was to save souls by preaching the gospel. If political change occurred in the process of contact and conversion, it was a by-product, not a central objective, and in many cases, no doubt completely unexpected.

There were a few individuals among the American missionary group of exceptional intellectual ability and educational background. To these fell important responsibilities for our early cultural relations with Japan. They served in a sense as the major "go-betweens" for the two societies. Their writings and lectures on Japan, even when reflective of "the missionary viewpoint," were the most accurate and scholarly evaluations of that society available. Both because of their understanding of the country and, generally speaking, their respect for it, this group became important not only in educating the American people but in helping to formulate American foreign policy. They constituted an important segment of the "Old Japan Hands" along with certain diplomats and others. It should be noted that a considerable part of our recent foreign policy toward Asia, including Japan, has been shaped out of the conflicts and compromises between such groups as the "Old Japan Hands" and the "Old China Hands," a fact that has largely escaped those who rush to put ideological rather than environmental labels on people.

This missionary elite, if so it may be called, played an equally significant role on the Japanese side. It contributed essays to Japanese magazines, some of which dealt with topics apart from religion, such as social welfare and political theory. Through the mission schools, many Western works were introduced, some in Japanese translation. This group had an influence upon Japanese intellectual life out of all proportion to its numbers, for even those who were bitterly anti-Christian felt compelled to deal with Christian writings and social theories.

OTHER REVOLUTIONARY FORCES

Despite what has been said about the influence of the missionary and Christianity on Japan, however, it would be hard to argue that other early American representatives such as the merchant shippers, engineers, and business men were any less radical in their own fashion. In many cases they were as zealous in promoting their belief in "modernization" as the missionary was in pursuing his campaign for conversion. By a variety of methods, these groups helped to forward the Japanese industrial and commercial revolution. Sometimes they were employed by Japanese for this specific purpose, but more frequently they entered Japan for private purposes and then provided an example by their mere presence and mode of operation. Here was "revolutionary activity" in its most natural and unconscious form, but revolutionary nevertheless, for as Japan borrowed and adapted from Western industrial techniques, her society underwent important changes at every level. Education expanded rapidly, factory production developed, and foreign trade grew by leaps and bounds.

Of course, the industrial revolution and the revolution in ideas that accompanied it were not the products merely of foreigners in Japan. There were other stimuli at least equally potent. Almost every government leader became personally acquainted with some part of the West and numbered some Westerners as his friends. Countless Japanese educators, business men, and professional men either received their advanced training abroad or engaged in Western travel at some point in their careers. Many who could not go abroad shared vicariously in the experiences of others, just as so many Americans have heard about Japan in recent years. Japanese articles and books on Western Europe and America soon were numbered in the thousands and covered every conceivable subject.

It is some measure of the power of Westernism in Japan that it not only created a new group of radicals but a new group of conservatives as well. Perry's expedition and its aftermath produced among Japanese conservatives a strongly defensive psychology. There was real and understandable fear of Western power. Fortunately for Japan, however, this fear did not produce complete immobilization. At first, hatred and blind reaction tended to govern; Westerners were murdered and so were Japanese who dared to call for new approaches. But among a growing number of the ruling elite, hatred gave way to curiosity and admiration for Western strength; this produced a desire to learn the secrets of Western power and hence a receptivity to change. Thus the Japanese "enlightened conservative" was born, and it is most significant that the Meiji oligarchy which governed Japan for many decades was composed mainly of this type. For the enlightened conservative, the ideal was some synthesis which would emphasize Western technology and Asian values. If such a synthesis was not possible in the terms of which he conceived, the modern Japanese conservative was nevertheless able to preserve many traditions in modified form while leading Japan toward urban, industrial growth.

During this period, the average American had only vague impressions of Japanese society and most of these were of its "peculiarities." One of the great problems of the early years was that many Americans found it difficult to take Asia seriously. To them, it represented a land of the curious and the bizarre, filled with upside-down customs, exotic foods with chopsticks, and strange people. Almost every side-show had its Wild Man of Borneo (often from Hoboken) or equivalent. However natural this emphasis upon the "unusual," it represented a substantial barrier to serious attitudes and policy. It was therefore significant that Japan became the first Asian country to impress itself upon some Americans in a new light. By the close of the nineteenth century most Americans who knew much about it took pride in the development of modern Japan. Indeed, Japan was becoming an American favorite in Asia. Any earlier resentment at Japanese "trickery" and "cruelty" was now giving way to approval for a nation that had shown such remarkable discipline and energy in following the Western pattern. Japan was regarded as the foremost disciple of progress in the Far East.

Our economic relations with Japan during the era supported these themes. As a result of a more standardized and reliable product, Japanese tea and silk were replacing the Chinese articles in the American market. We had not given up hope of four hundred million Chinese customers, but in fact, our trade with Japan was now more important and more promising. American private investment was also an increasing factor; with political stability assured in Japan, the ending of extraterritoriality and most other special concessions in the late 1890's did not disturb foreign investors. On the contrary, Japanese adherence to the gold standard and the phenomenal growth of Japanese industry encouraged more investment, leading up to the sizeable loans that were made during the Russo-Japanese War by British and American banking houses.

NATIONALISM

Meanwhile, within Japan, the tensions implicit in a program of rapid social change were reflected in attitudes toward Western societies including the United States. The greatest popular issue in Japan after 1880 was probably treaty revision and the attaining of legal equality with the west. On this issue was spent some of the old xenophobia, and those leaders accused of timidity in negotiations with the West faced real threats to their lives. Now Japanese nationalism was showing many diverse tendencies. The agrarian primitivists were fighting a stubborn if losing battle against modernization, taking full advantage of the many symbols which Japanese nationalism granted them through its mythology, and profiting from agrarian discontent. To this group, both the terms "radical" and "reactionary" apply in some degree. Its basic slogan was to be that of internal reform and external expansion, and both ends of this slogan were basically aimed against the West. As far as this group was concerned, the trend toward urbanism, industrialism, and liberalism was to be reversed. The "Oust the Barbarians" movement was to be expanded to include their ousting from all Asia.

The Asia for the Asians movement in modified form now received support from many quarters in Japan, and such Western concepts as independence and freedom could be used with considerable validity as weapons against Western actions. But Japanese nationalism in its more moderate vein, while innately expansionist and challenging Western imperialism, was fully dedicated to modernization, at least in its technical aspects, and had no desire to secede from the modern world. Actually it took considerable pride in the fact that the West now considered Japan a rising power eligible to sit at Western council tables.

Japanese nationalism has been affected by many developments, but one in particular deserves special mention, so important is it to the whole history of modern Japanese relations with the West. From the Meiji Restoration onward, there has been a tendency for Japan to react to the West in pendulum-like fashion. Periods of extensive borrowing and adaptation have been inevitably followed by eras when excessive "Europeanization" has come under sharp attack and a general retreat has been ordered. In the periods characterized by heavy cultural borrowing, Japanese leaders have tended to combine a rather condescending attitude toward many aspects of their own cultural legacy with the development of strong personal preferences for Western modes. Thus they have led the Japanese people in the acceptance of a wide range of Western ideas and institutions. Some of these have been serious; some have been trivial, but many of both types have been fads. Thus a Japanese intellectual would seize upon Ferdinand Lasalle and become a distributor of Lasalle's thought in Japan; a political leader like Ito would become greatly attracted to Bismarck and adopt even his mode of dress and cigar. In such manner, Western fads in clothing, music, books (and in more recent times even pin-ball machines) have enjoyed phenomenal vogue overnight.

When the inevitable reaction against such an era comes, it is easy to pick out the excesses and absurdities. Nationalism then presents its minimal and maximal demands. The minimal are to cast off the incongruities that do not fit the nature and character of Japanese society. The maximal are to purify the Japanese soul by exorcizing Westernism and its adherents from the body politic. It is in these latter periods that relations with the West undergo the greatest strain.

There is one additional aspect of this phenomenon that deserves mention. The periods of extensive borrowing also produced in Japanese society a distinct tendency toward compartmentalization. There was a great difference between factories modelled after the German system and those built along American lines; as a result a consolidation of techniques, not to mention an organic union, became complicated. Japanese intellectuals whose theories were learned at Heidelberg often had difficulty in communicating exactly with men who had studied at Yale. (This difficulty was accentuated when their intellectual contact was in the Japanese language.) Western education abbetted the intellectual factionalism that has run through Japanese life, and this type of factionalism had a direct bearing upon American-Japanese relations. Despite American influence in many aspects of Japanese society, Germany had the greatest influence of all Western states after 1880. This was equally true in the fields of politics, military organization, philosophy, education, and even business administration. But whether trained in Germany, England, or France, it was natural for the Japanese who had had an European education to regard many aspects of American culture rather critically.

There is no doubt that a considerable amount of the anti-Americanism in contemporary Asia is a reflection of European criticisms of American society expressed by Europeanized Asians. It is equally true, of course, that the United States in similar measure is responsible for some of the forms which anti-European sentiment takes in the Far East. From the beginning of Western contact with Asia, Western quarrels have been displayed prominently in that area; the present Russian-American conflict of words and deeds in the Far East has a long if not a distinguished tradition.

DETERIORATION OF AMERICAN-JAPANESE RELATIONS

With its victory in the Russo-Japanese War, Japan received new recognition from a somewhat startled Western world. Japanese successes were heralded in many American quarters as proof of Asian ability to make progress along Western lines and as a proper rebuke to Russian decadence. Accolades were given to the Japanese spirit of sacrifice and the extraordinary bravery of her soldiers. The United States paid its compliments in concrete as well as abstract form; as has been noted, our faith in Japanese development was underwritten with private loans during this period as well as words of praise. Yet in the aftermath of this war, American-Japanese relations deteriorated, and while there were many reasons for the change, probably the most basic lay in the fact that Japan was moving from the status of pupil to that of competitor. The dynamic qualities of our two societies were now to come into increasing conflict.

The issue of the Japanese immigrant was both a cause and a manifestation of this new era. After 1905, this question became a burning controversy, especially on the West Coast, and it remained as an irritant in some form throughout the entire period before the second World War. American opposition to Japanese immigration was compounded of various factors and sanctioned by many groups. Organized labor in the West, supported by its national organizations, saw Japanese workers as unfair competitors, willing to work for lower wages under any kind of circumstances and content with a much lower standard of living. Western agricultural interests also presented strong economic opposition to Japanese farmers for similar reasons.

Economic arguments, however, were supported by many other circumstances. Certain politicians and the press were quick to seize upon the Japanese issue and transform certain potential problems into political pay-dirt. Thus was the "Yellow Peril" theme born and carried to dangerous emotional heights by men who may have believed what they said, but in any case, found it personally rewarding to say it. All of the arguments against the Japanese were made more potent because they were a largely unassimilated group in American society. The problem of racial relations in any society is partially at least a problem of conformity. A rather strongly egalitarian society like the United States ironically may have considerable difficulty in being tolerant toward the noncomformist, whether it be an individual or a cultural group. Indeed, this is rather strikingly illustrated by trends in the position of the American-Japanese whose increasing Americanism has now produced an acceptance that could not have been imagined a few decades ago.

Before 1945, however, the question of anti-Japanese prejudice continued to plague the relations of our two societies. The crisis over an attempt by San Francisco to segregate Japanese school children in 1906 created lasting damage, as did the succeeding anti-Japanese actions centered mainly in California. Through the so-called Gentlemen's Agreement of 1907, the Japanese government voluntarily agreed to refuse passports to workers who wanted to come to the United States, thereby reducing some of the tension. But in 1924, the American Congress passed a permanent immigration act which excluded all aliens ineligible for citizenship, applying therefore to all Orientals including Japanese. Had the same provisions been applied to the Japanese that were applied to Europeans, namely two per cent of the 1890 census figures, it would have resulted in the entry of less than 150 Japanese per year. It is impossible to calculate the price that the American people paid for complete exclusion.

Among other results, the immigration restrictions played into the hands of the Japanese ultra-nationalists whose anti-Western and anti-American prejudices could match in many cases the anti-Japanese sentiment held by some Americans. This group began to forward a stereotype of the American that was decidedly unflattering. They depicted him as a sheer materialist, insensitive to matters of spirit and intellect, lacking in culture and refinement. A physical impression to match these qualities was also conveyed in many cases: the American was seen with coarse and bloated features; the hairy barbarian image was not completely gone. And a stereotype in kind acquired some strength in the United States. It caricatured the Japanese as specimens of physical weakness with heavy lensed spectacles and protruding teeth. "Japs" were castigated through this stereotype as deceitful and untrustworthy, and the camera in hand became a veritable symbol of the Japanese spy. If it is painful to recall these aspects of our past, it is also the most graphic method of calling to mind the deterioration of our cultural relations, especially in the period after 1930.

Fortunately, there were some representatives among both peoples who did not succumb to these crudities. Many individual and group contacts had been too long and intimate to be completely destroyed. Some of our missionaries, diplomats, and educators strove desperately to preserve a balanced outlook, particularly one that would separate policy issues from racial ones. The moderates in Japan more than matched these efforts in many cases, although both groups fought a generally losing battle. It proved almost impossible to preserve cultural cordiality and understanding in a period when the chasm in policies was becoming unbridgeable.

At the end of the 1930's Japanese society was once again moving in the direction of an intensive reaction against "Europeanization," particularly Anglo-American influences; and for most Americans, Japan was becoming once more an isolated and unfriendly citadel. This tragic era, however, could not erase the fact that by this time, Japan was irrevocably committed to the broad outlines of Westernism, despite the unique forms it sometimes assumed in that society and the almost frenzied efforts of certain Japanese to dislodge it. The Japanese industrial revolution itself was a major testament to that fact, but there were many other indications in the social, economic, and political fields. The doors that were forced open by MacArthur were vastly different from those pried loose by Perry, and this one massive fact is some measure of the cultural background of American-Japanese relations.

DILEMMAS OF AMERICAN POLICY IN ASIA BEFORE 1945

Before turning to the specifics of our pre-1945 Japanese policy, it may be helpful to suggest certain broad hypotheses concerning the background of general American policy in Asia. Admittedly, this is hazardous, but it is equally dangerous to view our policy toward Japan in isolation from our policy toward the rest of the Far East.

The United States has faced three historic dilemmas in its Asian policy, none of which has been "solved" or, indeed, is capable of easy solution. The first of these can be described briefly as a dilemma over our attitude toward change. Until the recent past at least, most Americans conceived of our role in Asia as very limited; throughout the whole of the nineteenth century, it was defined mainly in terms of trade and commerce. In reality, as we have seen, our real role was much more substantial during this period and quite revolutionary in its nature. We were contributing to major social and political upheavals. The American people, however, were not completely conscious of this, and more importantly for our immediate purposes, this broader role was not translated into national policy terms. Indeed, there was a certain paradox between the fact that the American role in Asia was strongly revolutionary and did much to undermine the old order, while American national policy was generally either laissez faire in character or supported the political status quo. To put this point somewhat differently, we have always found it difficult in Asia to adjust our policies to Asian revolutionary processes which we ourselves have done so much to stimulate. And where we have ignored those revolutionary processes or resisted them without posing any suitable alternative, we have frequently seen them turn against us.

The second fundamental problem in American Asian policy has related to both our values and our methods of achieving them. Such issues have often crystallized around the question of whether to rely essentially upon a policy of moral suasion or to undertake a more militant policy of sanctions or force. The latter might be labelled the general colonial position, so strongly was it held among the colonial powers of nineteenth century Europe. Its general outline ran something like this: the psychology of the Asian requires a policy of strength on the part of Western states because the Asian always regards leniency as weakness and acts accordingly. In the absence of any traditions of Christian humanism or indeed, any concepts of international law or proper relations between states in the Western sense, the Asian communities cannot be expected to respond in a Western or "civilized" fashion. Asian transgressions of civilized rules must be punished or they will be repeated endlessly.

The foregoing argument was often combined, of course, with the familiar concept of the white man's mission, a theory of comprehensive Western tutelage over the "backward peoples." It must not be forgotten that there were strong moral arguments presented on behalf of a forceful policy in Asia. Whether that policy was attuned merely to chastisement or to complete colonial control, presumably it was directed in part at least to passing on the benefits of Western civilization.

On the whole, however, Americans were very reluctant to accept this line of reasoning and its policy implications. For one reason, the element of validity held by the colonial argument was obviously greatest in the very early periods of contact between the modern West and Asia, during which periods the United States could not be very active in the Asian scene. With the passage of time, the very intrusion of Western ideas and values into Asia weakened colonial contention, at least in degree. In addition, of course, this theme ran counter to the rather deeply ingrained anti-colonialism of American society. It is true that we made our exceptions on a few occasions, notably the Philippines, but we were always uncomfortable in so doing, and we never really accepted the role—or the ideological premises—required of a major colonial power. Perhaps most important of all, the colonial thesis connoted a degree of involvement and responsibility that the average American did not wish to undertake.

From both a moral and a political standpoint, the more impressive arguments with Americans for a strong Asian policy were those later in time and more general in coverage, when they were timed and structured in such a fashion as to match American capacities and interests more closely. The new emphasis was upon the universal danger of militarist-Fascist aggression. In Asia, this applied particularly to Japan. Somewhat belatedly, perhaps, it was asserted that this form of aggression could not be checked by pious words, and that only a program of sanctions could bring about its control. Some argued that if economic sanctions were applied strictly and in time, military sanctions might be avoided. But the gist of the argument was that Fascist aggression had to be stopped whatever the risk, for the sake of the life as well as the moral health of the democratic world.

Despite the increasing potency of this latter argument, American policy in Asia before 1945 was characterized essentially by reliance upon what may be called moral suasion. Evidence of this fact can be seen in a wide series of policies ranging from disarmament and peace pacts on the one hand to nonrecognition and moral embargoes on the other. In the early period, our Asian policy of moral suasion was also applied to European powers, in an effort to effect the so-called Open Door Policy in China and stop European imperialism in this area; later, the policy was chiefly employed against Japanese expansion.

The attacks upon moral suasion as the basis of American policy in Asia were many, centering mainly around the simple charge that it was unrealistic and did not succeed in achieving the desired objective. Whatever its shortcomings during this period, however, moral suasion appealed to Americans because it seemed to represent minimum risks and maximum conformity to an American image of righteousness. Perhaps these two factors must go together in some degree. Certainly the more recent era of world responsibility has placed the United States under severe strains in trying to maintain the note of puritanism that has long been a hallmark of American foreign policy. It is curious, incidentally, that many of our Asian critics have missed this general point entirely. They persist in seeing our "errors" (from their viewpoint) in blindness, stupidity, or even immorality; it rarely occurs to them that the problem they are trying to define stems from the fact that there are still cases where we Americans appear more anxious to be righteous than right.

The third historic dilemma which American foreign policy in Asia has faced has been the choice of collective action versus "going it alone." Some might be inclined to think of this as essentially a postwar problem because of its importance in the last few years, but in reality it goes back to our earliest presence in Asia. Throughout the nineteenth century, most of those opposing collective action held that our interests were not sufficiently similar to those of Europe to warrant any such policy, and collective action with an Asian nation during this period was never seriously considered. Many Americans did argue that by clearly delineating our position from that of the major European powers, we would benefit both in commerce and in other concessions from appreciative Asian officials, and they cited evidence of the trust and gratitude that came to the United States in this fashion. Their opponents contended that Asian governments made no basic distinctions between one Western society and another, considering them all barbarians, and that the United States could only support its rights in the area efficiently by joining in a united front with other Western states. Thus, initially, there was a tendency for collective action to be coupled with a strong policy and unilateral action to be connected with moderation and an appeal to Asian friendship.

Later, these relationships underwent various changes. After the twentieth century began, collective action seemed a possible technique for saving what was left of independent Asia rather than a device for further bolstering Western prestige, though the two now went together in some respects. Ultimately, of course, the primary issue became whether to engage in collective action to deal with Japan, the new expanding power in this region.

While we dabbled in collective action from time to time in nineteenth century Asia, ordinarily we followed a unilateral policy. That policy often included sharp attacks upon European action. Long before the Soviet Union emerged on the scene, we were the chief gadfly of Western European colonialism in Asia. This did not prevent us from sharing many of the gains acquired by British and French arms, a fact that displeased the Europeans at the time and has been used against us by our Asian critics ever since. Ours was an understandable if unpleasant dilemma. While we usually did not want to join in the European campaigns against Asians and often criticized them in trenchant tones, we also did not want to accept a position less favorable than that which they subsequently acquired by military victory. Hence the formula of the most favored nation.

Even after 1900, we used collective action in Asia sparingly and with numerous reservations. It was never easy to reconcile completely American interests in this area with those of other major powers, European or Asian. And beyond this, collective action continued to imply in its most effective forms a degree of commitment greater than that which we (or most others) wanted to undertake in this area. In this later period, therefore, we were always seeking collective agreement, but with the hope that it would render collective action unnecessary. To the latter we would not be bound. Thereby we preserved the independence of American action, but could not preserve the peace.

THE ERA OF MORAL SUPPORT

In setting forth the three basic dilemmas that have historically troubled our Asian foreign policy, the writer has already suggested the broad outlines of American policy toward Japan prior to 1941. A few details need now to be supplied. It is possible to divide the entire period from 1856 (the date on which Townsend Harris, our first representative, arrived in Japan) to 1941 into four major periods on the basis of national policy trends.

The first period ended when Japan was finally able to rid herself of the unequal treaties and assume a fully independent status in the world, achievements essentially accomplished just before the Russo-Japanese War of 1904-05. During these years, American policy toward Japan was characterized mainly by friendly counsel and support, although our diplomatic influence was soon surpassed by the more important powers. Symbolic of both these facts was the ultimate abrogation of the unequal treaties. In 1878, we became the first Western country to agree to restore tariff autonomy to Japan, provided other Western countries concurred. However, Western agreement was not forthcoming until Great Britain signified her willingness to accept revision some twenty years later.

Our policy during this era gained us considerable popular support as a progressive young country willing to share its ideas and sympathetic to the cause of an independent Japan. But when Japanese leaders considered concrete methods of completing that independence and building from it toward regional power, they naturally turned to those Western countries capable of making this possible. We gave our good will, but the British gave an alliance that helped to change the whole course of Asia.

THE CHALLENGE OF JAPANESE EXPANSION

The inauguration of that alliance in 1902 can be termed the beginning of the second era of American-Japanese relations, so important was it in reshaping the policies of both parties. Great Britain had found that the security of her great empire demanded an end to the era of splendid isolation and during this period moved to cultivate the support of two rising powers so strategically placed as to offset various threats to the British Empire from any European bloc. To the United States, Great Britain offered her friendship and support on a wide range of matters; a new era of harmony replaced the old friction, and we became Britain's hope in the Western Hemisphere. And with Japan, the British contracted a formal alliance which established by implication their respective spheres of predominant influence and set the tone for Asian international relations for two decades.

That alliance signaled the entry of Japan upon the world stage as a major power, the first such power to come from modern Asia. It enabled her to concentrate upon two cherished objectives: the most specific goal was dominance in the northeast Asian area; the more general desire was to become spokesman for, and in some measure, leader of the broader Asian community. The former objective was defended by Japan with vigor and a wide range of arguments. The northeast Asian region was regarded as crucial to the development of the Japanese economy, and this theory grew stronger in proportion to the growth of industry and population in Japan.

While exceedingly important, however, the economic justification for Japanese hegemony was not the only one offered. The familiar messianic themes were popular, especially in Japanese nationalist circles. It was called the mission of Japan to fill the cultural vacuum of this vast region with the Japanese way of life. And it was also regarded as vital to Japanese national security interests that an area of political instability be safeguarded by Japanese power. Later, of course, the new focus of this theme became the Communist menace and the Japanese mission to stop Communism in continental Asia, especially in those areas of primary interest to her. Throughout the pre-1945 period, many Japanese spoke of a Japanese Monroe Doctrine for northeast Asia and sought to meet such American complaints as arose by making the comparison implicit in this phrase.

Had Japanese objectives excluded control of China below the Great Wall and stopped with the absorption of Korea and some control over the Manchuria-Mongolia regions, the ultimate conflict with the West would probably have been averted. Actually, the Western powers, including the United States, generally acquiesced in Japanese expansion during its early stages. From 1905 onward, we had qualms about Japanese aims in Asia, but only when the threats were against China proper did we try to adopt a policy of firmness.

Certain concessions were made by the American government in an attempt to further our own security interests in the Pacific. Having obtained the Philippines, we were now obligated to see to its defense. Consequently, we signed the Taft-Katsura Agreement with Japan in 1905, an agreement which in effect accepted Japanese control over Korea in exchange for pledges relating to our new possession. We could scarcely protest with vigor when the final annexation of Korea occurred in 1910. In similar fashion, we recognized the Japanese "special position" in the Manchuria-Mongolia region at an early date. The Root-Takahira notes exchanged in 1908 acknowledged this, and these were endorsed from time to time, as in the case of Secretary Bryan's note of March, 1915.

We were not prepared, however, to write off the territorial integrity and independence of China proper, nor abandon our historic "equality of opportunity" position. Our first challenge to Japan on these scores really came in connection with her so-called Twenty-One Demands. Japan had entered the first World War on the side of the Allies, and few wars have been so profitable to a belligerent or required such small sacrifice. On the one hand, she quickly overran German positions in the Pacific and on the Shantung Peninsula and thereby obtained new territories and influence in the Far East. On the other hand, her industries mushroomed, working night and day to fill those orders which Europe could no longer meet; it was during this period that industrial production in Japan finally surpassed that of agriculture.

It is small wonder that Japan felt opportunity was ripe to insist upon a greater role in China. The Chinese Revolution of 1911 was losing its original purpose and drive; China as the sick man of the Far East needed help, and Japan was prepared to supply assistance in a variety of ways. In 1915, the Japanese government confronted China with a long list of twenty-one demands, including a final category which might have reduced China to the status of a Japanese protectorate. We opposed some of these demands sharply but our opposition was diplomatic only. Secretary Bryan issued a lengthy note outlining our historical open-door policy toward China, stating that we would not recognize any action that impaired this policy or our treaty rights. The later Lansing-Ishii agreement disclaimed, in behalf of both countries, any ambition to infringe upon "the independence or territorial integrity of China," but it did recognize, while not defining, Japan's "special interests in China." The Japanese retreat from the twenty-one demands, however, cannot be attributed to our policy of moral pressure. More important was the reaction of the Chinese and above all, of the British whose support Japan needed to retain.

World War I had favored both the United States and Japan; both had gained enormously in economic strength and military-political power, while most of Europe suffered. But these were factors which could easily make for rivalry, and the end of the war climaxed this era with bitterness. At Versailles, our great idealist, Wilson, was unable to protect Chinese interests against various concessions to Japan to which our allies had already agreed. Nor was the American government able to curtail or control the ambitious Japanese program of intervention in Siberia which dwarfed that of the other Allies, suggesting in its scope and duration hopes of expansion in still another direction. These failures stimulated us to seek some substitute in the Pacific for the Anglo-Japanese alliance, an agreement that now seemed dangerous. Thus the first two decades of the twentieth century saw the stage set for American-Japanese rivalry, and also witnessed some of the preliminary testing of our respective positions and tactics. On the whole, the competition up to this point seemed to favor Japan.

THE ERA OF COLLECTIVE AGREEMENTS

The third era of American-Japanese relations comprises the decade 1920-1930. On the whole, this was a decade of disappointment for the Japanese expansionists and hope for the moderates; it was Japan's famous era of quasi-liberalism. But the frustrations suffered by Japanese militarism in the early years were turned into weapons of attack as the decade came to a close.

For the United States, this was an era when the American people wanted desperately to enjoy a standard of living which they had just discovered possible, without being troubled by foreign crises and war. In seeking a policy that would conform to it, the American government advanced a program of collective agreement concerning Asia, in the hope of avoiding the necessity for any collective action and as a type of alternative to continued involvement in Europe. One of our considerations was that of replacing the Anglo-Japanese Alliance with a framework more to our liking.

From the American viewpoint, the great accomplishment of the Washington Conference of 1921 was the substitution of the Four- and Nine-Power Treaties for the Anglo-Japanese alliance, and the establishment of the famous naval disarmament ratio among the five important Pacific powers. In certain respects, the results represented our effort to contain Japanese expansionist policy through supposedly binding collective agreements. This remained a key to a decade climaxed by the famous Pact of Paris or Kellogg-Briand Pact of 1928 in which more than fifty nations including Japan agreed to renounce war as an instrument of settling disputes. This was the American policy of moral suasion in its most expansive form.

It would be wrong to assert that American idealism had no impact upon Japanese society. On the contrary, the Wilsonian themes of self-determination, making the world safe for democracy, and the establishment of an international body to preserve the peace had a great influence upon the Japanese. Especially impressed were the intellectuals and students, but the whole aura of the early 1920's assisted the moderates in Japan. Moreover, the Siberian expedition failed, discrediting the militarists; and this greatly helped those who wanted to cooperate with the West on disarmament and a moderate China policy. In this period of liberal ascendancy in Japan, it appeared possible that the American objectives of achieving a peaceful Asia without any effort on our part might be realized, though the continued disorder in China was worrisome. At least, this third period represented a definite contrast to the earlier tempo of Japanese expansion.

THE SURGE OF JAPANESE AGGRESSION

The final period of prewar American-Japanese relations is too vivid to require much elaboration. After 1930, the tides of militarism rose rapidly in Japanese society, the product of liberal failures, economic distress, and world disorder. The Manchurian crisis of September, 1931, started that chain of aggression which finally culminated in global war. The Japanese defenders of the Manchuria policy used familiar arguments, all couched in terms of the national interest: the security theme emphasized the menace of Communism and the need to preserve law and order in areas so close to Japanese soil; the survival theme stressed the absolute need of an outlet for Japanese population and a source for raw materials; the messianic theme played upon the contribution which the Japanese way of life could make to the peace and prosperity of all peoples in the region. Once again Japanese society was gripped by a reaction against Westernism, particularly Western liberal institutions and ideas. The radical nationalists called for a new Restoration which would replace capitalism, urbanism, and cosmopolitanism with a revitalized soldier-peasant alliance centering upon the traditional values. The more conservative chauvinists were content with a "get tough" policy toward China and any Western society that tried to interfere. Both groups were anxious to reduce Western power in Asia at every level.

American policy during the period searched unsuccessfully for some answer. The Stimson nonrecognition policy proved ineffective as did his earnest efforts to encourage the League of Nations. To the average citizen of the Western democracies, Manchuria was a long way off and there were too many troubles near at hand. But if the quest for collective security failed, the attempt to establish security by a unilateral policy of neutralism was also increasingly unsatisfactory. The neutrality legislation of the mid-thirties demonstrated the fact that it is very difficult if not impossible for one of the world's great powers to "sit out" a protracted global crisis by pretending that it has no real interest in the outcome. By the end of the 1930's, there was very little personal neutrality in American society toward the world scene, and we found to our chagrin that the legal neutrality we had enacted was often of the greatest assistance to those we labelled "aggressors." A struggle then began in American political circles and more especially in the American conscience as to how far to move from a policy of mere moral suasion and how close to come to a policy of force—how much to abandon unilateral action and how firmly to join our policy and our fate with the anti-Fascist nations.

These issues were still being debated at the time of Pearl Harbor, although we had clearly moved away from neutralism and toward sanctions and collective action. There can be little doubt that our decision to freeze all Japanese assets in concert with other democratic powers in July, 1941, affected the timing of the war. This was the culmination of a series of economic sanctions to which we had brought ourselves, and Japanese leadership was now faced with the prospect of reaching an agreement with the United States or seeing itself grow weaker month by month, cut off from major sources of raw materials and other supplies. Our demands in 1941, interestingly enough, reflected in broad outline the historic position toward Asia that we had always held. We would have accepted the status quo in Manchuria, Mongolia, and of course, Korea, thereby recognizing the Japanese "special position" in these areas. But we held firm to the policy that Japan must abandon her position in China proper, which meant giving up the Wang Ching-wei government, recognizing only the Chiang Kai-shek regime, and removing all Japanese forces from China—in short, respecting the territorial integrity and independence of the Chinese Nationalist Republic.

The acceptance of these conditions by Japan would have meant the abandonment of allies who had staked their lives on Japanese victory and more importantly, acknowledgement of the failure of a policy that had cost Japan dearly in blood and treasure. Rather than make this sacrifice, the Japanese leaders accepted war, trusting in a German victory over Russia in the West and an ultimate peace that would give Japan the Asian leadership she had long desired. The emphasis had now shifted from "Asia for the Asians" to "The Asian Co-Prosperity Sphere," which meant Asia under Japanese leadership, or as many felt, "Asia for the Japanese."

THE WORLD CONTEXT

General world conditions also affected these past eras of American-Japanese relations. Throughout the entire period, Europe was the chief power factor in Asia. Indeed, much of Asia was a prostrate form across which the rival power conflicts of the West moved at will; Japan was the single important exception. Thus changes in European alliances and shifts in the European balance of power could and did decisively affect all the mutual relations of Asian and Western countries. After the first World War, to be sure, the power of Western Europe waned somewhat and the Asian nationalist movement spurted forward, but the real changes awaited World War II.

And since the world was largely European centered, important also were the ideological currents that spread through the Western world and were transmitted from there into both the domestic and the foreign politics of Asian societies. The period centering around the first World War was one in which Western-style democracy, with its emphasis upon human rights, parliamentarism, rationality, and science was having profound influence in such societies as Japan and China, especially among the intellectual classes. The Japanese decade of the 1920's shows evidence of this fact.

The experiments with Western political and economic institutions led to many bitter disappointments, and rival ideologies began to have their appeal. Marxism-Leninism as interpreted through the Bolshevik revolution already had began to threaten Western definitions of democracy and science and challenged the Western power position in Asia, as well. Russian Communists quickly recognized the opportunity in Asia to harness the nationalist movements to their cause. They concentrated upon this goal, unencumbered by any bonds of friendship to the colonial powers of Western Europe. In Japan, however, international Communism failed to score the sizeable gains it made in many other Asian areas partly because it was never able to capture and use the Japanese nationalist movement but rather had to fight it, and partly because the Japanese state was able and quite willing to use coercion effectively against its internal opponents. Thus it was mainly the Japanese intellectual rather than Japanese society as a whole that acquired an interest in Marxist thought, and even among these, very few sought to affiliate their society to the Communist world.

The influence of European Fascism upon Japan was much greater, as the period after 1930 indicates. The fact that there are many parallels in the problems and nature of so-called "late-developing" societies is well illustrated by the two societies of Japan and Germany, and this is one reason for the great influence of the latter upon the former throughout the entire modern period. Encouraged by common difficulties, that influence became steeply ascendant again after the rise of Hitler. Parliamentarism had produced a disappointing record in both societies, and economic conditions were a source of grave popular unrest. There was great appeal in a policy pledged to internal reform and external expansion. A militant union of the "have-not" societies was the national socialist answer to communism and democracy alike. The German-Japanese Anti-Comintern Pact of 1936 and the Tri-Partite Pact of 1940 between Germany, Italy, and Japan that created the so-called Axis powers had their background in these facts. Japan did not become a Fascist state of the pure German or Italian type because her traditions were different, but in its main trends Japanese militarism borrowed heavily from Fascism both in thought and in action. It is not surprising, therefore, that it followed Fascist techniques in foreign policy. In a time when the Western world itself was breaking up into warring camps, the course of international relations in Asia was certain to be affected.

The Japanese Defeat

The people of the United States were electrified on August 10, 1945, when the Japanese government through its Minister to Switzerland made public the offer to surrender, having earlier failed to get satisfaction in its secret overtures to the Soviet Union. The key passage in this surrender message was its acceptance of the terms of the Potsdam Declaration "with the understanding that the said declaration does not comprise any demand which prejudices the prerogatives of His Majesty as a Sovereign Ruler." Willing now to give up almost everything else, the Japanese conservatives still could not bear the thought of any action against the Emperor or the Imperial institution. Secretary Byrnes made a somewhat ambiguous but generally negative reply on the following day when he said, "From the moment of surrender the authority of the Emperor and the Japanese Government to rule the state shall be subject to the Supreme Commander of the Allied powers who will take such steps as he deems proper to effectuate the surrender terms." Byrnes stated also that the ultimate form of government in Japan was to be established "by the freely expressed will of the Japanese people." On August 14, 1945, after another traumatic conference in Tokyo with the Emperor in attendance, the decision was made to accept these terms. The war was over.

The crowded events of early August, 1945, constitute one of the most dramatic and significant episodes of world history. On August 6, the first atomic bomb was dropped at Hiroshima killing nearly eighty thousand people and inaugurating a new age for mankind. The second atomic bomb fell on Nagasaki three days later, again with tremendously destructive results. It will long be debated as to whether these actions were necessary and proper. There can be no question, however, that the hideous devastation of these two cities has been deeply etched into the Japanese mind, contributing to the spirit of pacifism, reluctance to rearm, and high sensitivity toward atomic-hydrogen experiments which figure so prominently in Japanese politics and foreign relations. Even before the atomic attacks, metropolitan Japan had been subjected to months of unending fire bombings on a massive scale; more than fifty per cent of Japan's three largest cities—Tokyo, Osaka, and Nagoya— were completely destroyed. The problems of food and shelter were critical beyond imagination. Millions had fled to the countryside where they existed under cramped and miserable circumstances. This was one war that did not pay for Japan, a fact the present generation seems unlikely to forget.

However, as Nagasaki was being bombed, the Soviet Union declared war upon Japan and proceeded to cut through the weakened Kwantung army. A long-standing threat had finally come to pass, although at this late date it could only add to the terror and bewilderment of the final days; it obviously could not affect the course of a war that had already been decided, something that the Soviet Union knew well when it marched into Manchuria. The Japanese press could only exhort the people to stand firm in the midst of the greatest crisis since the Mongol invasions of the thirteenth century. If the end was less dramatic than the Wagnerian climax to Berlin and Hitler, it was almost equally painful.

THE EARLY OCCUPATION

Immediately after the war, there was some talk that Japan and Germany would have to be occupied for twenty years or more, but actually the formal occupation of Japan lasted less than seven years, coming to an official close in April, 1952, with the application of the Treaty of San Francisco. The first phase of American postwar policy took place during the early Occupation and has been well denoted in terms of its objectives by the phrase, "punishment and reform." Before seeking to analyze this era briefly in policy terms, it is important to review those factors in the world scene and in the startling new pattern of cultural relations that gradually influenced and shaped it.

Our initial policy toward defeated Japan was based upon certain premises respecting postwar Asia and the world at large. It is necessary only to recall them in order to realize how greatly conditions were to change in a short period of time. In Asia, the Republic of China was marked by us for leadership as successor to Japan in power, and as principal spokesman, along with India possibly, for the Asian people. We had no qualms, therefore, about reducing Japan to the level of a lesser state. This was an era, moreover, when hope was still reasonably strong in continued Allied unity and the settlement of all issues among us by negotiation in good faith.

At the same time, however, some small clouds were gathering on the horizon even as we mapped out a program for Japan. Problems in postwar Europe between ourselves and the Russians were accumulating. The German occupation, with its quadri-partite division and questions of jurisdiction, was proving more difficult and less satisfactory than we had anticipated. We had not given up hope of general Allied accord but our impressions gained from the brief postwar experience in Europe bolstered our desire that the Japanese occupation should be primarily an American show; one which would avoid if possible the pitfalls of direct military government in favor of using, though not necessarily supporting, a Japanese government.

We accomplished both of these objectives, though not without some damage to relations with our wartime Allies, particularly the Russians. Neither the Far Eastern Commission nor the Allied Council could interfere with American policy. The Far Eastern Commission, sitting in Washington and composed of eleven nations, had the legal right to initiate or review basic policy for Japan; in practice it could do nothing without the concurrence of the United States, which together with Britain, Russia, and China, had to agree on policy. Since the United States was firm in supporting Occupation policy being formulated in Japan, the FEC played no important role. The Allied Council, sitting in Tokyo, consisted of representatives of the United States, the British Commonwealth, China, and the USSR; its role was supposedly advisory, but its advice was seldom requested and in general it was only a sounding board for ourselves and the Russians. Responsibility for the Japanese Occupation must lie with the United States for we made all the basic decisions. The Russians retaliated, it might be added, where they could, especially on the mainland of Asia—in China and Korea.

THE *GI* AND THE JAPANESE

The Occupation represented a new and colossal problem of cultural relations between Americans and Japanese. American representatives in Japan during the past seventeen years can be numbered in the millions, whereas in the previous ninety years they totalled only a few tens of thousands. The attitudes of these millions, along with the Japanese reaction to them, is a crucial factor in our mutual relations since World War II.

There was uncertainty everywhere as American troops began to move into Japan in September, 1945. Many Japanese feared for their lives, or at the very least, for their property and the honor of their women. Americans were prepared for violence and sabotage on an extensive scale. But these mutual apprehensions and fears were largely unwarranted; from the very beginning, Americans and Japanese were able to establish extraordinarily good personal relations with a minimum of unpleasant incidents. This fact was quite possibly the most significant single development of the immediate postwar period, because it was again one of those factors of cultural relations that was ultimately to exercise great influence on policies as well as attitudes.

Indeed, observers were quick to comment on the irony of a situation where we seemed better disposed in a personal sense toward our ex-enemies than toward some of our allies. No one has fully explored the reasons why Americans and Japanese have gotten along relatively well as individuals since 1945, and why feeling against Americans has not been at any time a really serious factor, despite more recent developments of a feeling against America. No doubt the initial psychology of both parties helped. Having expected the worst and gotten something very much better, there was naturally relief and even joy. The Japanese were particularly appreciative of the countless cases of individual American humanism and generosity in a period of great hardship for them. Chocolate bars and K-rations were as much symbols of American presence as the signs about Kilroy. And the sharing of food, which was an almost natural instinct in the average American when he saw suffering, meant a great deal to the hungry Japanese, even if they only heard about it second or third-hand. Moreover, Americans as a group seemed friendly, easygoing, and extroverted to the Japanese, in conspicuous contrast to their own highly formal and rather reserved and introverted behavior. Americans were unpredictable, uninhibited, and usually very amusing. They had such an obvious joy of life that this served as a kind of release from the immediate drabness of the Japanese scene.

To the Americans, on the other hand, the Japanese were a never-ending source of amazement. As individuals, they were extraordinarily polite, quiet, and submissive; but mass behavior in Tokyo subway and elevated train stations was a source of marvel even to veteran New Yorkers. Japanese customs were almost invariably quaint and highly entertaining, from Japanese-style baths to the numerous festivals and street parades. Perhaps the greatest appeal between Americans and Japanese was the attraction that some opposites have for each other. There are a few factors of similarity, however, that support the appeal. The Japanese, accustomed to arduous labor, were conditioned to admire the remarkable energy, creativity, and efficiency of Americans at work. And Americans were pleased with Japanese cleanliness and respected the Japanese handicraft artist.

There are, of course, other aspects to the picture. There have been many causes for annoyance and even antagonism on both sides, duly exploited by those who had a vested interest in ill will. The overwhelming majority of Americans in Japan have been young soldiers subject to the usual temptations. On the whole, they have acted well but it was inevitable that a certain number of incidents occur. The way in which these incidents were handled by the authorities, treated by the press, and received by the public is a good index of the trends of general reaction to the Occupation. Such an index would support the conclusion that it is inevitable that any foreign occupation of large-scale proportions will soon reach a point of diminishing returns in so far as both cultural relations and national policy are concerned.

No objective observer, however, could put the emphasis on the negative in speaking of the main effects of this mass exposure. A large majority of the Americans who were sent to Japan liked the country and the people. With few exceptions, they made no effort to acquire any profound understanding of the Japanese and they picked up a good deal of misinformation, which was duly scattered about the United States upon their return. At the same time, however, they could not avoid learning a great deal about Japan that was obvious, and as a result we as a people are vastly more informed about Japanese society than ever before. They also brought back tons of "souvenirs," and the present vogue for Japanese products, and even Japanese architecture, is traceable to their appreciation for important aspects of the Japanese way of life.

In similar fashion, bits and pieces of the American way of life have been transmitted to millions of Japanese in the last decade. Our gadgets and some of our customs are now commonplace, especially in urban centers. And on the whole, the Japanese have been satisfied with the American residents. If statistical evidence on this score is desired, one can turn to the various polls taken during the Occupation by Japanese newspapers. At the zenith point, approximately two-thirds of those polled regarded the United States as the foreign country they liked most, with the Soviet Union consistently leading the unpopular list. (Polls of 1961 indicate that the United States is still the most popular foreign country, although by a reduced margin, with some 44-48% of the votes, followed by Great Britain and Switzerland. The USSR still heads the unpopular column followed closely by the Republic of Korea and Communist China.) The same polls, however, showed that less than ten per cent of the Japanese people had had any personal contact with Americans, despite the large numbers in the country. This undoubtedly was due to such obstacles as the language barrier and the great differences in living standards. But if personal contacts were not as common as might have been guessed, personal observations and general impressions were omnipresent.

In summary, one might suggest that the great change in postwar American-Japanese cultural relations has lain in this fact: before 1945, cultural exchange was limited to the few; after 1945, it was conducted on a mass basis with millions of people of both societies having an unusual opportunity to see each other at work and play, to observe each other's customs and idiosyncrasies, and constantly to compare Japanese and American patterns. Seldom have two such different people been put together on such a large scale for so long a period of time. The results have been more favorable and rewarding to both countries than one could dare to have hoped.

INITIAL AMERICAN POLICY

The United States had begun to formulate policy for occupied Japan long before the war ended and some decisions regarding Japan had been reached in the form of Allied Declarations. That phase of American policy which has been called "punishment and reform" is spelled out in fullest detail in two documents on Initial Post-Surrender Policy sent from Washington to General MacArthur on August 29 and November 8, 1945.

For several years, these documents represented the "constitution" against which American occupation policy was tested. More specifically, this policy was to conform to two major objectives: "To insure that Japan will not again become a menace to the United States or to the peace and security of the world" and secondly, to help produce a peaceful government, supporting the objectives of the United States and the ideals of the United Nations, a government selected by the Japanese people themselves but preferably a democracy.

As can be seen, punishment took some priority partly because the Allies felt that the old had to be exorcised before the new could be born. Perhaps the most drastic punishment was the dismemberment of the Japanese Empire. This had already been decided by the Allies in their declarations at Cairo on December 1, 1943, Yalta in February, 1945, and Potsdam, on July 26, 1945. The net result of these statements was to reduce Japan to her four main islands "and such minor islands as we determine." The Republic of China was to receive back the territories taken from her, namely Manchuria, Taiwan, and the Pescadores; the USSR was to have restored her former rights "violated by the treacherous attack of Japan in 1904," namely southern Sakhalin and adjacent islands together with the concessions in north China and Manchuria; and the Yalta agreement also provided that Russia would receive the Kurile Islands. Korea was to be given its independence.

Thus Japan was reduced in size approximately to her boundaries at the time of the Meiji Restoration, with a population three times as great. Even the Bonin islands and the Ryukyus were taken from her, as were the mandated islands throughout the Pacific. She was now about the same size as the state of California in total land area, with about eighteen

The Japanese Empire, 1940

THE NEW YORK TIMES ·

CHART NO. 1

per cent of the land under cultivation or capable of being used immediately. Into this shrunken territory were soon to be poured some six and one-half million Japanese repatriated from overseas.

Disarmament was also high on the American agenda and was carried out with remarkable speed and thoroughness. Nearly four million military men were demobilized and the military administrative structure was completely scrapped. Swords were distributed as souvenirs rather than being beaten into plowshares, but the American emphasis during this period was upon long-range pacifism, as is well known. General MacArthur and many others encouraged the idea of Japan as a Switzerland of the Far East, permanently aloof from international strife. (Switzerland has always had a defense force.) The culminating event was the famous anti-war clause included in the new Japanese Constitution with

Japan Today

SOVIET UNION

KAMCHATKA

OUTER MONGOLIA

MANCHURIA

SAKHALIN

ATTU

KISKA

KURILE IS.

N. KOREA

S. KOREA

CHINA

JAPAN

Pacific Ocean

RYUKYU IS.

BONIN IS

TAIWAN

THAILAND

MARIANAS

WAKE I.

MARSHALL IS.

BURMA

PHILIPPINES

MALAYA

CAROLINE ISLANDS

NEW GUINEA

GILBERT IS.

REP. OF INDONESIA

ELLICE IS.

THE NEW YORK TIMES

AUSTRALIA

CHART NO. 2

our strong support, renouncing war as a method of settling disputes and abolishing Japanese military forces for these purposes.

WAR CRIMINALS

Allied policy also called for stern justice to war criminals and all those who were responsible for aggression. A famous section of the Potsdam Declaration reads as follows: "There must be eliminated for all time the authority and influence of those who have deceived and misled the people of Japan into embarking on world conquest, for we insist that a new order of peace, security and justice will be impossible until irresponsible militarism is driven from the world."

The United States fully concurred in this general statement. Together with the other Allies, we tried hundreds of Japanese from privates to generals—thousands if one includes the Russian trials—on charges of war atrocities. Many were executed or given long prison sentences. Perhaps the most famous American trial was that of General Yamashita in the Philippines, who was found guilty and executed for crimes committed under his command in the concluding period of the war. Most spectacular, however, were the long trials in Tokyo of some twenty-five top military and civilian leaders (twenty-eight originally), seven of whom were ultimately hanged including ex-Premier Hideki Tojo. One of the twenty-five, given the lightest sentence, subsequently became Foreign Minister, Mamoru Shigemitsu.

There were a few Americans who felt that these trials were setting a dangerous precedent and at least in some cases were based upon dubious law and morality. Was it possible, argued some, to discern accurately individual responsibility for the crimes being charged against the so-called Class A group, particularly in Japanese society? Those who favored the trials argued that however difficult, guilt must be established and the guilty punished as an obligation to our own war dead and a reminder to would-be aggressors in the future.

THE JAPANESE EMPEROR

The war crime trials brought one issue to the fore that split both American policy makers and American public opinion—the Japanese Emperor. One group agreed with the other Allies that the Emperor was defined as supreme sovereign of the Japanese state and had to be held responsible for the actions of his government. They warned that to allow the Emperor and the Imperial institution to go unpunished would be to leave the very core of militarism intact. The Imperial myth had been invoked by every ultra-nationalist and militarist group; his name had led the charge of suicidal troops. At no point had he taken serious action to stem the militarist tide.

But another group asserted with vigor that to oust the Japanese Emperor would be a serious political mistake and one not justified by the facts. This group was led by certain "Old Japan Hands," in contrast to the former element which had many "Old China Hands" among its supporters. It argued that in reality the Japanese Emperor had no personal power and was not responsible for state actions; indeed, he had personally opposed militarism, it was asserted, whenever his advisors would allow him to do so, albeit behind the scenes and to no avail. It was also contended that to remove the Emperor would jeopardize the entire Occupation by antagonizing some ninety per cent of the Japanese people, leading to a personalized Irredentist movement which most certainly would appear whenever the Occupation was over and might well sweep out all reforms in its wake. Rather, it was argued, use the Emperor on behalf of democracy and shift the Imperial institution into the kind of symbol represented by the British Monarchy. Needless to say, this latter group finally prevailed in what was undoubtedly the most important political decision made in the early period.

THE PURGE EDICTS

While the war crime trials were colorful and occasionally captured world attention, a much more broadly distributed punishment was carried out in the form of the purge edicts which began in January, 1946. In the course of the next several years, around two hundred thousand Japanese citizens were barred from public life and in some cases from important private occupations. The overwhelming majority of these were professional military men, but also included was a very high percentage of the top prewar conservative elite. Almost every veteran political party leader from the conservative groups was forced into retirement. While this retirement subsequently proved to be temporary rather than permanent, it nevertheless had important results. American policy served in some degree to recast the nature of Japanese conservative leadership. Legal power was denied the hard core of prewar professional politicians who had collaborated with the military and was given to men from the foreign office group who had some record of opposition to anti-Western trends. Thus Kijuro Shidehara, Shigeru Yoshida, and Hitoshi Ashida took over the reins of leadership in the postwar conservative parties.

The purge, of course, could not prevent the continuance of behind-the-scenes maneuvering and influence that had long been characteristic of Japanese politics. It did, however, weaken the conservatives sufficiently and cause enough disruption in their morale to make easier the passage of SCAP-sponsored legislation designed to alter Japanese society fundamentally. (SCAP stands for Supreme Commander of the Allied Powers and was used to designate both General MacArthur personally and the Occupation in general.) This was a period of radicalism for Japan, though radicalism largely in the American tradition, and one which has left its permanent mark upon Japanese society.

It is interesting to compare American tactics with Russian in this matter of dealing with those considered responsible for the war. The Russians were often exceedingly brutal by American standards; execution and enforced labor in the Soviet Union were the lot of hundreds of thousands in this category. Yet when it seemed desirable for strategic reasons, the Russians did not hesitate to "reindoctrinate" and use some ex-Fascists of relatively high rank. Perhaps they had had enough experience with political education to know that it could be very effective. Our policy, however, was curiously severe in its concept. We did not accept the idea of re-education in any part; rather we outlawed on a permanent basis those individuals considered guilty and, in the great majority of cases, guilt was established by category or association rather than on an individual basis. In reality, the Japanese purge was of relatively short duration, since depurging began on a large scale in 1949; within a few years practically all purgees were readmitted to public life. However, the program will continue to hold an interest to students of politics and psychology, especially when compared with possible alternatives.

THE DEMOCRATIZATION PROGRAM

Demilitarization, war crime trials, and purging were all essentially negative programs. The bulk of American energy during this early period was spent on more positive measures. We again played the role of revolutionaries in Asia, and on this occasion we had the opportunity and power to implant our ideas directly into policy: to shape Japanese institutions and to select Japanese leaders. Scholars will long try to decide how well we accomplished our objectives.

The American democratization program was certain to face a few fundamental problems. A kind of paradox is involved in attempting to establish democracy through foreign military government. In one sense, it can almost be said that Japanese politics under the Occupation reverted back to the Tokugawa period. General MacArthur's headquarters represented the *bakufu* or military administration in Tokyo, with MacArthur as the new *Shogun;* the Japanese government stood for the Imperial Court, which in the old days had resided at Kyoto and had done what it was told to do under the watchful eyes of the *bakufu.* The fact that Japan had had a long history of indirect rule and obscured responsibility may have made the American Occupation more acceptable but by the same token it made training for responsible government difficult.

On the one hand, the new Japanese political structure was to operate on the basis of the electorate's decision and in accordance with strict constitutional safeguards for individual liberties; on the other hand, SCAP had absolute power over any part of that government and did not hesitate on occasion to use it. No wonder the Japanese people were sometimes confused. Conservative Japanese governments were caused to pass the equivalent of a Wagner Labor Relations Act (much to their chagrin); but the score was evened when a later Socialist-led government was pushed into supporting the Japanese Taft-Hartley Law! Tutelage for democracy is never easy; foreign military tutelage undoubtedly complicates the problem.

The capacity of American society at this point to play a successful revolutionary role in Japan and its appropriateness as a prototype have not yet become clear. It was probably inevitable that the major reforms attempted would bear the strong imprint of American institutions and patterns. More specifically, the reform era represented the American New Deal, somewhat late and somewhat altered to Japanese requirements, but still strongly colored by that famous and recent epoch in American history. The questions of whether such a program could work effectively in Japan or, if it could, what modifications needed to be made and whether they were made are all points of vital importance. And with these questions, it is necessary to pose another: was democracy possible in Japan as we understood and knew that term, or at least, could there be a "Japanese-style democracy" that would still deserve the democratic label? The final answers to these questions cannot be given even yet. But before examining some hypotheses about this phase of our policy, let us look briefly at its major elements.

POLITICAL REFORM

The political reform program centered around the new Japanese Constitution of 1947, a document now under substantial conservative attack. In this case, as in many others, SCAP sought first to work through Japanese officials but finally felt forced to reject much of their product as too conservative and do a considerable share of the drafting itself. The resulting issue surrounding the Constitution therefore is whether or not it represents the real will of the Japanese people. Those who argue against it state that the Constitution was drafted essentially by foreigners at a time when Japan was not a sovereign state and had no real power of protest over its provisions. They insist that at least in some of its articles it lacks any conformity with the nature or needs of Japanese society and therefore must be amended or replaced. Those who now support the Constitution state that even though a considerable portion of it may have been foreign-drafted, it does represent the real interest and will of the Japanese people, as conservative-sponsored amendments would not, and this group also points out that there were some Japanese drafts that were equally radical, although they did not come from the government.

In any case, the Constitution of 1947 is in the great liberal tradition of the West, with the institutions it provides drawn from both British and American experience. The rather lengthy Preamble provides a fitting introduction to such a document, even if it borrows little from Japanese tradition. Could the American ideal be more adequately expressed for instance than in the following passage: "Government is a sacred trust of the people, the authority for which is derived from the people, the powers of which are exercised by the representatives of the people, and the benefits of which are enjoyed by the people"?

Under the new Constitution, the position of the Emperor is relegated legally to that of a symbol of unity rather than a sovereign and his duties are largely ceremonial. The essence of the new system is that of parliamentary government modified by the inclusion of a Supreme Court on the American model with the power of passing on the constitutionality of legislation. The upper house of the two-house Diet is called the House of Councillors, and unlike the old House of Peers it is wholly elected. The Cabinet is responsible to the Diet, or more precisely, to the lower house of the Diet. If it is not supported by the House of Representatives, it must either resign or dissolve the House of Representatives and call for new elections immediately.

The Constitution also includes one of the most comprehensive Bills of Rights to be found in any fundamental law. These rights, moreover, are absolute and not qualified as popular rights were in the old Constitution by the added proviso, "within the limits of the law."

The difference between this Constitution and the old Meiji Constitution of 1889 is not merely in the field of civil liberties, but in practically every aspect of government. As noted previously, the Meiji Constitution was drawn largely from Prussian experience (and subject to the same charge of foreign drafting, incidentally). It reflected the ideal of an Emperor-centered organic state, placing a high premium for its actual operation upon bureaucratic coordination and parliamentary dependency. Whatever the problems connected with drastic constitutional change, it is difficult to see how keeping the Meiji Constitution intact or making only minor modifications would have advanced the democratic cause. The trouble was not merely in the Meiji Constitution itself but also in the heritage connected with that Constitution, including the major concessions which even the Japanese prewar "liberals" had made on Constitutional theory. In taking this position, one is not forced to defend the present Constitution word by word, or to oppose any and all amendments. However, to contrast the Constitutional issues and arguments of today with those under the Meiji Constitution is itself a rather weighty argument supporting the basic type of change that took place.

Constitutional change was the broad framework for political democracy, but there were many additional measures taken. Rather extensive political decentralization was attempted, with local and prefectural government bolstered in its powers and responsibilities. Electoral reforms were carried out and woman suffrage was enacted, thereby more than doubling the number of voters. Some efforts at bureaucratic reform were also made. Thousands of Japanese officials from all echelons of government were taken to the United States and put into contact with various people in public and private life so that they might explore American methods and institutions first hand. Most of these American tours were short, of the exhausting ninety-day variety; but with modern means of transportation, a vast area could be covered before the weary teams returned home. It was impossible to assimilate everything, but pre-indocrination, interpreters, and various other aids were used and many Japanese articles and books testify to the value of these exchanges. Some trips, of course, were of longer duration and a different tempo.

ECONOMIC AND SOCIAL CHANGE

The proclivities and problems of American reform policies were also illustrated in the programs of economic and social change carried out under Occupational authority. The traditional Japanese family system was sharply attacked in a variety of ways, and equality for women was written into the new Japanese laws. Major changes in the educational system were ordered, affecting every aspect of that system including structure, curriculum, and basic objectives. The hope was that such actions would bring the home and the school into conformity with democratic values and actions.

Two additional reforms of key importance reveal some very interesting facets of American society in action in Asia. The land-reform program was one of the most radical undertaken up to that point in the Far East, yet it conformed in general with the American ideal of the family-owned farm. Inflation rendered the compensation formula for landlords almost meaningless and the program had the unplanned effect of bringing about a substantial change in the composition of the agrarian classes. In the so-called economic deconcentration program, another American ideal was pursued: the reduction of monopoly and encouragement of competition. But here, serious obstacles were met in the nature of Japanese society and ultimately this program settled for the reduction of certain family fortunes, a fairly strong attack upon the large cartels and trusts, and the establishment of anti-monopoly and trust laws patterned upon the American model.

The full effect of the American reform program as well as its wisdom are still being debated both in Japan and in the United States. The natural tendency for the Occupation at first to exaggerate its successes was followed by a more recent tendency to deprecate Occupation efforts, insisting that most changes that have occurred are merely the extension of prewar trends or that most of the reforms have only a superficial hold upon Japanese society and will soon disappear. Perhaps a position in between these two views is closest to the truth. There are many elements of contemporary Japan that still reflect the prewar period. At the same time, some of the changes either made or underway suggest an increasingly different Japanese society in the future, and not all of these by any means were implicit in the last stages of the prewar era. Perhaps the most substantial accomplishment of the Occupation was to shift the nature and power of pressure groups in Japanese society, and thereby produce many new possibilities in the domestic political scene. Under the reform program, the military class was decimated (at least for the present) and new groups such as organized labor were encouraged and allowed to expand. It remains to be seen whether such groups will support democratic values in the long run, but there can be no doubt that the tightly knit oligarchic controls characteristic of the prewar period have been decisively challenged.

One fact is clear about the past, whatever the future may hold. This first period found American policy receiving its greatest support coming from the Japanese liberals and those generally on the "left." Once more, we were an attraction for those who wanted to think in radical terms. The Japanese conservatives, on the other hand, now look back upon this period as one of their darkest and most dismal hours. They were not only powerless to stop what many of them considered to be foolish and dangerous actions; in some cases, as we have noted, they were forced to carry these into practice. Once certain ideological and political distinctions have been made, however, there remains one generalization which can be applied rather broadly with respect to Japanese attitudes in the early postwar period. Essentially, these attitudes were characterized by a rather high degree of self-criticism and another wave of eagerness to borrow and adapt from the West. Both of these factors encompassed many of the conservatives though naturally in somewhat different form and degree. Nevertheless, the period immediately after surrender was one of rather searching criticism of Japanese institutions and ideas. Led by an intellectual class that was at last free to speak its mind, the Japanese poured out their souls in articles, letters, and private conversations. Their analyses of past failures and shortcomings were by no means uniform, but there was little effort even in private to defend the past in bold and general terms. There was a search for new values, new concepts, and new institutions outside the framework of the Japanese past, and this undoubtedly assisted SCAP in its program of experimentation.

Policy Revision

After 1946, the United States gradually became aware of the fact that its original postwar premises concerning Asia and the world were no longer valid. We had foreseen one general trend, namely, the emergence of Asia as a dynamic world force and the end of the period when Asia had been merely the passive recipient of Western power. But we had counted upon a democratic China to serve as the great stabilizer and symbol of that Asia, and now the signs for Nationalist China were increasingly unfavorable. Indeed, all of Asia represented a power vaccum produced by the precipitous withdrawal or heavy reduction of Western power on the one hand and the almost pitiful weakness of the newly independent or reorganized Asian governments on the other. With political and economic unrest rampant in the area and the nationalist movements of South and Southeast Asia reaching a climax in many cases, with the old colonial powers their chief targets, we viewed the situation as critical. This was all the more true because our relations with the Soviet Union had rapidly deteriorated everywhere in the world, and we now strongly believed that the Soviet-led forces of world Communism would use any tactics to fill the power vacuum of Asia, building upon their footholds in China, north Korea, and other regions where they commanded some indigenous support. The era of the Cold War had begun and it affected our policy toward Japan as it did toward all other world areas.

In addition to factors connected with the external world, there were also factors relating directly to Japan that demanded attention. Two years after the war, the Japanese economy remained in the doldrums. Production was low and inflation was still rampant, producing a vicious price-wage spiral which threatened a complete collapse. In the fiscal year 1947, the index of mining and manufacturing production stood at only 43.2, the average of 1932-1936 representing 100. It must be remembered also that the population of Japan was steadily increasing. In November, 1945, the census showed a population of 72 million; after the large scale repatriations and postwar marriage boom, the population figures reached 80.5 million by 1948, or 21 per cent above the 1930-34 average. There were many statistical indications of the serious inflation. Perhaps the most graphic were comparative figures from the wholesale price and consumer price indices. Ministry of Finance figures using 1 as the index figure for the 1934-36 average, were 128 and 171 respectively for 1948. Such figures may not be very reliable but there can be no doubting the trend or its proportions.

These developments had an obvious effect upon the democratizition experiment, a fact that could not long escape American attention. They were also related to the costs that the American taxpayer had to assume in connection with keeping the Japanese people alive. Our contributions in all forms were close to four hundred million dollars a year. It is not surprising, therefore, that SCAP began somewhat belatedly to abandon its laissez-faire attitude toward the Japanese economy. At first, we had taken the position that the Japanese themselves had to straighten out an economic mess for which they were to blame. We stood by more or less idly during the early period while the situation grew progressively worse. Many wartime controls were dropped or poorly enforced. Military stockpiles were dumped on the market, and "black market" operations accounted for up to fifty per cent of individual expenditures. The government engaged in deficit financing by means of an enormous increase in the amount of Bank of Japan notes in circulation. The interactive effect among these factors was cumulative, and the economic situation, bad as it was, was threatened by further deterioration.

SCAP had the authority to intervene directly in the Japanese economy. It finally began to use that authority cautiously after Japanese government efforts proved insufficient. Beginning in 1947, we used various pressures in an effort to restore production, particularly in coal mining, and also to improve food collection from the farms. We were now exhorting the Japanese people, officials and citizens alike, to make heroic efforts to rehabilitate themselves. The new key word for American policy in Japan was "Recovery." This drive led up to the famous Nine-Point Stabilization Program, announced at the close of 1948. Through this program the United States sought to restore stability to the Japanese economy by such measures as a balanced budget, improved tax collection, credit restrictions, wage and price controls, trade expansion, production increases, and improved food collection. The Dodge Plan, as it was commonly called, achieved considerable success, and 1949 represented a year of relative price stability and accelerated recovery in many spheres of the economy, particularly in production.

There were a number of continuing problems, to be sure, and some were aggravated by the policy shift. Unemployment rose at first; and there was a definite relation between deflation and the scarcity of capital for reconstruction purposes. However, the Korean War, which broke out in June 1950, was to provide a major fillip to the Japanese economy. Japan served as a key center for American procurement demands, and economic recovery was greatly assisted. Indeed, the decade beginning in 1950 was a decade of phenomenal economic expansion for Japan, far surpassing the expectations of even the most optimistic observers. The Japanese rate of growth has been among the highest in the world. Along with West Germany, Japan illustrated that massive destruction may abet modernization, if there can be substantial external assistance, coupled with internal know-how, experience, and cultural adaptation to modern industrialism. American aid to Japan may have totalled as much as four billion dollars, although much technical assistance really cannot be figured in monetary terms.

REPARATIONS AND TRADE

Our efforts to support Japanese recovery extended into the field of Japanese foreign as well as domestic policy. Both reparations and trade policies were involved. At first, we had favored heavy reparations as some measure of repayment for damages and as an insurance against future Japanese ascendancy in the Asian area. The Pauley Report on Japanese Reparations issued in 1948 was a clear expression of this point of view. But the so-called Johnston Committee Report which followed shortly took a very much less drastic position, scaling down earlier recommendations for the dismantlement of heavy industry. American policy was moving toward the view that large reparations would have to be paid directly or indirectly by the United States, if the Japanese economy were not to be ruined. Our new position on reparations caused immediate friction with such countries as China, the Philippines, and many others that were demanding full compensation for Japanese wartime damage.

At the same time, Japanese trade began to assume a new shape. A very large percentage of trade was conducted with the United States as a natural result of American credits, the development of an intricate system of patent sharing and other forms of industrial interaction, and the drastic reduction of the northeast Asian market for Japan. In addition, Japan began to look to South and Southeast Asia with our encouragement. We urged the Japanese to rehabilitate themselves with the non-Communist countries of Asia so as to form an effective interaction for peace and prosperity. It was not easy to overcome the anti-Japanese sentiment in this area as a result of the wartime actions of Japanese. Immediately the charge was raised that we were supporting the old idea of Japan as a "workshop" for Asia, a concept which had complemented past aggression. The American answer was that Japan now posed no military threat whatsoever, but could make a basic contribution to those Asian countries desiring economic development.

In short, our new approach to Japan represented a striking contrast in many respects to the initial program of 1945. The new emphasis was defended, of course, in terms of our own self-interest. Its striking characteristic nonetheless was the extraordinary generosity that it represented, considering the bitterness of a few years earlier. Some of our allies even complained that a country seemed to be treated better if it had lost a war against the United States than if it had won a war with us. The United States was now playing the role of middleman between Japan and the outside world, supporting strongly the interests of the former. And as we advanced the cause of Japan abroad, we reconsidered priorities in the domestic scene. Wherever reform measures seemed to threaten recovery, they were restructured or abandoned. This was true not only of reparations but also of our economic deconcentration program and of various other measures. Our domestic program for Japan was now more conservative, in closer harmony with developments in the United States.

JAPANESE REFLECTIONS OF THE NEW ERA

It was now the turn of the Japanese conservatives to rejoice and the liberal and radical left to show their dismay. Despite its efforts to maintain an official nonpartisan position, SCAP was inevitably drawn into Japanese domestic politics. Now our favoritism for the conservatives, particularly the Liberals, became more pronounced. This led to frustration on the part of the Socialists, because they could not attack the Occupation openly and they had no way in which to meet its power. While certain broad trends in Japanese political and economic policy turned against them, they were forced to stand by lamenting the fact but without any real hope of capturing control. It was in this area that disagreement between the position of the United States and that of the

Japanese socialists came to a focus. This remains a serious and unsolved problem. We are still estranged from the main stream of the Japanese socialist movement.

Once again, however, setting political differences aside, a general trend can be observed. Together with the re-evaluation of American policy toward Japan, there occurred some re-evaluation on the part of the Japanese themselves. A retreat could be noted from the intensive self-criticism of the immediate postwar period. Certain "excesses" of American policy began to be criticized, and the considerable shift in that policy helped to confirm doubts of American omniscience that were now strong in all political circles. A growing disillusionment on the part of the Japanese intelligentsia was reflected in their journals. These trends did not represent any virulent anti-Americanism, nor indeed did the pendulum swing violently away from a psychology of dependence upon the West in general and the United States in particular. Through its spokesmen and chief organs, the Japanese people expressed gratitude for American economic aid and general benevolence. To most Japanese, we were still the *oyakata* (master or benefactor in a paternalist sense). But at the more articulate levels of Japanese society, nationalism had commenced its own recovery.

THE SAN FRANCISCO TREATY

The Korean War came as a great shock to Americans and quite possibly to the Communists also, who may have anticipated an easy over-running of South Korea without American defense of that area. But the United States decided to defend the South Korean Republic and obtained the support of the United Nations in one of the most crucial decisions since World War II. Immediately, military strategic considerations became paramount in American Far Eastern policy. American bases in Japan were the vital arteries through which flowed men and materials to Korea and from which came our aerial attacks upon the enemy. Okinawa was also of great importance. These were our "privileged sanctuaries," as some have tended to forget.

There was now great apprehension that the cold war would become really hot, and the Western nations watched Russian actions closely from day to day. It was in this atmosphere of world tension and bloodshed that the United States began negotiations with Japan and the non-Communist Allies for the end of the Occupation and the restoration of full Japanese sovereignty. Those negotiations were conducted primarily in early 1951. On September 8, a peace treaty with Japan was signed by forty-eight nations at San Francisco, coming into effect officially on April 28, 1952.

The United States faced many thorny problems in connection with this treaty, and the policies which it formulated concerning them set the tone of the period. Perhaps the key issues were three in number, all interrelated in some degree. Questions relating to the future security of Japan, and through Japan of the United States, were naturally given special emphasis. Japan as the only industrialized society of Asia was regarded as a likely target of Soviet aggression. It was also regarded by American officials as a vital link and northern anchor in our island defense perimeter around continental Asia. Increasingly during the period, the concept of an island "cordon sanitaire" had appealed to many Americans. The theory was that through such a defensive device we could make maximum use of American air power; and by maintaining bases from Japan through Okinawa and the Philippines, we could deter any aggression stemming from the mainland and protect the Pacific in depth. Certainly it was clear that without the Japanese bases, it would have been extremely difficult if not impossible to have fought the Korean War, and that war was not yet finished.

Consequently, the United States leaned heavily toward one of the two broad alternatives open on this issue, namely, toward the plan of a bilateral security treaty with Japan, providing for the continuance of American bases in that country and looking toward the gradual buildup of Japanese defense forces. The other broad alternative was that of a multilateral guarantee of Japanese territorial integrity by all the major powers, possibly through the United Nations, and a continued emphasis upon Japanese demilitarization. Those who favored the latter policy advanced many arguments. They contended that if Japan took to rearmament readily, it would create immediate repercussions throughout Asia, both in its Communist and non-Communist segments. The memory of World War II was still vivid. Such a development would also threaten Japanese democracy, a fragile flower at best, in the light of the long militarist tradition of that society. If on the other hand, Japan showed great reluctance to rearm, its value as a military ally would be dubious, and the resulting friction within Japan over rearmament would actually weaken the country as a political and ideological ally of Western democracy.

With the Korean War still active, however, and the Stalinist "get tough" policy finding expression in various forms, the Truman administration rejected these arguments in favor of the considerations outlined earlier. Mr. Dulles, its representative on the Japan negotiations, emphasized from the beginning the right of Japan to create a self-defense force to ward off aggression, insisting that this need not produce a revived Japanese militarism. Coupled with this defense of Japanese rearmament was an American offer to retain bases and troops in Japan, at least until such time as Japan could complete her own security arrangements. This became the basis for the Security Treaty which was signed with Japan at the same time as the Peace Treaty of September, 1951. In the Peace Treaty itself, Japan was given the right of individual or collective self-defense as a sovereign nation; it was also provided that bilateral or multi-lateral agreements with Japan could be made, permitting the stationing or retention of foreign troops in Japanese territory.

Another issue of importance was the degree to which Japan should be held to the "democratization" reforms of the Occupation. There were Americans and others who felt that Japan should be required to guarantee that she would not abandon those basic reforms which the Occupation had engineered, and it was also suggested that some form of continued supervision might be desirable to insure this fact. In the final analysis, the United States rejected this general line. Few stipulations regarding Japanese politics and economics were written into the Treaty, and these were almost exclusively of an international character. War criminals convicted by Allied Courts, for instance, could not be freed by Japan without the decision of those imposing the sentence. But basically, we decided on a "soft treaty" in this, as in most other respects. Our position was that Japan should become a fully sovereign nation and that any continued supervision or serious restrictions on her domestic policies might backfire. Behind this reasoning probably lay the fact also that some of those early reforms, such as the anti-war Article in the Constitution, no longer met with our own official approval, and we were not unwilling to see some changes made.

American policy toward Japan as exemplified in this Treaty did not always coincide with the policies of the other Allied nations. In the rather lengthy negotiations that preceded the San Francisco Treaty Conference, the United States consulted the nations represented on the Far Eastern Commission and some other powers, including of course the Japanese themselves. It was generally agreed that a treaty structured along the general lines discussed earlier should be ratified and rapidly put into effect. At the same time, however, there was little likelihood of American-Soviet agreement upon any Japanese Treaty. When the USSR rather unexpectedly stated that it would attend the San Francisco Conference with Czechoslovakia and Poland, we retained the view that this was a Conference to ratify not negotiate a treaty and acted accordingly, holding Communist oratory and delaying tactics to a minimum.

No important concessions were made to Japan with respect to territorial issues. Here we retained the wartime agreements but in a form that permitted some flexibility. Japan was caused to renounce her rights to Taiwan and the Pescadores but the recipient was not specified. This procedure was also followed with respect to the Kuriles, southern Sakhalin and adjacent islands, the mandated territories, Antarctic regions, and the Spratly and Paracel Islands. The article pertaining to the Bonin Islands and the Ryukyus, including Okinawa, was somewhat differently worded and will be discussed later.

Perhaps the softness of the Treaty was most apparent in connection with the reparations issue, and this caused some resentment among certain of our Allies. Some states, particularly the Philippines and Indonesia, wanted an ironclad guarantee on reparations written into the Treaty. In the final draft, however, there was only the pledge that Japan would negotiate on this matter with the Allied Powers desiring to do so. While the Article on reparations recognized the obligation of Japan to pay, it also stated that "the resources of Japan are not presently sufficient, if it is to maintain a viable economy, to make complete reparation for all such damage and suffering and at the same time meet its other obligations." The weakness implicit in this and other statements in the Article antagonized some of the Southeast Asians and jeopardized their support of the entire treaty.

Ultimately, however, the Treaty was accepted by all those present at San Francisco except the Communist bloc, although subsequently there were problems of ratification in Indonesia and the Philippines. In the spring of 1952, Japan was at peace with the Western democracies and their Asian allies, and she was shortly able to adjust her relations satisfactorily with most of the Asian neutrals. These developments were a source of great satisfaction to the American government. In the course of seven years, our policy toward Japan had undergone some amazing changes in an attempt to follow world trends, Occupation experience, and Japanese pressures. We had emerged as a champion of a "rehabilitated Japan" seeking recognition and equality for her at the world council tables. More than this, we were now looking to Japan as potentially one of our foremost political and military allies in Asia. We had offered her an alliance based upon continued economic and military assistance from us, contingent upon her own efforts toward self-defense. This was certainly a monumental shift from the days when we had promised to enforce the complete disarmament of Japan and called upon her to find salvation in pacifism. But it was at least equally striking that in considerably less than a decade, our general treatment of Japan had run the full gamut. From being a pariah, she had become an ally. This would not have been likely without the particular international trends and those generally favorable attitudes which have been previously discussed.

POSITION ON THE EVE OF INDEPENDENCE

It would be very misleading to imply that all Japanese had become enthusiastic about American policy. On the contrary, issues connected with this third phase of postwar American policy had continued and in some respects exacerbated earlier antagonisms. Among some of our policy critics were Japanese whose personal relations with Americans were friendly and who regarded themselves as closer to us in an ideological sense than a number of the official "pro-American" forces. Again, the cleavage was largely one that demarcated the liberal and radical left from the conservatives of all shades and hues. The former generally held to the desirability of an "over-all" peace, including a settlement with the Communists, continued support for Japanese demilitarization, and opposition to post-treaty American military bases. The average Japanese conservative, on the other hand, supported an immediate Treaty, alliance with the West, some rearmament, and acceptance of American bases. Within both groups, there were complex differences. Actually, the San Francisco Peace Treaty produced a serious split in Socialist ranks; the Right Wing was willing to accept it but opposed the Security Treaty, and the Left Wing opposed both treaties. In conservative ranks, also, opinion differed on the degree and timing of rearmament. Not all Japanese conservatives by any means were "pro-American," however that term may be defined.

Once again, a general condition overshadowing political differences within Japan served to keynote the period. The rise of Japanese nationalism on all sides and in many forms was the most pronounced characteristic of Japan during this third and final phase of the Occupation. Such a trend was of course inevitable in some degree after a long period of foreign occupation and control. The pendulum was swinging back. But the fascinating aspect of this new nationalism was the endless variety of its forms. In the prewar period, Japanese nationalism had been largely under the control of the conservatives. Now it was also a weapon of all elements on the left. This is one of the most significant developments in Japanese politics, and we shall deal with it more fully at a later point. Here we need only note the interesting fact that the shift in Japanese attitudes within seven years had been no less striking than the changes in American policy and, in part at least, an accompaniment to them. From intensive self-criticism and an attitude of dependency, the Japanese had moved to a renewed spirit of nationalism which ranged over a wide ideological sector but found some common denominator in its insistence upon Japanese sovereignty and independence.

Contemporary Issues

THE CURRENT WORLD BACKGROUND

Relations between the United States and Japan today can be more fully appreciated when viewed in the context of the modern world. What are some of the most basic trends of our times? First, the age of Western domination of the world is ending. Everywhere, new states are struggling to emerge and survive as Western imperialism fades away. Many of these states, especially in the Asian-African area, are having grave difficulties. Without sufficient time for an orderly evolution and marked by multiple deficiencies, these societies are occupied in a desperate battle against poverty, instability, and weakness. Generally, they represent regions of discontent, areas of political volatility, and power vacuums that threaten world peace.

It is natural that most of these new states gravitate toward "neutralism." Neutralism or non-alignment is an expression of nationalism in foreign policy. It is also a mid-twentieth century method of limiting commitments in international politics while maximizing the benefits derived from their status as a "floating vote." Both the democratic and the communist blocs have recognized the importance of the developing states. In this setting, moreover, Japan is one of the few non-Western states equipped by culture, ideology, and timing to play a unique role on behalf of the democratic bloc in terms of economic and technical aid. Together with Germany, Japan can be classified as a society that entered the modernization stream somewhat later than the first pioneers, but a society that has now had a legacy of nearly one hundred years of experimentation with and acculturation to industrialization. Today, Japan represents an advanced industrial society, albeit one with various premodern remnants, many of which have been adapted to the new order. But to some extent, this fact gives Japan increased compatibility with the Afro-Asian world and enhances her opportunities for constructive interaction.

Another trend of our times is the increasingly interdependent nature of the world. A major paradox exists today. Nationalism is still a vital force everywhere, and many peoples are striving to build nation-states where previously only tribalism or foreign rule existed. Nationalism has even survived communism. Indeed, it has flourished under that ideology as both the Soviet Union and Communist China make abundantly clear. At the same time, however, the age of classical nationalism—the totally sovereign state possessing no broader organic ties—is over. Today, various forms of regionalism and internationalism are indispensable. Nationalism can only be preserved now if it can be encompassed by some broader economic-political framework. It is in this general context that both the rationale and the stresses of the American-Japanese alliance must be seen.

Unfortunately, this is a lawless age. Never in human history have there been so many people in such intimate contact and with so few accepted rules governing their conduct. And international law is in a sad state of disrepair. Even national law has limited validity in many areas. Thus this is an exceedingly dangerous age, one in which the threat of war is still omnipresent despite the frightful cost that war now exacts. As a result, security issues cannot be ignored. We have not been able to reach any broad agreement, however, on the best methods of protecting the security and preserving the peace, even at the national level. It should not be surprising that these questions raise some thorny problems among allies. Military issues are the most complex and ticklish aspect of current American-Japanese relations.

Finally, this is the age of the common man. His beliefs, his commitments, his strengths are critical to every state, no matter what its ideological base. Today he will demand material progress. The common man of the world now knows how a man can live, the standard of living available to modern societies. Inevitably, he will exercise increasing pressure upon his leaders, no matter what ideological banners they fly, to provide him with a better life. No government can afford to ignore such pressures over the long run. This fact too has a direct bearing upon American-Japanese relations, because the Japanese common man is rising more rapidly than most others.

Present Goals of Japanese Foreign Policy

Against these trends, how are the goals of Japanese foreign policy to be defined? In setting forth the goals of any state, it is easy to oversimplify and to minimize inconsistencies. Japan presents a special hazard because that country does not have a "bipartisan" foreign policy. A socialist minority takes violent exception to the major policies pursued by a conservative majority. It is possible, however, to suggest several overriding considerations which govern present Japanese foreign policy and carry some measure of agreement across political lines. In the first place, Japan must give priority to economic considerations. Foreign policy must be used as an instrument of advancing the Japanese economy whereever possible.

A second consideration strongly felt in Japan today is the attainment of a more "independent" foreign policy which will permit Japan greater initiative and flexibility in her foreign relations and allow her to gain more standing in the world. Japan is still emerging from an era of subordination to American power. The Socialists of Japan insist that only through neutralism can Japan attain true independence. The conservatives do not believe that the goal of greater independence requires any severance of bonds with the West, and especially with the United States. Theirs is the call for partnership rather than subordination. Whether the conservatives are willing to assume the responsibilities of full partnership—and whether the United States is prepared to grant it—are important questions.

These are goals implicit in the situation of Japan, affecting citizen and policymaker alike. In the broadest sense, however, Japan represents a society where the primary goal remains undefined, a society in search of a purpose in the world. The certainty of the prewar period has been replaced by a strong element of doubt. What should take the place of the old messianic missions, the former claims of racial and cultural superiority? In the presence of doubts over fundamental questions like these, a mood of restlessness characterizes Japan, and especially the postwar generation. This restlessness may be conducive to creativity, or it may lead mainly to instability and a type of nihilism, Japanese-style. But it cannot be ignored.

ECONOMIC ISSUES

Since the Korean War, the Japanese economy has surprised all observers by its rate of growth. In the decade after 1950, the economic growth rate for Japan averaged an amazing 9% per annum. In the late years in the decade, it was even higher. By 1961, Japanese industrial production was three times greater than the peak prewar figure. Foreign currency reserves amounted to two billion dollars. Compared to the top prewar figures, the standard of living for the average Japanese had risen 30-40%. These are but a few indications of the recent prosperity that Japan has enjoyed.

It is possible to overemphasize the economic improvement. The Japanese living standard still does not compare with that of Western Europe, although the normal comparison for a Japanese to make is with his own earlier experience. The prosperity is uneven, and there are still depressed groups and classes in Japan. There are also some basic problems in the Japanese economy that do not lend themselves to easy solution. The Japanese population is now ninety-three million and, if present trends continue, it will not level off until it reaches at least one hundred and ten million. The present land area of Japan is equal to that of the state of California, and less than 20% of the land is arable. Yet 40% of the Japanese population is still employed primarily in agriculture. Each family must farm an incredibly small acreage.

In this situation, industrial expansion is a necessity, not a luxury. The past rate of industrial development has absorbed the surplus rural population. The total farm population has been reduced by nearly 6% in the five-year period between 1955 and 1960. It has also been possible for the Japanese farmer to share in prosperity. In part, this is the result of six bumper crops in recent years, continuous advances in scientific agriculture that have increased yields, and a government policy relatively generous in fixing rice prices. But it is also the result of opportunities for a large number of farm families to obtain subsidiary income through part-time (or part-family) industrial labor. Mechanization of agriculture, now rapidly advancing in Japan, has abetted this by reducing the need for hand labor on the farm.

In the next few years, over one million additional workers per year will enter the labor market in Japan. Industry must expand to absorb these workers in addition to offering subsidiary income to the agrarian population. Thus far, this has been successfully accomplished and, indeed, some labor shortages exist today.

One must also reckon with the basic structure of Japanese industry.

It resembles a pyramid with a broad base composed of a myriad of small and medium industries narrowing to a few giant concerns at the apex. Small and medium industry has played a major role in the rapid and successful industrialization process of modern Japan. It has enabled that society to make maximum use of its built-in resources, to utilize selected cultural forces on behalf of modernization. Yet that industry has its own problems. At present, about 60% of all Japanese industrial workers are employed in these small and medium industries, and it is unlikely that this percentage will be greatly lowered in the foreseeable future. To raise efficiency and to improve working conditions in this segment of the Japanese economy is one of the most important and difficult challenges confronting the nation.

The process of rapid growth requires keeping various parts of the economy in a sort of moving equilibrium. The high rate of investment may create excess capacity at some points and leave bottlenecks elsewhere. Expanding incomes may lead to inflation. And a country so dependent upon foreign trade cannot allow its imports to expand more rapidly than its exports. Thus, from time to time, the Japanese government has had to exercise economic controls over domestic credit and foreign trade in order to maintain economic health. While the high growth rate is partly the cause of economic strains and stresses, it also makes it easier to bring about whatever adjustment is needed, since excess capacity will not long be excess, and demand for labor keeps growing. In view of these and other problems, it is perhaps understandable that the phenomenal prosperity of Japan has confounded most experts. A persistent note of caution, even pessimism, has surrounded postwar predictions on the Japanese economy. Even now, the question "Can it last?" is recurrent at home and abroad. Thus far it has lasted, and the Japanese government is deeply committed to its continuance. The conservatives, somewhat defensive on issues of foreign policy, recognize that their political strength is heavily dependent upon domestic prosperity. In the general elections of 1960, the Liberal Democratic campaign slogan might well have been "You never had it so good, but we'll make it better!" In the course of that campaign, Prime Minister Ikeda promised the Japanese people that the national income would be doubled in ten years, and that in the same period they would attain a social security system equal to that of the advanced West. As initial installments on these promises, the conservatives pledged increased expenditures on housing, roads, and social security. There can be no doubt that the Japanese conservatives, mindful of a growing opposition and of the mood of their people, have accepted the welfare state as a legitimate national goal and have realized that continued prosperity is crucial to their retention of power. In the age of the common man Japanese prosperity is both an economic and a political necessity.

UNITED STATES-JAPAN TRADE AND ECONOMIC RELATIONS

To accomplish its promises, the Japanese government plans to maintain economic expansion at roughly the rate of 9% per year. This will require continuous vigilance. Guards must be posted against excessive inflation. Greater efficiency and balance must be achieved throughout Japanese industry. But above all, the pattern of expanding external trade must be continued. Despite the importance of the expanding domestic market, growth of the Japanese economy is highly dependent upon a steady increase of foreign trade. Japan must import about 80% of her industrial raw materials and some 20% of her foodstuffs. For Japan, continued trade expansion will hinge on many factors, but especially economic conditions in, and the accessibility of, the non-communist world. In this, as in other respects, the position of the United States is crucial.

As suggested earlier, the United States contributed greatly to the postwar recovery of Japan. In the initial postwar period, about $1,750 million was loaned Japan through the Civilian Supply Program, the assistance for Economic Rehabilitation in Occupied Areas, and the Surplus Property assistance program. The repayment of these loans was arranged only in 1961, with the United States settling for a sum of $490 million dollars or slightly over one-fourth to be paid over fifteen years at a compound interest of 2.5%. If all forms of American aid or financial support to Japan in the postwar period were totalled, however, the figure would be very much higher. Special procurement demand for military purposes at one point during the Korean War reached five hundred million dollars in a single year. While such expenditures have tapered off in recent years, substantial sums will be spent there so long as the United States maintains bases in Japan.

One result of extensive American assistance was the gravitation of the Japanese economy toward the United States. Other factors certainly contributed to this, notably the abrupt loss of northeast Asian markets, and the various obstacles—political and economic—to economic intercourse with southern Asia and Europe. In any case, Japanese-American economic relations have been both close and important in terms of trade, investment, and the transfer of technical know-how. Today, nearly one-third of all Japanese trade is with the United States, and the volume of that trade has skyrocketed. In 1960, Japan exported over $1,100 million of goods to the United States and purchased over $1,300 million of goods from her. Economic ties go far beyond trade. Some 80% of the one billion dollars of foreign investment in Japan is American capital, and there are some indications that the American market for Japanese investments has barely been tapped. In addition, about 1,350 agreements have been reached between Japanese and American industry regarding patent-sharing and other forms of exchange. This is an extraordinarily intimate and substantial economic relation for two countries to have with each other.

Inevitably, problems have arisen along with the many benefits. Japanese expansion into the American market has been extremely rapid, especially in certain fields. When Japanese textiles poured into the United States in the mid-1950's, major protests were fourthcoming from American producers. Certain southern states passed legislation discriminatory in intent. From New England came demands for fixed quotas or higher tariffs. Fearful of serious consequences, Japan cooperated in instituting a voluntary quota system whereby items "especially liable to compete with American products" would be restricted in volume. This system, in effect since 1956, did temporarily reduce American demands for protection. In 1960-61, however, another drive against Japanese textiles was mounted, with labor threatening a boycott of Japanese goods. The American argument can be summarized as follows: The American taxpayers financed new Japanese machinery, helping to rebuild the Japanese textile industry. The low Japanese wage level and this new machinery make Japanese imports possible at prices which American industry cannot possibly meet. While there is need for a sound Japanese economy, the American textile industry, which is already in grave trouble, should not have to bear a disproportionate share of the burden. The voluntary quota system cannot be enforced adequately, and in any case, it commences from too high a level.

The Japanese answer can also be put succinctly: American producers and workers exaggerate Japanese competition. All foreign textile imports into the United States amount to only 6% of domestic production, and the United States exports more textiles than are imported. Moreover, the Japanese share of imports has actually declined in recent years. Japan, enforcing the quota system, has dropped from 70% of the cotton textile imports in 1956 to 23% in 1961. Hong Kong, India, and Pakistan, having no such limitation, threaten to capture the American market. The unfair competition of Japanese "cheap labor" is also exaggerated. If wages are related to productivity, the labor cost differential between Japan and the United States is greatly narrowed. In broader terms, moreover, Japan normally buys several hundred million dollars more from the United States yearly than she sells to it. Japan imports approximately five hundred million dollars worth of agricultural commodities from the United States yearly. Japan therefore has a payments problem, since it is very difficult to earn dollars in other areas or ways, especially since the decline of procurement demand.

Since 1934, American trade policy in general has been directed toward lowering trade barriers, and American tariff levels have been greatly reduced. Stressing her own example, the United States has urged other countries to follow the same policy, on the basic theory that expanding foreign trade benefits all parties. In recent years, American trade has expanded rapidly, both in exports and imports. The result has been a rise in the demand for protection by those industries affected by imports. It has not yet been strong enough to reverse the basic policy, but specific cases like that of Japanese textiles threaten to undermine the general objective of trade expansion. The tuna industry, the pottery industry, and others have also protested vigorously. The Japanese in turn raise the question of how they are to meet the import requirements of rapid economic expansion if European nations discriminate against them by applying Article 35 of GATT (the General Agreement on Tariffs and Trade), thereby denying them most-favored-nation treatment; if political obstacles prevent their trade with China; and if their trade with the United States in the most promising fields is curbed. Can the slogan "Trade not Aid" be effectuated?

Several approaches to this problem are now being made. At the international level, the members of GATT are attempting to provide for an orderly flow of textiles between consuming and producing countries. And in conjunction with Prime Minister Ikeda's visit to the United States in June 1961, an announcement was made of the formation of a United States-Japan Committee on Trade and Economic Affairs. This Committee, consisting of various Cabinet level officials from both countries, will meet at least once a year with the purpose of discussing basic problems affecting trade, considering means of promoting broader economic collaboration, and exchanging views on the economic assistance programs of the two countries.

Behind the establishment of this committee lie issues other than Japanese imports to the United States. American producers have long complained about Japanese protectionism and various onerous restrictions in connection with foreign investment in Japan. The pressure upon Japan to abandon or reduce trade and investment barriers has grown stronger as Japanese prosperity has continued. The Japanese government has finally taken cognizance of these complaints and promised a program of gradual liberalization. However, there will undoubtedly be recurrent issues in these regards which the joint Committee should consider.

There is also the vitally important issue of assistance to the less developed areas. To the United States, this is of great political importance; to Japan, it is of both political and economic concern. Approximately 45% of Japanese trade is with less developed countries and this trade accounts for nearly 10% of the Japanese gross national product. Consequently, Japan has a real stake in the economic progress of these areas. She has long desired a triangular relationship involving American capital, Japanese technical know-how, and the needs (and products) of the late-developing areas. For its part, the United States has wanted Japan to invest more of its own capital in development projects in other countries.

By the end of 1960, Japan had extended some 665 million dollars in credits and pledges and an additional 100 million dollars in direct private investment. Moreover, Japan was committed to the payment of over one billion dollars in reparations mainly in services and materials in a period of from ten to twenty years. The United States would like to see loans to underdeveloped countries extended on a long term low interest rate basis without being linked to the donor's exports. It would hope that each of the advanced nations, including Japan, would contribute 1% of its gross national product to the cause of economic development. For Japan, this would amount to about 400 million dollars annually. Japan participated in the Development Assistance Group as the sole non-Western member, and now belongs to its successor, a subsidiary of the Organization for Economic Cooperation and Development. How fully she will participate in the economic assistance program remains to be seen.

Clearly, economic relations are crucial to the future of the American-Japanese cooperation. The forces of depression and protectionism could badly damage or destroy the common interest. On the other hand, the continuance of present trends could produce an era of even greater interaction and mutual advantage. Optimists believe that in the next decade, American-Japanese trade could treble, private investments and contractual agreements could greatly expand, and new methods of cooperation in aiding the backward areas could be developed. Whichever the path, economic relations are a central determinant to the future of American-Japanese good will.

CHINA POLICY

Before World War II, the China-Manchuria area accounted for 15-18% of the total Japanese trade, and in a great variety of ways, this vast region was vital to the Japanese economy. Today, Japanese trade with China is negligible. Many businessmen in Japan are not willing to accept this as a permanent situation. They recognize, of course, that political circumstances have greatly altered, and old trade patterns would not necessarily be duplicated. They are also aware of the possibility that China trade might never be as important to Japan as it once was. However, they believe that Japan could furnish chemical fertilizer, machinery, and other items needed by China more cheaply than either the Soviet bloc or Western Europe. These businessmen acknowledge that the Chinese Communists frequently have attached political strings to economic arrangements, but they maintain that if China trade supports a healthy, expanding Japanese economy, it will, on balance, help the cause of democracy. They would also point to the expanding trade between Communist China and other non-communist nations such as Great Britain and West Germany.

Skepticism remains in other quarters that the China trade will ever be significant for Japan. The already established and politically congruous trade contacts with the Soviet bloc, the uncertain ability of China to pay for large-scale Japanese trade, and the basic political obstacles are all cited as warranting pessimism. Other Japanese have envisaged an awkward situation whereby trade having been built up to a meaningful level, the Chinese Communists would use this to extract political concessions. Whatever weight there is in these arguments, the balance of Japanese political pressure has been strongly in favor of China trade. In an era when any trade expansion is important, Japan is prepared to welcome even modest improvements in Japanese-Chinese economic relations.

Pressure for improved relations between Japan and Communist China comes not merely from portions of the business community and for economic reasons, although such pressure is especially significant within the ruling conservative party. China policy is an intensely political issue in Japan, as it is in the United States, with the trend of the pressures reversed. Important Japanese pressure groups give their support to recognition of the Communist government as the only government of China, admission of Communist China into the United Nations and other international circles, and acceptance of the Chinese Communist position on a number of other issues. Politically, such pressure groups include all the socialists and a portion of the conservatives. In socio-economic terms, intellectual-student groups, organized labor, and selective professional-business elements are all involved.

Despite these mounting pressures, however, relations between Japan and Communist China have thus far been rather minimal and productive of many problems. For a time after the Korean War Peking appeared to solicit Japanese support through a moderately friendly policy. Private trade agreements were concluded, and repatriation of Japanese from China was arranged on a mutually satisfactory basis. By the spring of 1958, however, the Chinese Communists had switched to a "get tough" policy. The immediate issue was a refusal of the Japanese government to grant diplomatic privileges to a visiting Chinese trade mission and an incident involving the tearing down of a Chinese Communist flag. All trade was abruptly halted by the Communists and existing contracts were cancelled. A violent campaign of denunciation against the Japanese government was conducted. Epithets like "reactionary," "Fascist," and "running dog of American Imperialism" were used. The Communist leaders intensified their campaign to separate the Japanese government and people, employing the cultural mission technique. Hundreds of Japanese from all categories were invited to China, and most were given the red carpet treatment. Peking appeared to score its greatest triumph when it persuaded the late Inejiro Asanuma, then head of the Japan

Socialist Party, to sign a joint declaration proclaiming American imperialism a common enemy of the Chinese and Japanese people.

Cultural diplomacy, or as the Communists sometimes call it, "people to people diplomacy," has scored gains for Peking in Japan as elsewhere. Articles, interviews, and speeches by returnees have been generally favorable to the mainland regime, and these have been disseminated widely. Such gains, however, have been offset to a considerable extent by the "get tough" policy. Peking attacks on the Japanese government have boomeranged, supporting the conservative charges that Communist China seeks to interfere in Japanese internal affairs. Moreover, Peking now seems to be convinced that the Japanese Socialists will not come to power in the near future. Consequently, more attention is currently being given to certain conservative factions, and there are indications that the Peking government is prepared to experiment with a somewhat more moderate policy toward Japan, although the picture is cloudy and subject to change.

In the past, the Chinese Communists have insisted that relations can only be improved if Japan accepts three political principals: the abandonment of "a hostile attitude" toward the People's Republic (best indicated by scuttling the security treaty with the United States); full diplomatic recognition of the People's Republic as the government of China; and abandonment of any participation in "the two-China plot." In response, the Japanese government has asserted its willingness to develop "friendly relations," especially economic relations, with Communist China on the basis of equality and mutual noninterference in internal affairs. Japanese spokesmen have vigorously asserted that the security treaty is a defensive alliance, pointing to the fact that 230,000 Japanese and 50,000 American forces in the area currently confront over 3,000,000 Chinese Communist forces. They note the Sino-Soviet alliance, and also the new alliance that both the Soviet Union and Communist China recently concluded with North Korea. The present government has no intention of giving up its alliance with the United States. Neither does it intend to sever its ties with Taiwan, ties having both economic and strategic-political significance to Japan. Hence it will not meet the Chinese Communist demands, but it still hopes to obtain a gradual normalization of relations, beginning with an expansion of trade.

Japan has not been happy with the China policy of the United States which it has regarded as too unrealistic, negative, inflexible, and unilateral. Like many other countries, moreover, it has had increasing doubts that the American policy in its present form can long continue. There is no question that the Japanese conservatives favor a one China, one-Taiwan policy. Although they recognize the present difficulties in effectuating such a policy, they are convinced that in the long run it is a policy according both with the *de facto* situation and Japanese national interests. There are some indications that the United States and Japan have come closer to an understanding on the China issue since the advent of the Kennedy administration. Previously, there was much apprehension on both sides: Japanese fear that American rigidity would damage both the United States and Japan and create serious domestic problems for the conservatives, or that an abrupt shift in American policy would leave Japan in a poor bargaining position; American concern that at some point a combination of tempting Communist offers and internal political pressures would push Japanese policy in a direction opposite that of the United States.

As a result of the Kennedy-Ikeda talks and other activities, some mutual understandings have been reached, although differences of opinion and approach are also present. Both governments now appear to recognize the "special circumstances" involved in the China issue in each country. Both countries will refuse diplomatic recognition to Communist China at this time, with the understanding that consultations on this matter will be conducted frequently, so as to provide maximum unity and avoid embarrassment for either country.

In addition to the economic and political factors motivating Japan on China, there are also cultural factors of importance. The Japanese find it inconceivable that they should long be totally estranged from a people that have been so intimately connected with their whole history. Most Japanese have regarded modern China with a curious admixture of respect and condescension, and a belief that no foreigners can understand China as thoroughly as they. Respect for the great Chinese cultural legacy is combined with condescension toward a "backward society" of the twentieth century, hitherto unable to govern itself or achieve modernity. In degree at least, these views may be erroneous or dated, but they remain important in explaining the relative absence of Japanese fear with respect to Communist China, the continued feeling of rapport with the Chinese people, and the unwillingness to accept isolation from China as a permanent condition.

No such cultural ties bind Japan to the Soviet Union, the other major Communist power. On the contrary, to most Japanese Russia has always been a very foreign, hostile state. The period since 1945 has produced little to dissipate that view. The Soviet Union has pursued policies very harsh to Japan, whether the issue be repatriation of prisoners, economic recovery, or fishery and boundary questions. It is not surprising that Russia generally scores last in popularity polls, and that the Japanese Communist Party labors under a heavy burden. Perhaps a change of tactic has finally been signalled. In 1961, the Soviet Union dispatched Anastas Mikoyan, first deputy Premier, to Japan, the highest Russian official ever to visit that nation. Mikoyan's trip was scarcely an unqualified success. His suggestion that Japan scrap the security treaty with the United States produced immediate charges that he was seeking to interfere in the internal affairs of that country. It is clear that even if the Russians decide to woo Japan, the road is likely to be long and arduous.

THE MILITARY ALLIANCE

Unquestionably, the most basic issue facing Japan in the field of foreign policy is that of military alliance with the United States versus neutralism. It is an issue upon which the Japanese people have been deeply divided. Public opinion polls taken in 1960-61 indicated that about one-third of the people supported the alliance, an equal number opposed it, and the rest were undecided or disinterested. The appeal of neutralism in Japan is not difficult to understand. World War II brought tremendous suffering and destruction. Even today, the scars are omnipresent. Over 200,000 Japanese now living bear marks of the atomic bombings, and additional thousands carry injuries suffered during fire raids or on the field of battle. There is a strong belief, moreover, that with recent scientific-technological developments, war has become inconceivable for a society like Japan. Her population, approaching ninety-three million, along with the bulk of her industry, is heavily concentrated in densely packed urban centers. These centers are only minutes away from Sino-Soviet bases. Japan must import approximately 80% of her industrial raw materials and about 20% of her foodstuffs.

Pacifism flourishes on facts like these. But it will be recalled that it was also encouraged in the initial postwar period by American policy. Some Japanese find it puzzling that less than ten years after we insisted upon total disarmament we had begun to call for total armament. The reasons, of course, lie in the changed conditions in Asia and in the world, but some of the original arguments have had continued effect. The futility and horror of war, the danger of a revived Japanese militarism, and the waste involved in armament when social welfare measures are badly needed—these are the main issues raised by the opponents of rearmament. Supporters of the Japan Defense Force seek to answer these points and advance the case for limited rearmament. The right of self-defense, they insist, is the inalienable right of any sovereign state. Indeed, Japan can be truly independent, they argue, only if it possesses the means of self-defense, and only under such conditions will its words carry any weight in international circles. They also assert that since Communism does not really recognize neutralism or pacifism as legitimate, Japan as a neutral, pacifist state would be at the mercy of Communist unilateral decisions. Security guarantees given by the Communists would be abrogated when it served the interests of the Communist world. In addition, they argue that it is possible to develop a civilian-controlled defense force, properly indoctrinated and not susceptible to the old militarist urges; and that in her own interests, Japan can afford funds for limited rearmament and increased social welfare expenditures at the same time.

Closely connected with the rearmament issue is that of American military bases in Japan. In addition to the general neutralist arguments, opponents insist that such bases greatly increase the risk of Japanese involvement in any Asian or global war. They further assert that American bases on Japanese soil represent vestigial remains of the Occupation and make it impossible for Japan to control her own foreign policy. For the left, the issue of "American imperialism" is a potent one. There are also the elements of land alienation, noise and accidents, and GI incidents which have helped to make military bases the most controversial aspect of the American-Japanese military alliance. Once again, many Japanese have joined the government in supporting the continuance of bases. Some support has come for economic reasons—the American dollars expended in Japan in connection with such bases. The important arguments, however, have been political and military. If Japan rejects neutralism and lacks the military capacity to defend itself, it must assist American forces willing to defend it by affording them installations and bases. Japan must contribute to the alliance, and in lieu of massive military might, her only possible military contribution is facilities. Japanese spokesmen defending the military agreement with the United States have argued that war is less likely if a global balance of power can be maintained in this period, and that Japan has a vital role to play in maintaining that balance in Asia.

How are we to assess the present and future in terms of these issues of rearmament and military bases? It seems safe to predict that Japan will not be a major military ally of the United States in the foreseeable future. Rearmament will continue, with emphasis upon quality rather than quantity, utilizing the latest developments in conventional weapons and weapons carriers. There is almost no chance, however, that Japan will accept nuclear weapons, or allow them to be stored on her territory (with the exception of Okinawa) in the near future. There is also little likelihood that Japan will permit the use of her forces overseas, even in the service of the United Nations. Among other things, this would be unconstitutional, and it seems doubtful whether the Japanese conservatives will soon acquire the necessary strength in the Diet to repeal Article 9 of the 1947 Constitution, the so-called anti-war clause.

In all probability slow rearmament will continue in Japan, with emphasis upon short-term defense, that is, defense for a limited period, until the forces of the United States and other allies can be brought into play. Japanese forces supposedly would be prepared to deal with any internal revolution and to stave off external assault until aid were forthcoming. Meanwhile, under the terms of the revised security treaty, Japan will insist upon prior consultation *and approval* before American bases are used in connection with any military action. According to that treaty, Japan has the right to determine the location of bases and be consulted on their use.

The military aspect of the American-Japanese alliance may well continue to cause tension and could even produce a crisis of serious proportions. In the past, the American government has sometimes believed that Japan was insisting upon equality of treatment without a willingness to accept equality of responsibility. The United States has repeatedly urged Japan to assume a larger share of her own defense by appropriating more funds for the military program. The Japanese government in turn has argued that rearmament must be limited and for home use only, in view of the state of Japanese public opinion and the pressures for a higher standard of living. On all sides, there has been a pronounced reluctance to rearm at the rate desired by American authorities. At the same time, however, the conservatives have been vigorous in pushing for partnership in decisions relating to bases. Strenuous bargaining took place at the time of the security treaty revision, with Japanese spokesmen insisting upon much greater control over the location and use of bases.

The contention of American military men is that Japanese bases and facilities are vital to our military capacities in East Asia. The unanswered question, however, is whether these bases and facilities could actually be used in connection with any kind of military operation without very grave political repercussions. This is related to a broader question that should be under continuous study by a joint civilian-military group: in the light of rising political costs and radically changing military technology, can one justify fixed American bases in the populous areas of East Asia? In the long run, it seems likely that our defense posture in the Far East will be governed either by some type of disarmament-military disengagement agreement reached between the non-Communist and Communist blocs, or failing this, by the principle that most areas will be responsible for their own immediate, short-term defense, with the United States providing the major deterrent force and supplementary assistance to any nation attacked via its Central Pacific bases and such mobile units as atomic-powered submarines and aircraft.

OKINAWA

Meanwhile, Okinawa constitutes another issue that periodically disturbs American-Japanese relations. The United States occupied Okinawa after a bloody battle in the spring of 1945. For several years we ignored the area. Then began a feverish drive to make Okinawa an impregnable fortress, the center of American military power in East Asia. Substantial portions of the island were converted into airfields, bases, and installations of various sorts. A military administration was established, and military necessities—or desires—took complete priority. Probably a widening breach between American authority and the Okinawan people was inevitable in this situation. In any case, it occurred with our land acquisition and payment policies becoming a focal point of contention. On the part of the United States, a "don't give an inch" attitude was pursued until we had succeeded in building up a strong left wing movement among one of the most docile, conservative peoples in the world. Fortunately, that era is past. Our policies were finally changed in the face of imminent disaster. Okinawan politics today are relatively stable, thanks to acceptable land policies and certain political concessions. The issue of reversion to Japan, however, along with demands for fuller political democracy are matters of continuing interest to both Okinawans and Japanese. Actually, the basic issue would appear settled. The United States has long recognized that Japan has "residual sovereignty" with respect to Okinawa. The northern Ryukyu islands were returned to Japan some years ago. We have stated, however, that we will remain in Okinawa as long as there is a threat to the security of the free peoples of Asia. That could mean indefinite occupation. We have also resisted any arrangement whereby Japan acquired administrative control while we retained bases, on the score that divided jurisdiction on this small island would not be feasible. And we have continued to apply American military as opposed to civilian government, with the argument that since the only reason for our being on the island is military, the basic decisions should be made by military authority.

Many of these policies are not in accord with the desires of the Okinawan people. The Okinawans are Japanese in culture and inclination. Every poll taken in recent years has indicated their desire by an overwhelming margin to be reunited with Japan. As interim measures, they have also wanted American civilian government, expansion of local autonomy, especially popular election instead of appointment of the Okinawan chief executive, and more economic assistance from the United States. As might be expected, Okinawa has been a political issue in Japan. All elements in Japanese politics naturally advocate the reincorporation of Okinawa into Japan. The dominant conservatives, however, have been cautious in pushing this point too far, since they are aware of the fact that Okinawa serves certain military purposes (presumably the storing of atomic weapons) and represents certain military risks that Japan proper is not prepared to assume at this time.

Meanwhile, *de facto* reversion is taking place. There is constantly increasing Japanese-Okinawan interaction in such diverse fields as education, recreation, industry, and politics. The time will come when some form of *de jure* reversion will be required. Undoubtedly, if the transition is made with a proper sense of timing, the United States can continue to hold bases, although some adjustments in the full freedom currently allowed American military authorities will have to be made. The transitional steps would seem to be a movement toward civilian government, fuller Okinawan democracy, and implementation of joint American-Japanese action on behalf of economic development on Okinawa, as pledged by President Kennedy and Prime Minister Ikeda. Naturally, our Okinawan policy will continue to be governed in major degree by an appraisal of our military needs in the Far East and the suitability of fixed bases of this type. But political considerations will also have to be given full weight. The questions raised earlier in connection with Japanese bases also have validity here. In the final analysis, our Okinawa policy must be a part of, not apart from, our Japan policy. It must also be a policy soliciting the good will and support of the 900,000 Okinawans for whom we are still wholly responsible.

The General Picture

American-Japanese relations today bespeak the capacity of two peoples emerging from very different cultural backgrounds to communicate with each other in an increasingly effective manner as they both move toward the great goals of the twentieth century. As has been noted, trade and other economic ties between our two societies are of basic significance. We are now preparing to embark upon joint efforts for global economic development through the Organization for Economic Cooperation and Development. At bilateral and multilateral levels, American-Japanese economic interaction represents the vital center of our cooperation.

In addition, however, a growing network of cultural communications has been built. We and the Japanese have more to say to each other at present in such diverse fields as art and architecture, science, and the social sciences than would have been dreamed possible at the end of the War. In part this is a discovery of appealing facets of our different cultures, coupled with a willingness to accept change. In part it is the natural result of the increasing similarity of two peoples both of whom are dedicated to modernity. It would be difficult to overestimate the importance—real and potential—of this new trend. In the United States there has been an almost total disappearance of anti-Japanese sentiment, and wide-spread enthusiasm for Japanese art, architecture, handicrafts, and precision instruments. Japan has probably never made a deeper cultural impact at any time than she is making today on this country. In turn, we have affected almost every aspect of Japanese life in the last ten years— food, clothing, amusements, music, ideas, and even language. Social scientists and scientists are able to communicate with each other from our two countries with mutual profit.

We have only begun to realize the significance of this new trend. In the past, our diplomacy toward Japan has been timid and formalistic. We have taken refuge in the old doctrine that we should do business only with the government in power, seemingly unaware of the fact that our success—indeed our very survival—in this era depends upon doing business with as many people in a society as we can reach. The American-Japanese alliance is still too heavily dependent upon support from limited segments of Japanese society: conservative party leaders, the business community, and a portion of the bureaucracy. We need a policy of diplomacy in depth. We need to open channels of contact to the political opposition as well as the government in power, to labor and the intellectuals as well as to the business world.

It is also important that the image of the United States be recast in a more accurate light: we should be seen as a dynamic, revolutionary society in which the common man has risen higher in a generation than in any other society, and where culture has been brought to the masses in unprecedented degree. It is time to make known our symphonies, art galleries, our writers, and creative social scientists as well as our bombs. Significantly, Japan is the one ally according to the polls that feels that the United States is prone to military solutions in international politics. This is no doubt because of the great emphasis given bases and military forces. It is essential that we give equal emphasis to the great desire for peace which all Americans feel.

Because we have not pursued a dynamic policy of diplomacy in depth, nor paid adequate attention to the American image in the past, we have not taken full advantage of all the potentialities in American-Japanese relations. Indeed, anti-Americanism has grown in some Japanese circles, especially among intellectual and labor union groups. The fault does not lie entirely with us. The appeal of Marxism to these groups continues to be quite strong. Thus they receive mainly a stereotyped impression of the United States as "a mature capitalist country." They await a major economic depression in this country, and believe that the American economy is totally dependent upon armament-making. They are tempted to go overboard in describing American civil liberties issues, applying the word "Fascist" in loose and inaccurate senses. There is some indication that a number of Japanese left-wing intellectuals are now seeking a substitute for Marxism or at least some modifications of it. This trend can be greatly abetted by an intelligent, broadly-gauged American policy aimed at an appeal to all elements in Japanese society.

It must be emphasized, however, that there is very little personal anti-Americanism in Japan. Even among those groups who object to American policy, the doors of communication are open. As we have noted, there are many reasons why neutralism will continue to have an appeal in Japan. It is probable, however, that the American-Japanese alliance will remain intact. The indications are strong that the Japanese conservatives will stay in power for a considerable period. Their policy will be one of support for the alliance, albeit with an insistence upon greater partnership and our recognition of certain Japanese "special circumstances" and "special interests." For our part, we are anxious for Japan to assume a more active role in the world, finding her *raison d'etre* in services to the Afro-Asian world of both an economic and a political nature.

The American-Japanese alliance must find its real significance in economic, political, and cultural interaction rather than in military power. This need makes it no less valuable to our two countries and to the general cause of world peace and progress.

2.

The United States and Korea

◆ Shannon McCune

In 1950, Korea became a household word in the United States. It was the dramatic scene of naked Communist aggression in Asia. The overt crossing of the 38th parallel and the military advances, obviously planned well in advance and with support from the Soviet Union, awoke many Americans to the fact that militant Communism had grown powerful. The serious dimensions of the Korean War caused the drafting of American soldiers, the retooling of our factories, and the reimposition of economic controls. Korea stood as a symbol of the new position of America in the world.

The basic problem in Korea, despite the fact that a costly and devastating war was fought from 1950 to 1953, is today virtually the same as it was in 1950. Korea is divided by a truce line, crossing at a slightly oblique angle

74

◆ SHANNON McCUNE, formerly Provost of the University of Massachusetts and now Director, Department of Education, UNESCO, was born in Korea and has made it his special field of study and research. A geographer by training, he has taught at Ohio State, Colgate, and other universities. In 1950-51, he was Deputy Director of the Far East Program Division of ECA, and in 1954 while serving as a visiting professor at Tokyo University, he visited Korea again. He has written widely on Korea and the Far East; his *Korea's Heritage, A Regional and Social Geography* was published in the spring of 1956.

the 38th parallel. On each side a different government is in power. In the North is the Democratic People's Republic of Korea, a communist state which politically is closely following the lead of the Soviet Union. Economically and militarily, however, the Chinese Communists play a large role. Thus, it is dependent upon two masters. In the South the Republic of Korea was until the spring of 1960 under the strong hand of President Syngman Rhee. After his overthrow by a student-initiated and army-supported uprising, the moderate, democratically-inclined, but ineffectual government of John M. Chang was formed. This, in turn, was replaced after a turbulent year by a military junta pledged to eradicate corruption and create a strong anti-Communist state with elections in 1963. Each successive government has been dependent upon American aid for survival. Thus the avowed aim of United States foreign policy—the same as that of the United Nations: "The establishment by peaceful means of a unified, independent, and democratic Korea under a representative government"—is far from realized.

The Korean War, though it did not achieve the unification of Korea, did put the United Nations into the business of effectively meeting aggression by collective measures. Communist leaders bent on conquest in Asia were halted for a time. Thus in the larger perspective, though perhaps not in the limited range of the Korean peninsula, the war was an important episode in modern history, for through collective action under the United Nations a small nation was rescued after being overrun. What had appeared to some people as a polite bureaucratic debating society became an action agency meeting aggression by collective action and through military means. To Americans the role of the United Nations in the Korean War was of great significance. Many who had wavered in its support now became its advocates.

The basic American foreign policy goal in Korea was expressed for the first time in recent decades in the Cairo Declaration of 1943. This declaration, made originally by Roosevelt, Churchill, and Chiang, was later endorsed by Stalin at Potsdam. Mindful of the long domination of Korea by Japan, these leaders agreed that: "In due course Korea shall become free and independent."

In view of the present impasse in Korea on the major issue, five shorter-range aims have defined the United States foreign policy in the area since the Korean War:

(1) That we maintain the uneasy armistice but continue to keep militarily vigilant in Korea, not wishing to risk the recurrence of a Korean war;

(2) That, realizing that the growth of democracy and freedom is essential, we give moral support to the democratic forces within the Republic of Korea;

(3) That, recognizing the sacrifices made by the people of South Korea and the importance, not only locally but throughout Asia, of the rehabilitation of the war-torn land of Korea as a fact and as a symbol, we continue to furnish large amounts of economic aid both for relief and economic development;

(4) That, having in mind its geographical location and its economic limitations, we urge the Republic to achieve a peaceful and honorable relation with Japan and other free nations;

(5) That we remain willing to negotiate a Korean settlement, but only under the auspices of the United Nations, not unilaterally.

These limited aims are realistic and within our capabilities. The long-range American objective of a unified, independent, democratic Korea seems remote at this writing.

Korean Background

In 1950, Korea was a synonym for the meeting of Communist aggression through collective force. Unfortunately, however, Korea as a peninsula, as a nation, as a people, was relatively unknown, a *terra incognita*. Background knowledge of Korea, on the basis of which valid judgments could be made, was (and still is) sadly lacking.

GEOGRAPHY AND HISTORY

Korea lies in the heart of the Far East. It is a small nation, roughly the size of Minnesota and with some 36 million people, in close proximity to large neighbors in uneasy balance of power regulations. A peninsula with a broad continental base, Korea has been a passageway between forces based on the plains of North China and Manchuria and the islands of Japan. Yet the mountainous terrain and crude communication lines make it no easy road, rather a tortuous alley up and down which invaders spend themselves.

The geographically diversified peninsula long afforded isolation to the Korean people, who developed from waves of migrants in prehistoric times. Legends give the founding of Korea as occurring over four thousand years ago. (By the official calendar 1962 is the 4295th year of Tangun, the founder.) The Koreans evolved their own culture, language, and customs, but from time to time they borrowed (or had forced upon them) aspects of Chinese and Japanese culture and ideologies. To these they gave distinctive Korean twists. After a series of invasions by powerful neighbors—Tartars in 1011 A.D., Mongols a century later, Japanese in 1592, and Manchus in 1627—they withdrew into isolation and sought to preserve a hermit existence for some two centuries before their doors were forced open in 1876.

For centuries under the Confucian system of international relations, Korea was "the younger brother" nation of Imperial China. Had Korea developed a strong, well-knit national government under this benevolent system, she might have been able to maintain her independence. But a venal court, dominated by pedantic scholars and factious politicians, was divorced from the common people. A weak nation with a misguided reliance on Imperial China emerged from its isolation. Korea was easy prey for Japan. Following the Sino-Japanese War of 1894-95 and the Russo-Japanese War of 1904-05, Korea was annexed to Japan in 1910. Though appeals for help to preserve its independence were made at that time to the United States, these were not heeded.

Korea is an agricultural country. Four-fifths of the people are farmers; the rest are engaged in mining, forestry, industry, and services. The farmers cultivate small farms, the average holding being 2.5 acres. Many were tenants of large Japanese companies or Korean landlords. In 1938, over half of the farmers rented all of their land, and another quarter rented part. In recent years land reform programs in both North and South have changed the tenancy situation. The farming people live in villages for the most part, though in mountainous regions they live in isolated farmsteads cultivating poor fields cleared by fire. The mainstays of the Korean economy are the sedentary farmers who cultivate the valley lands, which can be irrigated and on which rice, the prize crop, can be grown. Forestry and fishing are subsidiary but important industries.

JAPAN'S KOREA

After 1910, Korea became a part of the developing Japanese empire, later to be known as the East Asia Co-Prosperity Sphere. The peninsula served as a source of raw materials—coal, iron ore, gold, copper, lumber, fish, and, most important, rice. It was a market for Japanese manufactured goods, though as the economy developed, Japanese firms built industrial plants in Korea. Railroads and highways opened up the country. Especially in the North, hydro-electric resources were developed; on this base chemical and other industries were established.

The Korean population grew rapidly from an estimated 13 million in 1910 to more than 24 million in 1940. This expanding population furnished manpower for Japanese exploitation. Not trusted (and with reason) in the armed forces of Japan, the Koreans worked in commerce and industry in areas conquered by Japan. They migrated as cheap laborers to the mines and factories of Japan itself. When World War II ended there were an estimated 2,500,000 Koreans in Japan, another million in Manchuria and North China, and additional thousands in Southeast Asia.

The Japanese impact on Korea was immense, not only on the economic development of railroads, commerce, and industry, but on the political and social structure. The Japanese ruled with a strong central regime and an oppressive police system. Social pressures, caused by latent nationalism, condoned the breaking of laws imposed from outside. In turn, Korean national customs and mores were undermined. Higher paid and responsible government and business positions were held by Japanese. Koreans had few educational or advanced occupational opportunities. Though there were some wealthy Korean landlords and merchants who managed to keep their property by collaboration with the Japanese, there was no large cadre of trained Korean executives and technicians.

THE 38TH PARALLEL

The jubilation experienced in 1945 by the Koreans over their release from Japanese domination was relatively short-lived, for their hitherto unified land was divided into two military occupation spheres, north and south of the 38th parallel. The use of the 38th parallel appears to have been based on a hasty American decision made in the Pentagon when plans were quickly improvised for the acceptance of the surrender of Japanese forces in Korea. For this limited purpose the 38th parallel was perhaps an adequate dividing line. But as a boundary between the two hostile regimes which subsequently developed, it was dangerous; as a basis of partition in their country, heartbreaking to the Koreans. It cut across the grain of the land like a knife and had none of those characteristics, natural or social, which give real meaning to a boundary line.

Though essentially unified as a peninsula, Korea shows important regional diversities, for example, in climate and agriculture. Generally, North Korea has a single crop economy, since bitterly cold winters limit the growing season. There is less arable land in the mountainous north than in the south which has more extensive plains. In South Korea, the winters, though cold, are not sufficiently severe to deter the cultivation of winter wheat or barley on some of the fields, and double cropping is a common practice. With greater food production, the carrying capacity of the land in the South is considerably greater than in the North. The population of South Korea in 1944 was 17 million people, twice that of the North. The mountainous North has more hydroelectric power resources and more mineral wealth. The two sections should effectively complement each other. Together, they make a more viable unit than does either section separately.

Soviet and Free World ideologies were set opposite one another dramatically in Korea. In the North, people's committees, to which militant Communists could be easily grafted, were recognized by the Soviet Army, and the Russians worked behind the scenes. Fronting for them was a Communist-dominated coalition of North Korean political leaders with new and well trained cadres based upon Koreans who had been in Russia and Communist China. The native Communist control gradually tightened so that the Soviet military forces were withdrawn in the confidence that the puppet regime would be completely subservient to Soviet wishes. Communist China and other nations in the Soviet bloc extended recognition to the newly formed Democratic People's Republic of Korea in 1948.

In the South, people's committees also sprang up but were not recognized. An American military occupation was set up, though there appears to have been an unfortunate delay before its lines of political and economic action were clear. Gradually more responsibilities were given to Koreans, but these were Koreans who worked for the American army. In contrast to the Russian system, American control was overt in the early years of occupation.

The situation of a divided Korea was contrary to the Cairo Declaration of 1943, and all agreed that it should be unified. But on what basis and under what ideology? At the Moscow meeting of foreign ministers in December 1945, a joint US-USSR Commission was organized to work toward the unification of Korea. The Commission held meetings during the spring of 1946 and again in the spring of 1947. However, progress was blocked by the adamant Soviet position to recognize as "democratic" only those groups which were in essence favorable to their aims. Thus, in the fall of 1947, the United States presented the Korean problem to the United Nations.

TWO GOVERNMENTS

The United Nations established The Temporary Commission on Korea to unify the country and to hold elections for a Constituent Assembly to form a Korean government. However, North Korea refused to recognize the Commission's authority or allow it to visit the North. The Commission observed elections held in the summer of 1948 south of the

38th parallel and certified that the government thereby established was the lawful government in that part of Korea where the elections were held and the only duly constituted government in Korea. Syngman Rhee was elected President of the new nation, the Republic of Korea (ROK), by an overwhelming majority of the Assembly. The United States and other nations gave diplomatic recognition to the new Republic. The American military occupation of Korea ended and American forces were then withdrawn.

Thus, two opposing governments faced each other across the 38th parallel in Korea during 1949 and the first half of 1950. It is difficult to assess correctly the relative strengths of programs of these regimes, for they were so different in their ideologies and practices. A very eloquent fact is that some two million Koreans fled from the North and made their way to the comparative haven of the South.

The Korean War

The Northern regime attempted to subvert the Republic of Korea by various means. Finally, after a strident call for "elections" to unify the peninsula, they massed an attack across the 38th parallel on June 25, 1950. At the urging of the United States, the Security Council of the United Nations acted promptly. (The Soviet Union had "walked out" of the Security Council some months previously on another issue and was, therefore, in no position to block this move.) The Korean War was on. General Douglas MacArthur was named Supreme Commander of the United Nations Forces. Large numbers of American troops were rushed to Korea. The devastated ROK forces were reorganized. Eventually, the onrush of North Korean troops equipped with Soviet tanks and heavy equipment was halted along the Naktong River in southeastern Korea, and a beachhead at Pusan was successfully maintained.

To the historian the Korean War has some remarkable parallels with military actions in the peninsula in past centuries. The Pusan-Naktong River gateway in the southeast was used by Hideyoshi's Japanese forces in 1592; the Ui ju-Yalu River gateway in the northwest was used by the invaders from China. The gross strategy—the movement of forces north and south between the two gateways with major battlegrounds on the west side of the peninsula and with diversionary movements to the northeast and the southwest—has its parallels in almost every military campaign in Korea's history. The general tactics in the Korean War— pushing spearheads up river valleys, infiltrating guerilla forces behind the lines, holding ridge crests which command important valleys—all have been used in wars in Korea throughout recorded time.

In September, 1950, after the build-up of their forces including added men and supplies from sixteen nations, the United Nations troops took the offensive. They landed in force at Inchon and broke out of the Pusan perimeter. The North Korean troops were quickly engulfed or driven back. Seoul was triumphantly retaken. Communist aggression had been met and defeated through collective action.

There then came an important though historically unclarified period. In October, the first ROK troops crossed the 38th parallel. On October 7, 1950, the United Nations General Assembly resolved that "all appropriate steps be taken to insure conditions of stability throughout Korea" as a measure designed for the establishment of a unified Korea, its long-range objective. Acting under the October 7th resolution, United Nations troops followed the ROK troops across the 38th parallel. (The question is perhaps academic but it is difficult to judge which came first, the resolution or the northward movement.) The United Nations forces captured Pyongyang and held the waist of the peninsula, extending spearheads along the coasts and quite far and deep into the mountainous areas of the northern interior of Korea. The North Korean Army was routed; victory seemed at hand.

The Chinese Communists, concerned that the war had come too close to their borders, sent troops across the Yalu in late October and started what General MacArthur called "an entirely new war." Against these massive Chinese forces the United Nations troops fell back. Seoul was lost on January 4th. After regrouping, the United Nations and ROK troops were able to recapture Seoul on March 14th and advance beyond the 38th parallel in the eastern part of the peninsula. By June, a year after the war had started, a solid battle line was formed across the peninsula, not very far from the line from which the original hostilities began. A military stalemate developed. A million or more troops faced each other across the line, constantly improving their defensive positions and making probing attacks. Finally on July 10, 1951, armistice negotiations were started.

In view of the continual threat that the Korean War might develop into a general world war, the United Nations forces were restricted to rather limited objectives: the repelling of the armed attack and restoring peace and security within the area. Military actions were confined to the Korean peninsula. The Communist forces, however, had a "haven" in Manchuria across the Yalu. There they were able to organize unhindered the Chinese Communist armies who entered the conflict when the Yalu region was approached. (In the same sense, the United Nations had a "haven" in Japan, which was never attacked by the Communists though at one time their air power was sufficient to do so.) However, the story of the Korean War might have been quite different if freedom of action had been allowed to General MacArthur—bombing across the Yalu, for example, or the use of atomic weapons. It appears that American leaders were not willing to take the risk that the Korean War might then have been but the opening chapter in a much larger and perhaps longer war history.

While the armistice negotiations dragged on from July 10, 1951, to July 27, 1953, the Korean War was far from quiet. Many bloody patrol actions and local battles took place, though neither side launched a major offensive. As time went on and more and more "digging in" was accomplished, the possibility of a successful breakthrough with conventional weapons diminished.

While the fighting along the front and the armistice negotiations at Panmunjom were going on, action relating to Korea was taking place at quite distant points. One of the pledges of Eisenhower's campaign for the presidency of the United States in 1952 was to bring an end to the fighting in Korea. At the United Nations, the General Assembly and the First Committee often had Korea on their agendas. Radio pronouncements of varying types came out of Peking, Moscow, Washington, and other capitals.

The first positive action as a result of the armistice negotiations occurred in the spring of 1953, when an exchange of sick and wounded prisoners was arranged. On June 8, a general agreement on repatriation of prisoners was reached. Shortly thereafter, the ROK appeared to connive in allowing some 25,000 anti-Communist North Korean prisoners to break out of their POW camps, and this almost wrecked the negotiations. Finally the armistice was signed on July 27. It set up a military demarcation line across Korea and provided for a demilitarized zone to extend two kilometers on each side of the line.

A minor but significant point is that the armistice was a military one. The signators were Lt. General Harrison, an American, for the United Nations Command, and General Nam Il for the North Koreans and Chinese. The countersigners were General Clark for the United Nations and General Peng and Marshall Kim for the Chinese and Koreans. ROK troops served under the United Nations Command and were bound by the armistice. As a consequence, the ROK makes the point that in all non-military respects, they are not bound by the armistice.

The exchange of POW's was one of the most difficult problems in the immediate post-armistice period. Many more prisoners were reported to be held in the South than in the North. An elaborate process was developed for interviewing prisoners, managed by Indian troops. Provision was made for the POW's to choose whether they should be repatriated, go to some neutral nation, or stay in the land of their captors. As a result of the process, 75,000 Communist troops were returned in exchange for 12,750 United Nations soldiers. Another 75,000 North Korean troops elected to remain in South Korea, and 14,000 Chinese Communist troops who refused repatriation were sent to Taiwan. A small group of 88 Koreans was given the privilege of going to India, where they were, to some extent, men without countries; some subsequently went to Brazil. There were 21 Americans and one Briton who elected to stay with the Chinese Communists, and 327 South Korean troops elected to stay in North Korea. In general, Operation Big Switch worked rather smoothly, though while it was progressing there was a great deal of recrimination on both sides.

POLITICAL STALEMATE

The armistice agreements recommended that

> in order to insure the peaceful settlement of the Korean question . . . a political conference of a higher level of both sides be held (within three months) by representatives appointed respectively to settle through negotiation the questions of the withdrawal of all foreign forces from Korea, the peaceful settlement of the Korean question. . . .

Though preliminary meetings were held at Panmunjom to arrange such a political conference, nothing developed. The Communists insisted, for example, that the Soviet Union be included as a "neutral" participant. To this the United States would not agree.

In August, 1953, Secretary Dulles held conversations in Korea with President Rhee and Foreign Minister Pyun about a military security pact. This was formalized in October in Washington, and consent to its ratification was given by the Senate on January 28, 1954. Many Americans are probably unaware of the significance of this document. It commits the United States to "act to meet the common danger" in the event of "an armed attack" on Korean territory. On the other hand, it binds the hands of the ROK from taking unilateral military action without consultation with the United States.

In addition, the sixteen nations who had fought in Korea under the United Nations Command issued a statement in August, 1953, pledging themselves to renew the war if Communist aggression again occurred. They warned that in the event of renewed warfare "in all probability it would not be possible to confine hostilities within the frontiers of Korea." The effectiveness of this warning is hard to estimate. It does put on the record the fact that if renewed aggression takes place in Korea, it is likely that war will spread to the mainland of China.

Hopes for the settlement of the Korean problem at a political conference were revived when at the Berlin Conference in February, 1954, the foreign ministers of the United States, France, Britain, and the USSR agreed that a conference should be called at Geneva on April 28th. To this conference were invited those nations whose troops had fought in Korea plus the Soviet Union, which technically had not had forces there. Other problems were also to be discussed such as disarmament and the Indo-Chinese situation.

The Geneva Conference was held from April 26 to June 15, with obvious and basic disagreement concerning Korea between the two sides. This situation was well epitomized in a declaration by the sixteen nations on June 15, 1954:

> The Communist delegations have rejected our every effort to obtain agreement. The principal issues between us therefore are clear. Firstly, we accept and assert the authority of the United Nations. The Communists repudiate and reject the authority and competence of the United Nations in Korea and have labelled the United Nations itself as the tool of aggression. Were we to accept this position of the Communists, it would mean the death of the principle of collective security and of the United Nations itself. Secondly, we desire genuinely free elections. The Communists insist upon procedures which would make genuinely free elections impossible. It is clear that the Communists will not accept impartial and effective supervision of free elections. Plainly, they have shown their intention to maintain Communist control over North Korea. They have persisted in the same attitudes which have frustrated United Nations efforts to unify Korea since 1947.
>
> We believe, therefore, that it is better to face the fact of our disagreement than to raise false hopes and mislead the peoples of the world into believing that there is agreement where there is none.

The Korean behavior during the conference has not been fully appreciated. The North Koreans generally followed the lead of the Soviet Union and Communist China, though occasionally they took a more adamant position from which they retreated. The ROK representatives, on the other hand, acted with considerable independence from that of their allies. The ROK had not signed the armistice agreement. They had come reluctantly, insisting that nothing would come of the conference. Nothing did—but whether or not something would have come with a different attitude on their part is hardly worth conjecturing. At the end of the Geneva Conference, the solution of the Korean problem seemed no nearer than in 1947. In fact, the opposing positions had hardened and the continuing development of separate economic, political, and ideological institutions tended to undermine the possibility of unity.

RECENT EVENTS

In the ensuing years little progress has been made toward the resolution of the unification problem. Statements are made at various times; in the United Nations meetings, Korea is discussed occasionally, but no gain can be recorded. Within the Korean peninsula, nonetheless, events of note continue to occur. Both in the North and the South leaders call for the reunification of Korea—"March to the Yalu" has been a rallying cry on the streets of Seoul. "Free our land from American imperialism," unreal as it may sound to American ears, has been shouted in Pyongyang.

The truce line is being kept. Both sides remain vigilant and alert in their defensive positions though there are constant complaints of violations from both sides. ROK troops have been trained to take the place of the United Nations soldiers. The ROK troops number roughly three-quarters of a million and are stationed along the line and throughout South Korea. There are less than 50,000 United States troops in South Korea, generally situated in reserve positions to the truce line. In the north, the line is held by an estimated half-million North Korean troops. The Chinese Communist forces are reported to have been withdrawn beyond the Yalu river, but they comprise a massive ready reserve in Manchuria.

On both sides economic rehabilitation has been speeded, though with different aims. The Soviet Union, Communist China, and other Communist countries have signed economic aid and trade agreements with the Northern regime. The United Nations organized a special rehabilitation agency (UNKRA) through which some 125 million dollars of aid was channeled to South Korea before it closed its operations in 1960. The regular United Nations agencies continue to give modest support to programs in Korea. In addition to its large share in the United Nations programs, the United States is carrying on unilaterally in Korea one of its largest economic assistance programs. On the political scene the Communists in the north have strengthened their monolithic control over the people, though some token minor parties are included in the coalition in titular command. There have been occasional purges of political leaders and changes in cabinet ministries. In 1961 Kim Il-sung, the Premier, journeyed first to Moscow and then to Peking (the order is significant) and signed treaties which will assure Soviet Union and Chinese Communist support in case of aggression by South Korean forces.

In the south there was a great deal of political activity. Syngman Rhee was never without a vocal opposition, though this was silenced through assassination or arrest if it became too radical. In the election of May 1956 his hand-picked candidate for Vice-President was defeated by John M. Chang (Chang Myun), an opposition leader. The government of Syngman Rhee had many weaknesses; graft, corruption, and disregard for civil rights became more and more blatant. The rigging of the 1960 elections and the increasingly harsh police interference with the rights of the citizens to protest precipitated a violent reaction, the student-led riots of April. The Korean armed forces, withholding support from the Rhee regime, assured its downfall. Syngman Rhee was allowed to leave for retirement in Hawaii; and a new regime with a titular President, Yun Po-sun, and a Premier responsible to the legislature, John M. Chang, came into power following new and notably free elections. This new regime, though pledged to clean up graft and corruption, was riven by internal frictions and was not effective in mobilizing the people to solve the pressing economic problems.

The groups within the Korean armed forces, who in the spring of 1960 had swung their support to the overthrow of Rhee, became increasingly concerned by the ineffectiveness and liberal tendencies of the new political structure. For example, individuals and small groups were openly discussing acceptance of negotiations with the Communist regime in the north. Undoubtedly some of these groups were being infiltrated by Communists, though the extent of this is difficult to determine. The Army authorities were worried, also, by the amassing of fortunes by some Koreans through unexplained means and, on a broader basis, by the lack of a vigorous economic program which would benefit the rural areas of Korea.

As a consequence, a military junta with the support of the armed forces seized power in a bloodless coup d'état early in the morning of May 16, 1961. Though the titular President, Yun Po-sun, was kept in office, the cabinet of John M. Chang resigned and the houses of the legislature were dissolved. A Supreme Council for National Reconstruction was headed by Lt. Gen. Chang Do-yung. His power, too, was relatively short-lived, for on July 3rd he resigned and there emerged the real power of the junta, 44-year-old Maj. Gen. Park Chung-hi. Subsequently John M. Chang and some of his colleagues were arrested for alleged graft. General Chang and some of his military associates were arrested for plotting the assassination of General Park. On August 15th, the military junta, headed by General Park and with former general Song Yo-chan as Premier, announced that they expected to accomplish their reforms in two years and would turn over power to a civilian regime in the summer of 1963.

The Present United States Position

In the decade since the Korean War the official United States position in regard to Korea has been little changed. Korea is becoming somewhat of a forgotten word on American lips. The potentiality of renewed Communist aggression there seems remote to the average American. What is important is that the fighting was stopped. He seems to think that the basic issues are settled (or are insoluble); he would like to forget Korea.

The official American view seems to be that the peace should not be broken in Korea either by the Communists or by the ROK. Where the

United States can take action, for example, in deterring ROK action or bellicose remarks, it does so. The United States is bound by the Mutual Defense Treaty to come to the assistance of the ROK in the event of armed aggression. It has strongly supported the economy of the South and given military supplies to the ROK troops which have replaced American and the other United Nations forces. On the other hand, the United States has tried to limit the development of economic and military strength of the North through limiting the expansion of trade and through the terms of the armistice. When these are broken, as in the case of the military buildup, we apparently do little but protest. The Truce Commission has proved to be quite impotent as a control factor over Northern Korea. Probably the continued existence of two regimes dividing Korea, with large forces facing each other across the truce line, is recognized by most Americans as unsatisfactory. Yet the alternative of taking vigorous action involving heavy commitments and unpredictable risks seems to have few supporters.

With the present division of Korea, American actions are related almost entirely to the Southern regime. The Northern regime is still considered as a belligerent in the Korean War. Its strictly Communist-controlled government, the Democratic People's Republic of Korea, is headed by Russian-trained Kim Il-Sung. Military leaders have been emerging with more power; for example, General Nam Il is now Foreign Minister. North Korea is clearly part of the Soviet bloc. It has been receiving aid from the Soviet Union, Communist China, and the East European satellites. It has a powerful, poised military force. New generations of Korean students and soldiers are being indoctrinated along Communist lines. Though there undoubtedly are some latent divisive forces within the regime between the Chinese and Russian-trained leaders, these have not been of major concern. The mutual-assistance treaties signed with both in the summer of 1961 give clear indication of continued support by the Soviet Union and Communist China. Collectivization of agriculture has been increased notably since 1953. The state-owned mines, industrial plants, and transport facilities have been repaired since the destruction of the Korean War. Cities, especially Pyongyang, the northern capital, have been reconstructed, the streets widened, and large apartment blocks and public buildings erected. Though much of the economic development is for the ultimate benefit of Communist China with which close economic links have been forged, ideological lines appear to be drawn from Moscow rather than Peking. The independence of the 'tiger hunters,' as the north Koreans have called themselves for centuries, has virtually disappeared.

In contrast, the Republic of Korea is no satellite or docile ally of the United States, and American dealings with South Korea, though close, have often been strained. To be realistic, America's strategic need for

Korea is very slight, certainly when compared to the ROK's need for American aid. Yet the Korean government has often acted as though it considered itself absolutely indispensable to America. Korea's strategic position on the periphery of the Communist world has certain value, but the Korean War proved that the peninsula is no easily used base for military operations and is difficult to defend.

In its grave problems, the new Republic of Korea has had varying support from the United States. Korea is still divided, and the Communist threat, though not so evident since the armistice, is none the less very real. Internally, many factors including the inexperience of government officials and businessmen, the pressure of population upon the land, and the overwhelming war destruction have resulted in chaotic instability. These internal problems have no easy solutions, though the resilient and resourceful Korean people are tackling them with courage. The newly established military junta's emphasis upon national reconstruction and a five-year economic reconstruction plan to begin in 1962 is in answer to the obvious need to stabilize the economic situation. However, such means and such personnel may not be adequate to the long-range task. Outside aid, correctly applied and used, can be of great assistance. The attitude and efforts of the United States are being watched closely by other Asian nations threatened by Communist aggression. Korea is a showcase of American action. It behooves Americans to recognize this. What they do or do not do in Korea may have widespread repercussions in Asia. Support of the ROK is thus of more than local concern or significance.

The Growth of Democracy

When the regime of Syngman Rhee, which had become less and less democratically-inclined, was overthrown, there were high hopes for the development of a more truly democratic regime acting responsibly for the people of Korea. Unfortunately, this did not take place. The emergence of a military junta to power in Korea seems to have dashed many of these hopes. This may account for some of the immediate adverse reactions of American military authorities and of United States Embassy personnel in Seoul to the new regime. However, the American authorities in Washington accepted the establishment of the political power of the junta as a fait accompli and expressed a desire to work with it in the reconstruction of Korea. Actually, in Asia there have been a series of countries faced with external pressures and with the lack of political stability, due in part to the absence of an educated and sophisticated electorate, which have gone under the power of military juntas or leaders in recent years. A "White Paper" entitled "The Military Revolution in Korea" and issued by the junta on July 5, 1961 concluded thus:

The Korean people therefore have no tradition of and no experience with real democracy. The most important tasks facing the present Government are to create an atmosphere that will permit the emergence of true democracy in a form that will be workable against this background and to teach through all informational media democratic theories—most especially that real freedom and individual liberty can only exist if citizens understand their democratic duties and responsibilities and are willing to accept these duties and responsibilities as the price of liberty.

The military junta subsequently announced that it hoped to accomplish this task of creating an atmosphere favorable to democracy in less than two years so that elections could be held in the spring of 1963 and a new civilian government could succeed to power in the summer.

The possibilities of this being accomplished so quickly cannot be viewed with optimism. There has been virtually no tradition of national democracy in Korea in recent decades. Under the Japanese, the government continued in a more efficient manner the autocratic, centralized pattern which it had under the earlier Korean Royal Court. The police and other instruments of control suppressed democratic or liberal tendencies. The liberation of Korea in 1945 found a people politically naive. Holding elections for government officials responsible to the people was a new thing. The Communist, infiltrating under the guise of liberal movements, attempted to institute their own forms of totalitarianism. Counter organizations were developed, often youth groups, modeled on the Hitler Jugend pattern.

The welter of political parties gradually merged after the elections of 1948 into two conservative coalitions. Personal politics was the dominant characteristic. The "Liberal" party was headed by Syngman Rhee, a complex individual, who despite his old age was typically Korean in his resilience in the face of adversity, his volatile nature, and his deep-seated antipathy to outside interference. His stubborn strength was of great benefit during the dark days of the Korean War. He was adroit in handling potential political opponents in the early days of his power, but he became increasingly separated from political realities as he entered his mid-eighties. Bribery and police force became the methods of handling political affairs rather than political and economic leadership. Assisting his party were the national police, not at all democratically inclined. Many of their high officials were trained by the Japanese, and they continued to use the harsh methods they had learned from their masters.

The revolt against the Rhee regime in April, 1960 was sparked by students—young people who were inspired in large part by American democratic ideals. The key factor in the success of the revolt, however, was the action of the Korean military forces in supporting the students and effectively negating the hated national police. One of the personal tragedies of this chaotic time was the mass suicide of Lee Ki-poong, the Vice-President and political heir of Rhee, and his family, including his son who had been "adopted" by the Rhees. The Army leaders did not attempt to seize power; the martial law commander, Lt. Gen. Song Yo-chan, supported the care-taker government of Huh Chang while new elections took place.

The Democratic party, long an opposition coalition, swept the elections but quickly dissolved into factions over which Premier John M. Chang was not able to exercise control. His administration was unable to clear out corruption in high places, to counter the economic instability, and to prevent Communist infiltration. The fresh winds of freedom sometimes became of gale force. The device of student riots was used for less noble purposes. A peculiar phenomenon was the growth of newspapers and periodicals, many of which were only mimeographed in give-away issues and were used for personal blackmail! There were, however, many dedicated Koreans who had refused to take active political roles under Syngman Rhee who emerged from academic circles with sincere desires to aid in building democratic strength. Unfortunately, time was short and the economic stability required to make their efforts successful was sadly lacking.

It was into this volatile political situation that the military junta moved in May 1961. In its beginning days the junta, too, evidenced the personal factionalism which has been a hallmark of Korean political life for centuries. The leaders are relatively young; tested and trained during the Korean War, they constitute the cream of Korean youth. Though some (including General Park) were originally trained by the Japanese, most of them have been greatly influenced by the American army and know its traditions of civilian control of the government. Having exercised political power, the colonels and generals may be reluctant to retire at the end of their announced two-year period of democratic tutelage.

Despite the great interest of the United States in the development of democracy in Korea, it is obvious that it must grow from the inside. Nevertheless, American prestige and influence can be used in this direction. There is one strategic opportunity in working closely with the ROK armed forces and through their training programs seeking to instill democratic ideals. Through aid to education and cultural activities much may be accomplished. This may be done effectively through nongovernmental channels as well as by government programs.

ROK-JAPANESE RELATIONS

There is another sphere where improvement would be of great value, that is ROK-Japanese economic relations. Korea could again produce

a surplus of rice which could be bartered with Japan for needed manufactured goods. The proximity of Japan and Korea, six hours by boat
ferry, lends itself to easy intercourse. Relations between the two countries deteriorated to a very low point during the period of Rhee's control.
He, personally, had spent a lifetime of opposition to the Japanese and
could hardly be expected to cooperate happily with his hated enemies.
The Koreans remember with bitterness their years of subjugation to
the Japanese. Though they have vastly superior forces at present, these
are related to a threat from the North, and the Koreans fear a military
buildup of Japan. They resent the slighting statements which are made
from time to time by Japanese; they insist on being treated as equals.
Counter property claims on both sides are very great but are not realistic.
The Japanese property in Korea was taken over by the American Military
Occupation and subsequently vested in the ROK. The Japanese claim
some recompense for this. The Koreans claim that not only should this
property be given to them as a form of reparations but that the offices
and investments in Japan of companies which operated in Korea should
be turned over to them. There is a significant minority of Koreans in
Japan, numbering some 600,000 persons. This group has been rather
thoroughly infiltrated by Communist elements and many of them declare
their allegiance to North Korea rather than the ROK. Through the
agency of the Japanese Red Cross almost 150,000 Koreans have been
repatriated to North Korea despite the opposition of the South Koreans.
The citizenship rights of the Koreans remaining in Japan are not clear.
They have objected violently to the imposition of Japanese educational
systems for their children and wish to have special privileges in Japan.

During the American occupation of Japan and Korea a line was drawn
beyond which the Japanese fishing boats were not to operate. This line
was continued by the United Nations command and is now the so-called
Peace Line. It extends as far as 60 miles from the peninsula in some
places. Japanese fishing boats entering the Korean side of the line have
been fired upon and captured. Naturally there have been strident protests from Tokyo. A small island, Tokto (or Takeshima in Japanese),
in the Sea of Japan not far from Ullong Island, has been claimed by both
Japan and Korea. It is now in possession of the ROK and a few lonely
Korean guards are posted there. Actually it has little value other than
some seaweed beds around it. However, it has been the scene of a succession of irritating incidents, the tearing down of flags and markers
by both sides, for example. In the museums of Japan are numerous
art treasures of Korean origin which the Koreans would like to have
returned. These are typical of the many minor but irritating issues which
stand between Korea and Japan.

There has been trade between Japan and Korea in recent years, but
most of this has been under rather special conditions. For example, some
of the aid goods which America has furnished to Korea were procured

in Japan. There has been direct smuggling and indirect trade via Hong Kong. Legitimate trade channels have been blocked for the most part, yet it is clear that a considerable volume of trade could be developed which would be of decided benefit to both.

Under the regime of John M. Chang in 1960-61, some trade with Japan was developed in other than American financed military goods and strategic commodities. There was also a great increase in visits by Japanese business, political, and cultural leaders. Economic rapprochement, even to the extent of Japanese investments in mining and other enterprises, appeared to be developing. The attitude of the military junta to the Japanese is not yet clear, though it would appear that a strong anti-Japanese line similar to that of the Rhee regime will not prevail. It is obvious that the United States should continue its efforts to help resolve some of the issues, for it is to their mutual advantage that Korea and Japan live at peace and carry on trade with each other.

UNITED STATES ECONOMIC AID

The ROK is rightly concerned over the future development of its economy. Even before the Korean War, American aid for relief and economic development had amounted in total to some $400 million. In the wake of the war's destruction, estimated at over three billion dollars in productive goods and facilities, and the continuing heavy government expenditures for defense, it is not surprising that the Korean economy is shaky and serious inflation a constant threat. Therefore, short-term economic aid measures in the form of relief supplies and consumer goods for currency generation and support, have dominated the post-Korean War aid programs.

United States economic assistance from 1954 through June 30, 1961 is reported to have totalled roughly $2.4 billions. Much of this was in the form of raw materials and essential commodities—including U. S. surplus agricultural products—to bolster the economy. The local currency proceeds of the sale of these items has financed the Korean economic development program and paid a major portion of the salaries, supplies, and services of the Korean armed forces. Some aid did go to long term productive enterprises, such as fertilizer plants, glass factories, and the like which could save foreign exchange, and to more basic developments, railroad lines into coal fields, expansion of electric power generating facilities, and harbor improvements. Despite the huge aid programs, economic growth has not been sufficient to provide self-sustaining overall improvement of conditions for the Korean people.

Many economic plans and blue prints have been drawn up and some of them have been implemented in part. The United States military and aid agencies and the United Nations have all provided large sums at various times. However, difficulties in Korea including corrupt and inefficient governmental practices interfered with carrying out the program effectively. (After the military revolution, thirteen businessmen publicly admitted to having evaded the payment of the equivalent of over 33 million dollars in income taxes.)

The military junta in mid-July announced both an Emergency Economic Program and a Five-Year Economic Reconstruction Plan. These may not be hampered by some of the adverse factors of the past but certain basic economic difficulties still face Korea. For example, the Korean population is increasing in recent years at an annual rate of 2.9 per cent. While the economic growth of the seven years from the end of the Korean War (1953-1960) averaged 4.7 per cent, the net growth was only 1.9 per cent on a per capita basis.

The desire is great for higher standards of living, miserably low for decades. Koreans, having witnessed mechanized warfare, are not content to practice a primitive unmechanized civilian life. Aggravated by a large influx of refugees from North Korea prior to and during the Korean War, unemployment is a chronic ill. In 1960, 26.1 per cent of the population was reported as unemployed; because of the current agricultural practices underemployment, always difficult to measure, is also prevalent. With the constant threat of renewed aggression from North Korea and the need to keep an alert military establishment along the Armistice Line, government expenditures (largely military) in 1960 took over 10 per cent of the total expenditure of gross national income.

The latest five-year plan has as its ultimate goal "to establish a foundation for a self-sufficient economy through investment in key industries, elimination of obstacles to sound development of domestic industries, promotion of exports, establishment of import-substitute industries, and improvement of the international payment balance." The specific objectives of the plan are to step up the rate of economic growth to an average annual rate of 7.1 per cent, to reduce unemployment by about one-half, and to reduce the deficit on foreign account. Emphasis is placed upon increasing the total amount of investment. Although domestic capital formation is to be greatly expanded, the five-year plan counts on $927 million from United States defense support and economic aid and $424 million from foreign loans and private investment.

It is important to American prestige and to the preservation from Communism of the area for which we fought, that there be a real demonstration of political development and economic progress in the Republic of Korea. It is apparent that this can be achieved only with outside help. If the objective is accepted, the whole machinery of aid to economic development must be utilized—technical assistance, training, cultural interchange, trade expansion, and a substantial flow of capital. The prospects for private foreign investment in Korea are certainly slight, except perhaps in mining ventures, and the main flow will have to come through public channels. Aid of course is a necessary condition, but the essential requirement is for domestic efforts of a new intensity and quality. At present, an annual decision is made as to economic aid. The Korean situation raises clearly the question as to whether or not the United States, if it wishes to do so, can engage in such an undertaking on a continuing basis, with all the increased effectiveness which would flow from setting up an objective and pursuing it with some constancy on a longer-term basis.

THE MILITARY SITUATION

Finally and inescapably, there is the problem of the armistice and the military stalemate. The armistice has lasted since 1953. The ROK government, though not technically a signatory to the agreement, abided by its terms. The sixteen governments of the United Nations command reaffirmed in a statement of May 28, 1956, "their support of the armistice agreement and their intention to contribute to peace in the area." Both the Communist and the United Nations forces have complained often and bitterly over violations of the agreement to the Military Armistice Commission. In more recent years they have erected very formidable defenses along the line so that the line is more and more an effective defensive position. However, with the mobility of modern aircraft and the existence of new weapons, it is obvious that the defensive line offers no sure protection for either side. It is at best an uneasy peace which reigns along the truce line.

In South Korea there has been a massive United States military assistance program. This has been devoted mainly to training and keeping alert the Korean Armed Forces which now number roughly three-quarters of a million troops equipped with modern weapons. There has been a withdrawal of some of the United Nations forces, particularly the smaller units from some countries. Defensive positions and lines of supply from rear bases have been improved; the roads and railroads of Korea are now able to carry much greater supplies in case of emergencies. The United States defensive positions in Japan and more particularly in Okinawa have been strengthened so that Korea is not in itself so significant militarily as it was at the time of the Korean War.

During the coup d'état of the military junta, the United Nations Command was seriously weakened in prestige by the unilateral use of some Korean armed forces, technically under the UN Command, in this political action. There has been a return of these forces to the UN Command, but grave doubts have been raised as to whether or not the Korean forces are under effective control. The military junta has made some major shake-ups in the Korean armed forces. A number of military officers have been used for civilian posts in the government in Korea; more than ten of the highest ranking officers have been sent out of Korea as ambassadors. Others have been retired whose sympathies were not with the junta or who had not been so active in its support as was wished. (Thirty generals were retired in ceremonies on one day, July 8, 1961.) The emergence of General Park as the strong man of the junta and the accusation of General Chang, his predecessor, of plotting and "fomenting factionalism" reveal the rifts which are present within the Korean armed forces. The direct intrusion of the military into domestic politics results in an Armed Force which must be concerned with the many facets of economic and social life in addition to its task of defense and which faces, therefore, the danger of a weakening of military purpose.

The Korean War is not over. There is only an armistice and a truce line that divides a hitherto unified country. The same explosive situation which brought the United Nations and the United States into a major military conflict on the side of the ROK in 1950 could flare up again without warning. In addition to aid for economic development, the United States is faced with the problem of providing not only direct military support but also economic support whose proceeds can be used to provide local funds for the Korean armed forces.

Conclusion

Through the years the United Nations has served as a forum for the discussion of Korean problems. The United Nations Commission for the Unification and Rehabilitation of Korea continues to observe the Korean scene. It reported to the United Nations General Assembly in 1961 that "the prospects of unification, on which a full measure of stability and sound economic progress in Korea largely depend, remain remote." The ROK is not a member of the United Nations, though it holds membership and takes an active part in the activities of a number of the United Nations specialized agencies. (One of the tallest buildings in Seoul is a cultural center, UNESCO House.) In the spring of 1961 under the regime of John M. Chang vigorous efforts were made to have the Korean situation debated anew at the United Nations General Assembly. Various factors (including crises in other parts of the world that crowded it off the agenda) negated these efforts for more positive negotiations. With the military junta taking control, there appears to be a hardening in the anti-Communist attitude of the ROK and as a consequence negotiations seem more remote. After their long experience in the tents at Panmunjom, the Korean military puts little faith in negotiation by compromise. The United States should continue to urge the solution of the Korean problem within the United Nations framework; at some point of time, this may involve a renewed General Assembly debate or even a new Geneva conference, though this seems remote, particularly if rightful ROK participation is expected.

Any new conference would probably be faced with the same questions about elections which were discussed at Geneva. How "free" would an election be in North Korea under a Communist regime? For what positions should elections be held? The United Nations General Assembly in 1959 after reaffirming the objectives of the United Nations in Korea called upon "the Communist authorities concerned" to accept these objectives and to agree on the holding of "genuinely free" elections. There is no reason to feel that answers are more readily to be found than before. A conference would not solve the Korean problems, but it would have the advantage of probing anew the position of the Communist world in one of many crucial spots.

This approach rests on the assumption that the Korean problem, "the frustration of the hopes of the Korean people for unification of their country" as the sixteen nations termed it, should only be discussed under the auspices of the United Nations and not unilaterally. Paul-Henri Spaak, Belgian Minister for Foreign Affairs, said at the conclusion of the Geneva Conference:

> I believe that after a time, when the inevitable passions stirred up by the fighting and cruel war which has divided Korea have died down, the parties will be able to meet again and renew discussions together . . . reexamining the conditions in which we shall at last be able to achieve the desire which all of us share and which has been reiterated incessantly during the Conference, namely, a democratic, independent and united Korea.

So long as the assumption is made that this is a United Nations matter, any forward steps must be taken under United Nations auspices; otherwise (in the words of Spaak) it would result in "the terrible end of collective security and the United Nations." This does not prevent corridor discussion, of course, but it does emphasize the fact that in this instance the problem is in United Nations hands. This may require more effective techniques for collective consideration and collective negotiation than have yet been developed.

The United Nations in 1950 acted in the face of the aggression launched against the Republic of Korea. It dealt with that problem but it has not moved on, though Lester B. Pearson of Canada, President of the General Assembly in August of 1953, urged it to do so "toward political settlement and reconstruction in a free, democratic and united Korea— a goal which the Korean people have fought so valiantly to reach. Such a settlement could in its turn lead to a solution of outstanding issues in the whole of the Far East."

Having set unification as the goal, it is important to realize that this same problem exists in Germany and Vietnam. In all three instances, the passage of time is widening the gulf between the divided regions. Different economic structures, political institutions, and ideological exposures are increasing the problems of reintegration. One cannot be blind to the fact that unification may not be achieved. In that case, the line of policy must be to protect the independence of the free sector and contribute to the rapid building of its political, economic, and military strength. Such a program for Korea seems to be essential, but it will be difficult, costly, and long-term.

3.

The United States
and Communist China

◆ A. DOAK BARNETT

The rise to power of a Communist regime in China has created entirely new problems for the United States in its relationship with the Far East. In the years since the Chinese Communists established their People's Republic of China, a tremendous revolution has taken place within China, and the balance of power in the Far East has been fundamentally affected. The transformation of China from a weak nation playing a relatively passive role in world affairs into a unified totalitarian society with growing military power and ambitious international aims is certainly one of the most disrupting and disturbing developments since the end of World War II.

Traditionally, China-policy has been the key to United States relations with the Far

98

◆ A. Doak Barnett has written extensively on China for the American Universities Field Staff, Chicago Daily News Foreign Service, and Institute of Current World Affairs. He is the author of *Communist China and Asia: Challenge to American Policy* and many other writings on China. Formerly of the State Department, he more recently has been a Research Fellow at the Council on Foreign Relations and Program Associate of the Ford Foundation. He is now Associate Professor of Government at Columbia University.

East. Prior to 1949, the United States supported the Nationalist Government as an important ally in the hope that China would develop into a strong, unified, and democratic nation, friendly to the United States. Since 1949 the strengthening and unification of mainland China have proceeded rapidly, but under a regime which is both totalitarian and intensely hostile to the United States. Instead of being a power vacuum, Communist China, allied with the Soviet Union, is now the strongest nation militarily in Asia, is exerting a wide influence on surrounding areas, and is making an energetic bid for world power status. The pre-1949 basis for United States policy in the Far East has been drastically altered.

The adaptation of American policy to meet this new situation has been based to a considerable degree on improvisation, and it is still difficult to define a workable, long-term policy toward the Far East. The situation itself creates problems of the first magnitude, but the difficulty of reformulating United States policy has been complicated by a widespread American reluctance to face the realities of the new situation. Specifically, many Americans persist in viewing the Far East with nostalgic memories of the hopeful potentialities inherent in pre-1949 China rather than on the basis of a realistic appraisal of China as it exists now, and as it is likely to develop under Communist rule.

There is a legitimate basis for differences concerning the means by which the United States should attempt to meet the challenge presented by Communist China, but a first prerequisite for any rational approach is an understanding of the character and dimensions of that challenge. It is important, therefore, that United States policy be based upon a careful appraisal of the Chinese Communists' revolutionary strategy, the basis of their political power, and the profound revolution which they are engineering. It is even more important that United States policy be based upon a realistic assessment of the impact of Communist China on the international scene.

Strategy of Revolution

Although the pressing need now is to analyze contemporary Communist China rather than to re-examine past history, a few brief comments on the Chinese Communists' successful struggle for power are necessary as prologue to an examination of the present situation.

Much has already been written about the Communist revolution in China from 1921 to 1949, but a tendency to exaggerate external influences on China has often obscured rather than illuminated the fundamental character of the internal revolution in modern China and the strategy by which the Chinese Communists utilized existing revolutionary forces to achieve power.

International influences did affect domestic developments in China significantly, but the basic reasons for Chinese Communist success cannot be attributed either to the effectiveness of Soviet assistance to the Communists in China or to the failure of the United States to give sufficient arms and diplomatic backing to the Chinese Nationalists (Kuomintang). The influence of both the Soviet Union and the United States on the struggle within China was marginal. The United States actually had a much greater influence on developments in China before 1949 than the Soviet Union did, but large-scale American military and economic assistance to the Nationalists was not sufficient to prevent their defeat. Nationalist failure was due primarily to the domestic shortcomings of Chiang Kai-shek and his government. It is true that the Chinese Communist Party from its inception borrowed its ideology from abroad, received encouragement and support from the Russians, maintained continuous ties with the Soviet Union, regarded Moscow as a source of guidance, and identified itself with a Soviet-led world revolution. But within China the Chinese Communists largely fought and won their own revolution.

The establishment of a Communist regime in Peking in 1949 was actually the product of a century of revolution and the culmination of twenty-eight years of Communist struggle within China. Communist victory in this long struggle was neither preordained nor inevitable; it was the result of the Nationalists' failure to solve such national problems as an agrarian crisis, runaway inflation, administrative corruption, and political disunity, and of the Communists' success in exploiting the resulting situation.

One of the basic prerequisites for a successful Communist revolution, unless it is the result of external aggression, is a national crisis of serious proportions. This certainly existed in China.

RISING REVOLUTIONARY PRESSURES

Since the middle of the 19th century, China has been in a state of ferment. The political, economic, and social impact of the West after the mid-19th Century coincided with growing overpopulation, serious agrarian problems, an ideological soul-searching. The collapse of the Manchu Dynasty in 1911 was symbolic of a general process of disintegration. China was then in urgent need of reintegration, but instead it experienced almost two decades of near chaos during which the country was fragmented into numerous warlord regimes and lacked any effective central government.

Several basic revolutionary pressures became increasingly intense during this period. One was the growth of peasant dissatisfaction, unrest, and rebellion, caused by many factors including the shortage of agricultural land and the increase of landlordism and concentrated ownership. Another was the development of nationalism, emphasized particularly by a new class of Chinese intellectuals, products of a Western type of education, who demanded a strong, united, modernized China.

The Chinese Nationalist Party which came to power in the late 1920's was a product of these revolutionary forces; and during the Nationalists' early years in power the majority of Chinese desiring reform and modernization centered their hopes upon the Nanking regime. But the Nationalists were unable to satisfy existing revolutionary urges or to achieve national reintegration and stability.

Japanese aggression in the 1930's was a major reason for the Nationalists' failure. The Sino-Japanese War had a devastating effect upon China. Economic conditions deteriorated. Inflation sky-rocketed. Political disintegration set in. In the difficult wartime situation, the Nationalist regime was barely able to stave off defeat; it neglected the urgent economic, political, and social problems confronting the country. During this period the Nationalists steadily lost both their own vitality and popular support, and by the end of World War II their regime, although one of the victors, was in fact close to defeat. The Japanese War and the disorder it created provided the Communists with revolutionary opportunities which they were able to exploit. Only a heroic internal regeneration within the Nationalist camp might have halted continued deterioration in the postwar period; this the Nationalists proved incapable of accomplishing.

THE PATTERN OF REVOLUTION

The Chinese Communist Party, founded in 1921, was a small and relatively unimportant political force in China during the first decade or so of its existence. Its early strategy of revolution was based upon the traditional Marxist idea of urban, proletarian uprisings, an idea with little relevance to China where the urban proletariat was small and weak. Under instructions from Moscow, it formed a shortlived alliance with the Nationalist Party in the 1920's and attempted to achieve power by attaching itself to the Nationalist-led revolutionary movement. But this strategy was unsuccessful.

In the late 1920's, the Communists struck in many places in a wild attempt to seize power, but this resulted in defeat after defeat, forcing the Communists out of the cities and into the countryside. Defeat also forced, however, a basic revision of their revolutionary strategy in which Mao Tse-tung played the leading role, and it was the new strategy which was to lead ultimately to their success.

The Chinese Communists now label their revolution "the classic type of revolution in colonial and semi-colonial countries" which outlines, they assert, "the path which must be taken by the peoples of all colonial and semi-colonial countries in their fight for national independence and people's democracy." It is of considerable importance, therefore, to understand the essentials of this strategic blueprint which the Chinese now hold up as a model for revolutions elsewhere.

Two features of the Chinese Communists' strategy are of central importance. One was their decision to concentrate efforts on the peasantry. From the late 1920's onward, the Chinese Communists proved that where serious peasant dissatisfaction exists it can be exploited to organize a strong revolutionary force. They did this by making "agrarian reform" of some kind a basic plank in their revolutionary platform at all times. With complete tactical flexibility, they pursued land policies, varying from moderate reduction of tenants' rents to violent expropriation of landlords' holdings, which they believed most likely at a particular time and place to attract peasant support and consolidate Communist power in rural areas. No moves toward collectivization were made until after they had achieved power.

Another basic feature of the pattern of revolution established by Mao and the other Chinese Communist leaders was the concentration on building an army to fight a revolutionary guerilla war—what was called "armed revolution against armed counterrevolution"—rather than relying simply on political organization and maneuver or subversion. Control of definite geographical areas in the countryside was required in order to provide bases from which this revolutionary army could operate. Peasant soldiers operating from such rural bases, so-called "liberated areas," were the core of the Chinese Communists' revolutionary strength and the primary means to their success.

The Chinese Communists organized an effective Leninist type of party organization, which has become standard throughout the world Communist movement. The Party was built up as a disciplined elite, a hard core which organized the "masses," manipulated other groups, and controlled the whole revolutionary movement.

The Communists in China also disguised their ultimate goals and concentrated at every stage upon limited tactical objectives. The revolution was conceived of as one involving several stages, each leading to the next. Specifically, the Chinese Communists stated that their immediate goal was merely "new democracy" and that "socialism" would not come until later. This strategy of revolution by stages is fundamentally Machiavellian. The Communists could not have gotten very far in China if from the start they had emphasized their final objectives. During and after World War II they were able to attract support and, equally important, to minimize fear and resistance by sponsoring so-called "new democracy," supporting popular causes, and appealing to both reformism and nationalism in China.

THE UNITED FRONT CONCEPT

Another important feature of Chinese Communist strategy was the concentration of attacks, before 1949, on a relatively few "enemies" of the revolution and the attempt to include as many people as possible within a "united front" or "class coalition" under Communist control. The Communists prior to takeover of power defined their enemies in China as "imperialism, feudalism, and bureaucratic capitalism" or, in non-Marxist terms, foreigners and their influence, landlords, and private businessmen profiting from their government connections, all of whom were the objects of genuine, widespread Chinese resentment. The Communists tried to convince the Chinese people that no one else would suffer from Communist policies and that urban workers, peasants, petty bourgeoisie, and even patriotic capitalists should support their class coalition. At the same time, they encouraged divisions and antagonisms among non-Communist groups, infiltrated and subverted the Government, and did everything possible to weaken the opposition.

All of these factors contributed to Communist success in China. The Chinese Communists built up formidable military power in rural areas. At the same time, they helped to accelerate the disintegration already in progress in Government-held areas of China. By 1948, Communist armies were able to challenge the power of the Government directly, and when their armies began taking major cities and spread from North to South in 1949, Nationalist opposition crumbled.

China was really a political vacuum when the Communists took over in 1949, and the startling rapidity of changes within the country since then is only understandable if this fact is recognized. Important segments of two key groups in China, the peasants and young intellectuals, had been won over by the Communists, but most of the population accepted the change of rule passively. The majority neither assisted Communist takeover in any positive way nor actively opposed it. They merely abandoned the Nationalists and waited, with feelings ranging from hopefulness to apprehension, to see what a change of regime would mean.

They have seen the most tremendous revolution in Chinese history.

The Communists' Initial Achievements

It is impossible in a short space to give a comprehensive survey of all the great changes which took place in China in the first few years after the Communists' takeover. Even a brief listing of some of the major results may, however, suggest the broad sweep of historical trends which are sometimes overlooked in the current preoccupation with day-to-day headline events.

In a brief span of time, the Communists reunified China and re-established what can legitimately be called a Chinese empire, conforming for the most part to the traditional outlines of past Chinese empires. For decades prior to 1949, China was divided and weakened by civil war, provincial regionalism, warlordism, and separatism in its minority-inhabited borderlands. Soon after 1949, the Communists established unified control and imposed stern order over the whole country, destroying local concentrations of military or political power. They extended centralized Chinese administration effectively to Manchuria, Inner Mongolia, Chinese Turkestan, and Tibet.

Organized opposition to the Communists within China virtually disappeared. The Peking regime ruthlessly suppressed all possible opposition leaders and groups, liquidating considerable numbers of people in its campaigns against counter-revolutionaries. Whole social classes which stood in the way of the regime's aims were "eliminated" in a social and economic sense. The landlord class was dispossessed. The intelligentsia and business classes were subjected to tough "reform" campaigns. The peasants and workers were brought under tight control.

National leadership was changed almost in its entirety. From the central government to the villages, old leaders of state and society were pushed aside and largely replaced by Communist-fostered cadres. The new leaders are Communist Party members, government and army bureaucrats, and others working for them.

In the years since 1949, the Communists have established a very strong political structure in China. Despite many internal problems, the present regime, run by a disciplined party-army-government apparatus, is doubtless the strongest in Chinese history. Decisions made by the regime's leaders affect almost every aspect of people's lives, and the power of the regime reaches down and controls the mass of people, even at a village level, to a degree unprecedented in China.

Although political power in the past has been centralized and authoritarian in China, the Communists have established the first genuinely totalitarian regime in Chinese history. Almost the entire population has been organized into groups under Communist control and regimented in a way many people formerly believed to be impossible in China. An atmosphere of discipline, dynamism, "struggle," and tension pervades the country.

The Chinese Communists have attempted to impose a new national ideology on a country with one of the longest unbroken traditions of culture and philosophy of any nation on earth, and they have had some success. The whole population has been the target for intensive propaganda and indoctrination in Marxism-Leninism and the "Thought of Mao Tse-tung." Under an elaborate system of thought control, free expression of ideas has been suppressed except for a few brief intervals. The youth is being educated for socialism and trained for service to the state.

In the economic sphere, ownership and management have undergone revolutionary changes. After a cautious start, when the Chinese Communists first stressed land redistribution rather than collectivization, and the coexistence of state and private enterprises rather than nationalization, the Communists then rapidly accelerated their program of complete socialization. Collectivization of agriculture and socialization of industry and commerce were virtually completed in 1956, and were followed by the communes in 1958.

Wealth and property have been radically redistributed in a general economic levelling process. There are no longer significant concentrations of private wealth in China. Now the Communists are siphoning off the nation's product above minimum consumption needs to devote to national industrial development under state control. Austerity has been imposed as a way of life for the whole population.

The Chinese economy, which was in a confused state in 1949 after years of war and civil strife, was stabilized and rehabilitated within a relatively short period of time. The Communists brought inflation under control, restored former production levels of existing enterprises, and then embarked on a very ambitious development program.

The program of economic development is aimed at industrialization, and this has become the central element in the entire domestic program. The Communists are trying to mobilize, in a manner comparable to wartime mobilization in other countries, all available manpower, resources, and skills to support industrialization and general economic development. They appear determined to build a heavy industrial basis, whatever the costs or sacrifices involved.

In still another aspect of its national life, China's military power has been greatly expanded and modernized and now constitutes a force which cannot be ignored even by the major powers. In a basic sense, the Communists are militarizing China, and they are teaching the younger generation the glories of military service in behalf of the new China. They have announced that they intend ultimately to manufacture nuclear weapons.

The Communists have basically changed China's international orientation. For many years before 1949, China looked to the West for ideology, politics, and economic relations. All this changed in 1949. Communist China allied itself with the Soviet Union, Soviet influence began replacing that of the West within China and China's economic relations shifted toward the Soviet bloc. The recent increase in Sino-Soviet tensions has not to date affected this basic shift in China's international posture.

Communist China clearly has emerged as a major factor in international relations, not only with respect to the rest of Asia, but also in relation to the Middle East, Africa, and Latin America. Although the regime has won only partial international acceptance, it has increasingly made its power and influence felt in the underdeveloped world by military action or pressure, diplomatic maneuver, and political subversion.

Any real history of the past twelve years in Communist China also would have to devote attention to the social and cultural revolution which has been carried out. Changes of tremendous significance have been taking place in the role of the family in society, the status of women, the pattern of individual and group behavior. Education has been radically changed. Reform of the language is being attempted, with the ultimate long-term aim of substituting phonetic writing for traditional Chinese ideographs. Literature and the arts have been revolutionized. These and countless other aspects of the social and cultural revolution are making an indelible mark on Chinese society, changing the lives of over 650 million people, the largest single group of human beings in the world.

In short, the China of today is a very different country in many basic respects from the China of 1949. However, certain of the developments are most significant to an analysis of Communist China viewed in the context of world affairs today. For this purpose three aspects of the Chinese Communist regime will be examined in more detail: its political control, its economic development program, and its international position and policy.

Political Control

The Communists' rapid success in establishing tight totalitarian control over the huge amorphous population of China must rank as one of the phenomenal accomplishments of the Peking regime as well as one of the most disturbing developments in recent political history anywhere. On the basis of the best estimates of Chinese "national character" before 1949, it was widely believed that no regime could really discipline and control the Chinese people. But the Chinese Communists have done it. Borrowing Soviet techniques of political organization and manipulation, adapting some and refining others, they have effectively brought the entire population of China within the grip of their political, social, and psychological controls.

This demonstration that the masses in a huge overpopulated, underdeveloped nation can be effectively regimented by the Communists' "organizational weapon," in spite of traditional social and cultural resistances to modern totalitarian methods, adds a new dimension to political power. It is important, therefore, to understand the techniques and organizational apparatus by which this remarkable political feat has been accomplished.

COMMUNIST PARTY DOMINANCE

The locus of all real political power in China today is the Communist Party itself. Its members now total roughly 14 million or about 2 per cent of the total population. They comprise an elite which directs all the other institutions—army, government, mass organizations—which exercise control over the common people.

Political terminology is often misleading, and an organism such as the Chinese Communist Party bears almost no relation to a political party in the Western sense. It is first of all a state within a state. No serious attempt is made to disguise the fact that the top echelons of the Party possess primary decision-making power. The Party does not tolerate any real political opposition. It maintains its own functioning bureaucracy from the national capital to the villages. The government and other institutional bureaucracies merely implement Party policies, and at every level they are directed by Party members.

The Chinese Communist Party is also a semi-military type of ruling caste. Under "iron discipline," its members must obey orders from above unquestioningly, maintain strict security about Party matters, and function within a clearcut hierarchy of rank. They define their tasks in quasi-military terms and wear standard clothing almost like uniforms; many live a barracks sort of life. They are transferrable anywhere in the country and their lives are fully controlled by the Party. The Party has some of the characteristics of a religious brotherhood. All members must learn the orthodox ideological dogma and an enormous amount of time is spent studying it.

The Party's organizational structure, based upon Lenin's principle of "democratic centralism," is monolithic and completely centralized. "The individual obeys the organization, the minority obeys the majority, the lower ranks obey the higher ranks, branch organizations obey the Central Committee."

Organization is not merely a means to an end; it is really an end in itself, because it is the basis for creating the "new socialist man," a collective-minded servant of Party and state. The Chinese Communists assert that "the life of a Party member belongs to the Party."

Recruitment of new members from the masses is selective and careful. Candidates must be recommended by members in good standing, undergo indoctrination and severe testing during a probationary period lasting several months at a minimum, and then be approved by several levels of the Party hierarchy. This process of selection, screening, and testing has kept the membership a tightly-knit body.

The mass membership of the Chinese Communist Party is grouped into several hundred thousand small units which are in direct contact with every level of society and are scattered all over the Country. These basic branches, organized in any factory, mine, village, enterprise, urban locality, army unit, office, school, or other institution where there are three or more members, are run by elected committees under a secretary.

THE LEADERSHIP

The national hierarchy is built upon regional Party Congresses in every administrative division into which China is divided. Each Party Congress is elected by lower-level Party organizations and each elects its own committees and secretaries, who must be approved by higher authorities. In this hierarchy, although personnel, reports, and suggestions move upward, all major decisions flow downward.

Real power even within the Party is concentrated wholly in a handful of leaders at the top. Periodically a National Party Congress meets and its principal function is to choose these leaders by electing the Central Committee. However, such national Congress meetings have been relatively infrequent.

Far more important than the Party Congress as a governing body of the Party is the Central Committee which in mid-1961 had 95 regular and 94 alternate members. These persons corporately make almost all major policy decisions, and individually they occupy virtually every top position of power in the government, army, and other organizations, as well as in the Party itself.

Top authority in the Party is in the hands of two even smaller bodies, chosen by the Central Committee and headed by Mao Tse-tung, Chairman of the Party—the Politburo and its Standing Committee. Mao, Liu Shao-chi, Chou En-lai, Chu Teh, Chen Yun, Lin Piao, and Teng Hsiaoping made up the Standing Committee of the Politburo; the Politburo itself has nineteen regular and six alternate members. This small group of men has virtually unlimited power in China.

One of the important sources of Chinese Communist organizational strength is the competence and unity of this group of leaders. The members of the Central Committee are tough, capable, revolutionary leaders with long experience and many common ties. Most of them joined the Communist Party in its early days and have held leading posts in it for many years. The internal unity of this group has contrasted markedly with the factionalism within many other Communist parties. Mao Tse-tung established personal supremacy in the Party by 1935. Only twice in the twenty-six years since then has his leadership been seriously challenged and both of these attempts failed to split the Party. The most recent of these challenges, in 1954-55, definitely shook the Party and resulted in a purge which victimized two Politburo members, Kao Kang and Jao Shu-shih, but the Party was not basically weakened by the purge.

Purges at lower levels of the Party have been more frequent and have played an important role in weeding out the Party's membership, maintaining discipline, and enforcing orthodoxy. There is, in fact, almost constant "inner party struggle" within the Party, keeping the organization in that state of tension which the Chinese Communists consider necessary to insure effective performance by Party members.

Needless to say, the Chinese Communist Party does have many internal problems. Some are primarily administrative: shortages of personnel for new and more complex tasks as they have arisen, conflicts between new personnel and old Party members, tensions between higher levels of Party authority and the overburdened rank and file, bureaucratism and corruption, and others. Some have been political problems: tensions between centralized Party authorities and regional Party leaders, and rivalries between leaders involving clashes of personal ambitions. Quite clearly there also have been significant differences of views within the top leadership on both domestic and foreign policies. Since 1956-58, such differences seem definitely to have increased.

Some of these problems could develop into serious weaknesses or even splits in the future. There is a real question as to how the problem of successor to Mao will eventually be handled. But to date none of these problems has prevented the Chinese Communist Party from becoming and maintaining itself as a disciplined, effective elite, directed by capable, purposeful leaders who control the entire country and its huge population.

MILITARY TAKEOVER

Political and military power have been inseparable in modern China and the Chinese Communists' internal position rests upon military control of the country. As already pointed out, a revolutionary army was the spearpoint of the Chinese Communists' revolution. The military campaigns of this army, rather than popular civilian uprisings, put the Communists in power. Under the Party's control, the army remains one of the most important instruments of enforcing the Party's will in China.

Units of the Communists' so-called People's Liberation Army accomplished the initial takeover of power throughout the country. Troops moved into cities and villages alike, eliminating remnants of armed opposition, conducting mopping up operations, and everywhere putting on an impressive show of force to demonstrate the power of the new regime to the populace. This was an extremely important fact, for it demonstrated to people throughout China that Party members had behind them, at their call, effective military force.

The first period of Communist power in China after 1949 was one of open military rule, which only gradually gave way to civil administration. Scattered armed resistance to the Communists continued in isolated areas of the country for at least two years. The Communists' army was engaged during this period in clean-up operations against organized units and gangs, and it systematically disarmed the whole population by collecting even the small weapons traditionally kept by many peasant families. In the villages, after establishing initial control, the Communists organized armed peasant militia units directed by the Party to assist in maintaining order and suppressing opposition.

During this period the whole country was divided into regions run by Military and Administrative Committees. Most of these regions were headed by generals who had commanded the units which "liberated" them; and the regional boundaries were determined for the most part by the configuration of areas occupied by various army units. For several years the Military and Administrative Committees remained the highest local authority in most of the country. It was not until 1954, in fact, that the Great Regions covering most of the country were dissolved and the generals heading them reassigned to new duties.

At a national level, too, the army had a unique status during this period. Army organizations were not placed under a ministry subordinate to the Government Administration Council or Cabinet; instead a People's Revolutionary Military Council with status equal to that of the Cabinet was set up. After the adoption of Communist China's first formal constitution in 1954, this Military Council was replaced by a less important advisory group, the National Defense Council, and military affairs were placed under a newly organized Ministry of National Defense subordinate to the State Council, the new Cabinet body.

THE MILITARY COMPONENT OF COMMUNIST RULE

With the stabilization and regularization of the Chinese Communist regime, two types of military units have been differentiated. Under the Ministry of National Defense, there are regular army units comparable to the national armies of other countries. Separate from these, however, there are several hundred thousand troops, perhaps close to half a million, organized as so-called Public Security Troops. These are also regulars in the sense that they are trained, full-time soldiers, but they are assigned to local areas and their primary function is maintenance of law and order. Although control of these troops is shared by the military authorities and the Ministry of Public Security, they have come increasingly under the direction of the latter. In short, they are primarily military units with internal police duties, stationed all over the country in every province and county. At the county level they are now called People's Armed Police, which more clearly indicates their function.

All military organizations in China are infiltrated at every level by Communist Party members. Soldiers receive intensive political indoctrination. Political commissars, with rank equivalent to that of their counterpart commanders, are assigned to all important military units and Party cells function within the units. The whole army is enrolled en masse in some political organizations such as the Sino-Soviet Friendship Association.

The Communist Party uses the army domestically for many nonmilitary purposes. Some troops are used as laborers on transport and other public works projects. Some engage in farming; a few are used on industrial projects. During the collectivization and communization programs many soldiers were sent into the countryside to help Party "cadres" organize the peasants.

Military power is, therefore, extremely important in domestic rule in China. This is not an entirely new situation; the Nationalists also used the army as an internal support for its political power. But the army is now a far more effective prop for Communist rule than it ever was for the Nationalists. There are several explanations for this fact. The Communists have established genuinely unified and centralized control over all military units, eliminating local or personal units which previously existed. They have accorded their troops privileged status and good treatment, thereby helping to keep up morale. They have indoctrinated their soldiers, creating an army with high political consciousness, whereas formerly soldiers in China were often nonpolitical mercenaries of dubious loyalty to any political regime. There were some signs that the programs of collectivization and communization led to some concern about the morale of rank and file troops, most of whom are of peasant origin, but if there were adverse effects, they seemed to be temporary.

In short, the Chinese Communists not only possess a strong Party organization which functions all over the country, they also effectively occupy the country in a military sense. In addition to the highly political regular army, local Public Security Troops, People's Armed Police, and People's Militia provide nationwide military support for the regime.

GOVERNMENT ADMINISTRATION

The machinery of government is, of course, the principal administrative channel through which the Communist Party gives effective expression to its will. Formally, the present government in China represents a "united front." Selected representatives of the minor pro-Communist political "parties" still tolerated in China take part in the Government.

The bureaucracy still includes civil servants who are not Communist Party members. But the Communists' control of the government is complete and the bureaucracy implements Party policies.

The Communists first established a central government in China in the fall of 1949. In September, a Communist-appointed body called the People's Political Consultative Conference met in Peking and endorsed the Communists' Common Program and several organic laws which were to serve as the provisional constitutional basis of the regime for the first five years after the People's Republic of China was proclaimed on October 1, 1949.

By late 1952, the Communists began to feel a need to regularize and legitimize the government and they set in motion steps to draft a constitution and hold national elections. After unexpected delays, these preliminaries were finally completed in 1954; in September, the constitution was adopted and the government was reorganized on a more permanent basis. Government in the Soviet Union provided a model for the Chinese Communists but the Soviet pattern was modified in many details by the Chinese.

Several basic characteristics of government in Communist China today should be underlined. First and foremost is the extreme centralization of power and authority. Under the principle of "democratic centralism," all levels of government are controlled in almost every respect by higher authorities. There are no reserved powers or autonomy at a local level; orders are passed downward. At the same time, it is true that there is a wider mass participation in government affairs than in any past period in Chinese history. More people than ever before take part in activities such as elections and meetings of representative bodies, but their participation in politics is rigidly controlled and manipulated.

The administrative bureaucracy is undoubtedly the largest in Chinese history. It is by no means efficient in an administrative sense and it is plagued by bureaucratism. However, the Communists appear to have largely overcome traditional problems of local insubordination, corruption, evasion of responsibility, and inaction which have afflicted so many Chinese governments in the past. The apparatus of government, under the watchful eye of the Communist Party, effectively translates policy decisions of Communist leaders into action at a village level all over the country.

GOVERNMENT STRUCTURE

The structure of government includes a hierarchy of elected representative bodies called People's Congresses, separate and distinct from the Party Congresses, at every level of administration from the villages to the central government. Ordinary citizens participate in "elections" only at the lowest level, where they "vote" by show of hands rather than secret ballot on single lists of candidates prepared by the Communist Party. Congresses at higher levels are elected by the congresses of the levels below. In any case, the congresses only meet infrequently and exercise almost no real power. Their main function is to endorse key personnel in the government councils and other functioning bodies. The Communists attempt to make the congresses important in a symbolic and propaganda sense, however; they assert that the meetings of these bodies are an indication of the solidarity of support behind the government.

The National People's Congress holds periodic sessions at which it approves Communist policies and elects the Chairman of the Republic and other top government leaders. But although it is called the "highest organ of state power," it does not operate really as a legislature. It does, however, choose from its own membership a Standing Committee which possesses all the powers of the Congress and is one of the most important bodies in the government, having primary "legislative power."

The Chairman of the Republic is the symbolic head of the state. He does not function within any of the key governmental organs, but he can coordinate all top government leaders by convening special meetings called Supreme State Conferences. He nominates the Premier of the State Council, who is formally elected by the People's Congress.

The State Council or Cabinet is the most important organ of day-to-day administration in the government and all ministries and comparable bodies come under it. The Premier and sixteen Vice Premiers form what is in effect an "inner Cabinet" which can exercise most if not all of the powers of the whole Cabinet. The State Council not only administers the country at a national level but also controls and directs all regional or local governments in China. It rules by decree, issuing various types of decisions, orders, and administrative regulations which are binding on all lower levels of government and substitute for legislation on most matters.

The leaders of the Communist Party occupy the key posts in the government structure. Mao Tse-tung, Chairman of the Communist Party, was Chairman of the Republic until 1959, when he was succeeded in the top governmental post by Liu Shao-chi. Since 1949, Chou En-lai has been Premier of the State Council. All sixteen Vice Premiers are members of the Communist Party Central Committee. Central Committee members spread throughout the whole government structure and their control over the government as well as the Party constitutes a complex system of interlocking directorates.

THE DICTATORSHIP

The Chinese Communists refer to their government as a "people's democratic dictatorship" and a dictatorship it certainly is in reality.

They also refer to it as a "coalition government," however, and they continue to maintain the facade of a united front, giving some "representation" in the People's Political Consulative Conference to such minor parties as the Revolutionary Committee of the Kuomintang, Democratic League, and National Construction Association. But the United Front Department of the Central Committee tightly controls and effectively manipulates the non-Communist groups. Actually, the Communists could easily dispense with such forms of "cooperation" with non-Communist groups in China but they still find them to be convenient devices for indirect control, providing certain psychological advantages over open one-party dictatorship.

Party dominance of the government is transparent, therefore, despite the window dressing. A handful of Party leaders controls the central government, which in turn completely controls all local governments, even in the so-called "autonomous areas" which have been set up in minority-inhabited areas. Many of the most important policies of the government are actually announced by the Party Central Committee before the government formally adopts them. An article in an official Chinese Communist publication states simply that "the will of the Party must be executed by Government organs." The government, in fact as well as theory, simply executes the will of the Party and it does so very effectively.

CONTROL OF THE MASSES

Centralized, authoritarian rule is really nothing new in China; it is the traditional pattern of government. The most radical innovation under the Communists is the extension of political control under the party-army-government apparatus to such a degree that virtually every individual in China is tightly enmeshed in a system of close totalitarian supervision. This is new; it is, in fact, unprecedented in Chinese history. The Communists have created an amazingly complex web of organizations which have a tremendous impact upon the lives of ordinary people throughout the country.

Party members control or direct all the numerous governmental and nongovernmental strands which go to make up the control net-work at a grassroots level, but they are aided by many non-Party followers. Throughout the country there are numerous non-Party "cadres" or political workers who function within the framework of Party discipline even though they do not hold Party membership cards. In addition the Communists foster large numbers of "activists" (persons who emerge from the population to work with the Communists either because they genuinely support present policies or because they are motivated by opportunistic personal aims) and place them in positions of responsibility. These "cadres" and "activists" not only add to the number of persons on whom the Party can rely to run all sorts of organizations but they also provide a reservoir from which new Party members can be recruited. The "masses" are enveloped by the whole organizational web of control whether they like it or not. They are brought into organizations of many sorts and find themselves not only ruled by the apparatus but also drawn into it as participants.

From the start, one important component of the control network has been made up of residents' groups. The citizenry of China was soon organized by the Communists into small groups which are easy for the authorities to supervise. In cities, households were grouped into Residents' Teams. These in turn were represented on Residents' Committees often controlling several hundred families. The function of such groups has been to "mobilize residents to respond to government calls and to observe laws" and to help "direct mass security work."

The police in China have small posts called Security Sub-Stations throughout the cities, which control the residents' organizations. The police also check all population movements and register all persons in their districts. Absences from home must be reported as must overnight visitors. The police regularly visit the homes of residents under their supervision.

The large and ubiquitous regular police force in Communist China is organized into a centralized national bureaucracy under the Ministry of Public Security. In addition to the uniformed police, there are secret police who are active and effective in the background even though less in evidence in China than they were in the Soviet Union during the Stalinist period. There are at least two major secret police organizations; one is under the Ministry of Public Security and the other is directly controlled by an innocently labelled body called the Department of Social Affairs of the Communist Party Central Committee.

Several other government organizations assist the police in keeping close check on the population. The Ministry of Control in the central government maintains a separate nationwide organization to scrutinize all public employees and to ensure enforcement of directives and orders from above. The People's Procurator General's Office, on a par with the Cabinet in the government, has a wider function; its offices all over the country are responsible for investigating enforcement of laws and policies and their implementation by the population as a whole; its personnel are also the government's prosecutors in the courts. The nationwide court system, including provincial and county courts under the People's Supreme Court, has also played an active rather than passive role in enforcement of laws and policies; the courts have not only conducted trials but have also sought out cases to be tried.

Under these various government agencies an extensive system of subsidiary citizens' groups has been established which constitutes a nationwide system of organized informers. At various periods the police have organized groups called Public Security Committees, while both the

Procurators' and Ministry of Control's offices have appointed informers called, respectively, Procurators' Correspondents and Control Correspondents. The role of all such persons has been to check and report on everyone within a certain organization or district. The regime has also encouraged anonymous denunciations of any suspicious activity by the public.

In terms of both political and economic control, the most startling innovation in China has been, of course, the communes. First introduced in 1958, the communes provide the regime with an unprecedented degree of control in both rural and urban areas. Although some of the most extreme original features of the communes have subsequently been modified, they still represent an almost Orwellian control mechanism.

All of this adds up to an omnipresent institutionalization of investigation, mutual surveillance, and organized informing which breeds an atmosphere of suspicion and makes every individual feel under continuous scrutiny by other ordinary citizens as well as by official personnel.

THE ROLE OF LAW

The role of law and the courts is far different in China than it is in the political system of a democratic country. Law is viewed not as an entity separate from politics but as a "legal weapon" for implementing the program of the Communist Party. One of the clearest statements of this to appear in Chinese Communist writings stated simply: "It is impossible to talk of justice in isolation from Party principles. Whatever agrees with Party principles is just; whatever disagrees with Party principles is unjust."

By abolishing all previous laws when they came to power in 1949 the Communists created a legal vacuum which only slowly has been filled. A good many specific laws, regulations, and decrees that have been published are phrased so broadly that they provide legal justification for almost any action the Communists wish to take against those whom they consider political enemies. For example, regulations on punishment of "counterrevolutionaries," a vague and flexible term, have permitted the death sentence for such offenses as resisting taxes, labor service, military service, or grain collections, for alienating the people from the government, and even for conducting allegedly counterrevolutionary propaganda or spreading rumors.

Among the major innovations which the Communists have added to the court system have been special People's Tribunals, set up on an *ad hoc* basis all over the country to administer "revolutionary justice" during major nationwide campaigns such as land reform and campaigns against counterrevolutionaries. These mobile bodies toured through cities and villages during these campaigns, conducting emotional, mass public trials and executions in which the public was compelled to take

part so that they would be "educated" to understand Communist policies. In the trials which these tribunals conducted in the early years of
the regime, the number of victims executed certainly amounted to hundreds of thousands and may well have totalled several millions.

The penal institutions of the Chinese Communist regime include a
system of forced labor, labelled "reform through labor," administered
by the Ministry of Public Security. Almost every city and county has
groups of these unpaid forced laborers at its disposal, while large working groups of them are controlled by the national authorities; they are
of considerable economic importance to the regime. This kind of penal
forced labor, inspired by Soviet practices, is new in China; the Communists also have conscripted temporary *corvee* labor on a huge scale for
public works, a practice which has a long tradition in China.

MOBILIZATION METHODS

The Chinese Communists also organize the population in a more
positive sense in institutions through which the people can be actively
mobilized to support Communist policies. Virtually the entire population has been brought into Communist-controlled mass political organizations of numerous sorts. It would not be much of an exaggeration
to say that virtually everyone in China belongs to one or more of these
organizations which the Communists regard as "transmission belts" between themselves and the masses.

Such organizations are set up for the most part on the basis of specific
social, economic, or occupational groups. Practically every identifiable
group in China is organized—peasants, women, urban laborers, children,
youth, students, different groups in the arts and professions, even businessmen. The local branches of each organization attempt to include all
persons of a specific group and are directed by centralized, national bodies.

The ability of the Chinese Communist regime to mobilize the mass of
the population to take part in directed activities rests to a considerable
extent upon these mass organizations. Each of them conducts frequent
meetings, indoctrinates its members, serves as a channel for propaganda,
and sponsors activities of many sorts. Through these organizations, the
energies of active supporters of the regime are put to work, while others
are subjected to constant, organized, social pressure to conform and sub-
mit.

In a society organized in this fashion, support for official policies is
mobilized, opposition is suppressed, while noninvolvement and neutrality are made extremely difficult.

PROPAGANDA AND INDOCTRINATION

The efficiency of instruments of coercion which the police-state apparatus in China possesses should not obscure the fact that the Chinese

Communists rely to a great extent upon persuasion in dealing with the Chinese population. A tremendous amount of energy is devoted to propagandizing, educating, indoctrinating, and in effect trying to convert the Chinese people. The fiction is consistently maintained that virtually everything people are forced to do is done "voluntarily," and the spectacle of people "enthusiastically" doing things which are obviously in conflict with their own personal interests is one of the most remarkable phenomena observable in China. Actually, the line between coercion and persuasion is so blurred as to have little meaning in China today. The populace is persuaded to take "voluntary" action, but the Communists' persuasiveness rests to a considerable degree on the instruments of coercion they possess, the periodic campaigns of controlled terror they have conducted, and the undercurrent of fear which permeates Chinese society under Communist rule. Nonetheless, the Chinese Communists' efforts at mass persuasion are impressive.

The propaganda machine in Communist China is huge and its primary mission is to convince people within China of the correctness of Communist policies. There is no doubt that a significant proportion of the younger generation, nurtured in a controlled environment, indoctrinated in school, and subjected to an intense barrage of propaganda in whatever they do, is being deeply influenced by the communists' efforts to change the thinking of a whole nation. The psychological impact of propaganda and indoctrination on the older generation is more problematical, but some older people's thinking has certainly been influenced and outward conformity with official ideology is almost universal.

In 1957, when Peking's leaders briefly permitted genuinely free expression of opinion, they were shocked by the resulting flood of criticism against the regime which came not only from intellectuals but also from various other groups, including youth. They quickly reimposed controls, but that episode made it very clear that conformity does not necessarily mean agreement. However, the goal of the Chinese Communists' propaganda efforts is, in any case, effective thought control. The regime has established a firm grip on almost all conceivable media for communicating ideas, using them to propagate the official "correct" line on every possible subject and excluding unorthodox, undesirable ideas.

The daily press, supplemented by the radio, is of great political importance. The official line emanates from primary sources such as the Peking *People's Daily* and New China News Agency and is then disseminated all over the country. Careful reading of the press is considered to be a political obligation, and coverage by newspapers and radios is maximized through devices such as collective reading and listening groups. The limited output of the motion picture industry is almost wholly devoted to propaganda. Numerous official magazines are widely distributed. The state-controlled publishing and printing industry pours out tremendous numbers of propaganda pamphlets and books. Most novels and plays center on propaganda themes of current importance and writers' organizations define what these themes should be.

Propaganda is not limited to these obvious media, however. It is also injected into painting and poster art, dances and songs, and even into the Chinese equivalent of comic books. Traditional operas have been revised to include political messages. Village story tellers have been given material outlining new tales to tell. Diaries are printed with Communist aphorisms on every page and political slogans have been knitted into women's garters.

Despite the Communists' expansion of primary education and sponsorship of widespread adult literacy training, illiterates still make up a majority of the population and great emphasis has been placed upon oral propaganda and agitation. Immediately after achieving power, the Communist Party organized a nationwide oral propaganda network which ultimately, it claimed, will contain one per cent of the population. Oral propagandists operating at a village level "deliver propaganda to the door"; they are even advised, without a trace of humor, to get ordinary people to "replace family gossip with talk on current events." They use public meetings and speeches, slide showing, picture exhibits, simple plays, group singing, and informal conversation to propagandize the populace.

The organized propaganda apparatus is so extensive that the Chinese Communists have claimed that during special campaigns they can mobilize 15 per cent of the total population to propagandize the remaining 85 per cent.

One of the unique features of Chinese Communist rule is group indoctrination on a very large scale. Contrary to some opinion, the techniques labelled "brainwashing" by Westerners are not restricted in their use to inmates of Communist jails or labor camps. Although prisoners of the regime are subjected to indoctrination in its most intensive forms, similar techniques showing great psychological insight into means of manipulating and controlling men's minds are used in small study groups to which millions of ordinary citizens belong. These study groups usually average ten or twelve members. They meet regularly in places of work or residence, often for an hour a day, to read, listen to talks, and discuss materials provided by the official propaganda agencies of the regime. Generally each group is headed by a leader who makes regular reports to higher authorities. Discussion within the groups is often prolonged and intense. Members can and in fact are expected to raise doubts about the official "correct" view on any subject; but when this happens all other members are expected to argue in favor of the official line. The final objective is mutual agreement and unanimous support of the official line. Every member of such a group must take an active part;

one cannot be passive or silent. The result is described by some Chinese as a situation in which there is "neither freedom of speech nor freedom of silence."

A strong semireligious aura surrounds Chinese Communist propaganda and indoctrination. They put a premium on conversion, confessions of past errors in beliefs or behavior, and positive expressions of belief in Communist dogmas and catechisms. However, it is difficult to assess the real effects upon people. Although many undoubtedly just give lip service to the Communists' creed, many are undoubtedly genuinely influenced in their thinking. Whatever the real psychological impact, the Communists' propaganda and indoctrination are eminently successful in obtaining surface conformity with the official ideology. People who are not converted are at least intimidated.

POPULAR SUPPORT

The effectiveness of the Chinese Communists' totalitarian apparatus of political control is indisputable. It is not a simple matter, however, to judge the real attitudes of the Chinese people toward the present Communist regime. Some visitors to China report impressions of popular support and enthusiasm; others report sullen regimentation. Probably reports of both types contain elements of truth. Since convincing evidence on general Chinese attitudes is impossible to obtain, any estimate must be based to a large extent on guesswork.

There is no doubt that the Chinese Communist regime, despite its totalitarian character, does have a basis of support which is by no means small. There are millions of people in China who work for the regime in its myriad organizations and who have a vested interest in it. Although their financial rewards are small, they acquire power, status, and prestige in return for their support. In China, also, there are clearly many people who, although undoubtedly objecting to some Communist policies, apparently accept the proposition that China requires violent social surgery to change and develop the country and that totalitarian methods are therefore justified. There are certainly many Chinese whose intense nationalism has led them to accept totalitarianism and justify its necessity because they want to see China acquire national power and international prestige. In addition, the Chinese Communist regime appears to have attracted positive support from a significant proportion of the youth of the country who are being taught that the Communists' policies are inevitable and right, historically unavoidable, and desirable. Active support of the regime comes from all of these sources.

POPULAR OPPOSITION

It is the opinion of this writer, however, that active supporters of the regime constitute only a relatively small minority of the total population and that a large majority of Chinese dislike Communist rule and have been alienated by Peking's policies. The outpouring of criticisms during the "100 flowers" period in 1957 gave some indication of the types of resentments and frustrations that exist under the surface.

The Communists' performance has been far different from the slogans and promises used before 1949. Their ruthlessness, totalitarian control, and use of violence have disillusioned millions who were once hopeful about what a change of regime might bring. They have undermined the position and attacked the interests of groups making up a great majority of the population. They have alienated most of the peasantry by communization, the majority of businessmen by socialization, and many intellectuals by campaigns of "thought reform." The Communists have clearly, in fact, come to rely increasingly on repression and control, and decreasingly on voluntary support. It is a reasonable guess, therefore, that the majority of Chinese, if they were now offered a choice of regimes—a choice they have never in history been given—would reject the Communists, and that if there were some practical political alternative which they believed achievable—which there is not at present—they would probably choose to be ruled by another group of leaders.

While there is undoubtedly widespread dissatisfaction and dislike of the Communist regime in China (serious food shortages during 1959-61 certainly contributed to increased popular dissatisfaction), there is still no significant organized opposition or any immediate possibility of such opposition developing. In fact, the Communists have violently suppressed all signs of active opposition as soon as they have appeared. For several years after 1949, some anti-Communist guerrillas fought the regime in outlying border regions and subsequently a few guerrilla enclaves held out elsewhere in mountain hideouts. There have been a few short-lived and ineffective peasant explosions against the regime. Anti-Communist underground activity has continued on the part of secret societies and groups such as Taoist religious orders, as well as on the part of a few underground elements still linked to the Chinese Nationalists. And there has been a major revolt in Tibet which was ruthlessly suppressed. But none of these has presented any serious challenge to the Communists' control.

The principal form which existing dissatisfaction with the Communist regime in China can take, actually, is passive resistance to Communist policies. This kind of opposition creates problems for the regime and the magnitude of such problems could grow, but it does not now constitute any serious threat to Communist power in China.

In short, what could be called effective organized opposition does not now exist. Those opposing the Communists do not have any real leadership, program, or organization. Although there are some supporters of the Nationalists still left in China, most evidence indicates that the Nationalists were so discredited on the mainland by their performance and their defeat that there is no widespread hope—to say nothing of expectation—that they will return from Taiwan. It is completely unrealistic to expect a revival of support for the Nationalists.

The power structure which the Chinese Communists have established is clearly capable, therefore, of suppressing active opposition at present; it will only become incapable of doing so if it is seriously split or weakened from within.

Economic Development

Soon after consolidating power domestically in China, the Communists initiated an ambitious program of economic development and they are now engaged in the tremendous task of trying to catch up with the more advanced industrial nations. Their aim is to compress the industrial revolution into a few short years and to transform China from an agricultural into an industrial nation. At the start, the Chinese Communist program was clearly Stalinist, but since 1957 they have increasingly adapted and modified Soviet practices and have evolved many distinctive policies of their own. Their program, in any case, is one in which building heavy industry to provide an industrial base for national strength and power is the central focus of national life. To this end, living standards are sacrificed and the population is forced to accept the prospect of severe economic austerity for the indefinite future.

The Chinese Communists are attempting to force the pace of industrial development in every way possible. They have set very high production goals for their major heavy industries and they appear determined to outstrip other competitors in Asia in heavy industrial development. The long-run significance of this development is very great indeed. It seems destined to alter in a fundamental sense both the character of the Chinese nation and the economic basis for China's position in world affairs.

Its significance is heightened by the fact that it is taking place during a period when the desire for economic development has become a universal urge in the underdeveloped areas of the world. Leaders of underdeveloped nations are searching for answers to the problems of development and undoubtedly will be influenced by all major experiments now under way. The Chinese Communist program is a test of Communist methods in one of the most important overpopulated preindustrial economies in the world. It is not the only experiment in progress, however. India, for example, has chosen another path. The relative success of the economic programs in Communist China and India will have a great impact on leaders of underdeveloped areas elsewhere. The India program stresses steady, balanced development of all sectors of the economy, improvement in current levels of consumption, and an important role for private enterprise under overall state planning, while the Chinese Communists' program emphasizes rapid construction of heavy industry, national military power, complete government control of the economy, and ruthless total mobilization of manpower. There is no doubt that they will be compared and judged on the basis of their results.

The Chinese Communists are pushing their industrial program with energy and complete singleness of purpose. They have encountered difficulties of many sorts, some extremely serious, but because of their effective totalitarian control they have been able to push steadily ahead; despite all problems and obstacles, they have already made notable progress in industrial output. In agriculture, however, they have encountered increasingly serious problems.

EVOLUTION OF ECONOMIC POLICY

The Chinese Communists' concept of revolution by stages is well illustrated by the great changes in their economic policies between 1949 and the present. Their long-range twin goals of "socialization" and industrialization (and, of course, ultimately "communism") have been clear from the start, but their methods of achieving them have undergone a rapid evolution over the years.

In 1949 many observers were impressed by the seemingly unique "moderation" of Chinese Communist policy. Mao Tse-tung's program at that time, outlined in *On New Democracy,* called for a long period during which state and private enterprise would coexist. Although the state would rapidly take over large-scale enterprise, the Communists promised that private business would be allowed to exist and even to develop further in other sectors of the economy.

The Chinese Communists did start cautiously in their approach to the economy; in 1949 they were not yet ready for a frontal assault on private ownership. In rural areas they were preoccupied until 1953 with eliminating landlordism and redistributing the land; "agrarian reform" policies in this period involved violent revolution in the villages but not collectivization. In the cities during this same period a great deal of industry and commerce was left in private hands, even though the Communists took over large-scale Chinese as well as foreign enterprises, imposed firm indirect control over the entire economy, and took preliminary steps toward socialization.

The Communists' main economic aim between 1949 and 1952 was rehabilitation; they restored production in existing enterprises, repaired transport, revived trade, controlled inflation, achieved price stability, and initiated a few large-scale public works projects. They themselves now distinguish between this first "period of reconstruction" and the "period of construction" or development starting in 1953.

By 1952 the rehabilitation process had been fairly successful despite the severe strain of the Korean War on the Chinese economy, and the Chinese Communists prepared for the next major stage in their economic revolution. Peking's leaders decided to launch their industrialization program with a Five Year Plan starting in 1953. They also decided to make a tactical redefinition of their overall economic policies and formulated a new theoretical statement on economic policy which they labelled "the general line of the state for a period of transition to socialism." This policy statement, unveiled to the public in 1953, was quite different in tone from previous writings on "new democracy" which had emphasized gradualism; it called for more rapid steps toward both industrialization and socialization.

THE FIRST FIVE-YEAR PLAN AND SOCIALIZATION

China's first Five Year Plan got off to a start on January 1, 1953. However, it was not until after the death of Stalin, in the latter part of the year, that an agreement was concluded with the Russians on the level of Soviet aid to China and a truce was signed in Korea which enabled the Chinese Communists to crystallize plans and concentrate their resources and energies on domestic development. At the start, economic planning was rudimentary; China did not actually complete and publish a final version of their first Five Year Plan until mid-1955 when the plan period was already half over, and this version was soon outdated.

In this initial period the Communists did, however, set production targets for various sectors of the economy and started industrial expansion. But they immediately encountered numerous problems, the most serious of which was the lag in agricultural output. Agricultural production fell far short of the goals set for it in the first two years of the Plan, and this fact undoubtedly was a major reason for Peking's decision to speed up socialization in order to achieve overall state control of the economy as rapidly as possible. In late 1953, a complete state monopoly of the food market and nationwide rationing of basic food staples were instituted. Immediately thereafter, the Chinese Communist Party Central Committee decided to accelerate nationwide agricultural collectivization, emphasizing at this stage the organization of producer cooperatives which had been established experimentally during the previous two years. Similarly, it was decided to crystallize as definite national policy past experiments in organizing businessmen into so-called "state capitalist," semi-socialist forms of organization.

One of the distinctive features of socialization during this period in China was the concept of achieving both collectivization of agriculture and nationalization of business in several stages, in order to minimize the disruptiveness of the "transition to socialism." In agriculture, peasants were first grouped into small mutual-aid teams and then organized into producer cooperatives, in which they retained theoretical land ownership even though farm management was collectivized, before the final establishment of full collective farms in which private ownership was eliminated. This step-by-step process effectively reduced peasant resistance to collectivization. Socialization of industry and commerce also proceeded in stages. Private businessmen were brought under increasingly close control of the government through various stages of so-called "state capitalism," finally being grouped into "joint state-private enterprises" prior to outright nationalization. This process enabled the Communists to put businessmen to work for the government, in effect converting them into state employees, and it thereby helped the Communists solve their lack of experienced, competent personnel in economic fields.

From late 1953 until mid-1955, the process of organizing peasants into producer cooperatives and converting business into "state capitalist" forms went on steadily, with successive speedups and slowdowns, but generally at a moderate pace.

Then in mid-1955, in response to serious agricultural problems, Mao Tse-tung himself took the initiative in demanding much faster socialization, and a tremendous burst of organizing activity took place in the second half of the year. By the end of 1955, almost the entire peasantry had been brought into the producer cooperatives, and by the end of 1956 most of the cooperatives had been converted into full collectives, on paper at least. In late 1955, a similar speedup in organizing businessmen took place, with an energetic drive to convert remaining private enterprises into "joint state-private enterprises." By the end of 1956 this too was largely completed. The regime's entire timetable was drastically altered; socialization was virtually completed before the end of the first Five Year Plan.

THE FIRST FIVE-YEAR PLAN—OVERALL GROWTH

While these tremendous institutional changes were being engineered, the Chinese Communists were simultaneously struggling to achieve very ambitious targets for production increases and overall economic growth.

The first Plan called for roughly doubling the value of gross industrial output and increasing by approximately one-quarter the value of gross agricultural output. At the end of the plan period, Peking declared that both of these overall targets had been exceeded. Gross industrial output, it claimed, had increased during the five-year period by close to 120 per cent (over 200 per cent in capital goods and 85 per cent in consumer goods produced by modern machine industry), while gross agricultural output was alleged to have increased by almost 25 per cent.

It is extremely difficult to evaluate Peking's official claims. While the statistics issued during 1954-57 were considerably more accurate and reliable than those which have appeared more recently, especially since the start of 1958, many of the official claims regarding accomplishments during the first Five Year Plan were either inaccurate or somewhat misleading.

But even if Peking's official claims are substantially discounted, it is clear that the Chinese Communists were able to initiate a significant process of rapid overall economic growth during their first Five Year Plan. A number of economists in the West have made independent estimates of Communist China's rate of growth during the 1952-57 period, and although their estimates vary in details, they nevertheless indicate that Communist China's gross national product increased during 1953-57 by an average rate of perhaps 7 or 8 per cent a year—a rate considerably above that of most underdeveloped nations and perhaps close to double the rate achieved by India during the same period.

RATE OF INVESTMENT AND LIVING STANDARDS

Rapid growth of this sort requires, of course, a high rate of investment. The Chinese Communists themselves state that the rate of "accumulation"—i.e., total national savings—averaged 23 per cent of total product per year during their first plan period. Independent estimates by economists in the U. S., using Western rather than Communist concepts, indicate that perhaps close to a fifth of China's gross national product went into gross domestic investment during the first Plan.

What all of these figures mean is that the Peking regime, through taxation, profits from state enterprises, and many other forms of compulsory savings, siphoned off a large part of the nation's economic product to invest in development, and kept the current standard of living at a very low, although equalized and fairly stable, level.

The Chinese Communists frankly state that any hope for a general rise in living standards must be postponed; "the small betterment of today," they assert, "must be subordinated to the big betterment of tomorrow." It is possible that some industrial workers in China, a relatively small group, may have improved their livelihood slightly since Communist takeover, but this has been more than counterbalanced by the sharp decline in the economic position of business, commercial, and other urban groups.

It is difficult to judge accurately what has happened to the peasant mass of the populace. Some reports indicate that peasant incomes have actually been reduced, but most peasants' former living standards were so low that no great reduction was possible while permitting survival. It is almost certain in any case that little significant general improvement in peasant living standards has taken place. In an agricultural country such as China, the main burden of supporting a rapid industrialization program of the type now underway must inevitably be passed on to the peasantry.

The low priority on raising living standards in China is justified by the Communists in the name of industrialization, but not all of the economic burden on the population is due to the economic development program. The Communists are currently supporting a large military establishment, and the cost of building and maintaining military power is high. The cost of maintaining domestic control is also high. The Chinese Communists are supporting the largest bureaucracy in Chinese history, and the payroll of millions of unproductive bureaucrats, even on low salaries and with remarkably little corruption, is huge.

SOVIET ECONOMIC AND TECHNICAL ASSISTANCE

The present industrialization program in China is a boot-strap type of operation in which the Peking regime must rely primarily on China's own financial resources. However, the Chinese Communists could not have carried out their first Five Year Plan without various types of assistance which the Soviet Union provided. The entire initial development plan was based, in fact, upon Soviet promises to help construct key industrial projects in China by providing large-scale technical assistance and by selling to China essential equipment, mostly on a barter basis.

In a series of commitments made in 1950, 1953, 1954, and 1956, the Soviet Union promised to help Communist China construct 211 major projects, by providing essential technical assistance and by selling to the Chinese the necessary machinery, equipment, and supplies. By the end of China's first plan period, these Soviet promises involved commitments to provide equipment and supplies to the value of about $2 billion for the 211 projects. Subsequently, in August 1958 and February 1959, the number of so-called "aid projects" was increased by 125; Soviet commitments to sell equipment to China were increased accordingly.

The entire Soviet "assistance" program really might be described as "trade not aid." The Chinese have paid for what they have received from the Russians, and this has led to a very close trade integration between China and the Soviet bloc, involving a radical international reorientation of the Chinese economy. Prior to World War II, China's trade was almost entirely with Western countries and Japan; less than one per cent of China's trade was with Russia. Since 1949 this pattern has completely changed. Currently, approximately three quarters of Communist China's trade is with Soviet bloc countries (about one half of it with the Soviet Union alone), on the basis of barter agreements negotiated annually.

Soviet technical assistance was also extremely important to China's first Five Year Plan. In 1955 Peking's top economic planner revealed the extent of Chinese dependence at that time on Soviet experts and advisors. "On the 156 industrial projects which the Soviet Union is helping us to build," he said, "she assists us throughout the whole process from start to finish, from geological surveying, selecting construction sites, collecting basic data for designing, supplying equipment, directing the work of construction, installation and getting into production, and supplying technical information, right down to directing the manufacture of new products."

Although during the second Five Year Plan period, the number of such experts was greatly reduced, Premier Chou En-lai in late 1959 revealed that up to that time 10,800 experts from the U.S.S.R. and over 1,500 from the other East European communist nations had worked in China.

The Chinese Communists have had to pay for this Soviet assistance. As far as is known, Moscow has not given Peking a single free grant for economic development, and even its loans have been small. Only two Soviet long-term loans for economic development have ever been publicly announced—the 1950 loan of $300 million and the 1954 loan equivalent to $130 million. Both of these loans were completely used up by 1957, the end of the first Five Year Plan period, and Peking began at that time to encounter increasingly serious balance of payments problems, as it tried simultaneously to pay back past Soviet loans, to develop substantial foreign aid programs of its own, and to continue importing large amounts of needed equipment from the Russians. (When Communist China encountered critical agricultural problems in 1959-60 and was unable to pay with exports for a sizable proportion of its current imports from the U.S.S.R., the Russians did agree in early 1961 to allow them five years to make these payments, thus giving them, in effect, substantial trading credits.)

REGIONAL DEVELOPMENT

The regional distribution of development projects in China has been of great interest and importance ever since the first Five Year Plan was initiated. Manchuria was the only region in China containing the beginnings of a heavy industrial base before Communist takeover and has to date been the center of greatest industrial construction activity. The Chinese have rehabilitated and expanded Japanese-built industries there and have begun construction on many important new ones. The industrial developments at China's "steel capital" of Anshan, at Mukden, Changchun, Harbin, and other centers, make Manchuria the most vital region in China's economic plans.

In the rest of China, however, a conscious and significant alteration of the industrial map of the country has been undertaken. Important new industrial centers are being built deep in China's interior in areas of Northwest and Southwest China. These include two entirely new iron and steel centers which, it is claimed, will eventually rival Anshan— one at Paotow in Inner Mongolia and the other at Tayeh in the middle reaches of the Yangtze River. In Northwest China, industrial bases are slowly developing at Lanchow, Sian, Taiyuan, and elsewhere. In the Southwest, considerable activity is under way at Chungking.

Shanghai and the other major light industrial areas near the coast formerly developed largely by foreign investment continue to be China's main centers producing consumer goods, but the most spectacular development of new industries is in the interior where very little modern industry existed before.

There are economic explanations for this planned redistribution or dispersion of industry in China, but the strategic significance of the shift is also very great. The relative proximity of the new industrial centers to the Soviet Union and their distance from China's fairly vulnerable coastline are factors of real military and geopolitical importance.

The current development of transportation in China, as well as the industrial shift to the interior, also reflects the importance of strategic factors in the thinking of Chinese Communist leaders. Many of the new roads and rail lines should be evaluated in strategic terms.

Before 1949 the only rail link between China and Russia was in Manchuria. A second has now been built, the Tsining-Ulan Bator railway connecting with Siberia via Outer Mongolia. A third, the Lanchow-Sinkiang line which will connect with the Turk-Sib line in Soviet Central Asia, is nearing completion. In addition, an important new trunk system has been built within China to provide a rail connection between the country's remote Northwest and Southwest regions, linking many of the new centers of projected industrial development. The Chinese Communists have already completed motor roads to Lhasa, providing the first modern transport connection with Tibet, and they plan to build a new railway that will in time be extended to Tibet. Chinese railway construction has also included many short lines of strategic importance such as the Hanoi-Kunming line linking Indo-China and China, and the Yingtan-Amoy railway in the coastal area opposite Formosa.

There is no doubt that by the end of the First Five Year Plan period an important start had been made toward the primary goal of industrialization. In key industries they had, in fact, initiated an almost phenomenal rate of industrial growth which, if sustained, promised within a relatively short period of time to lift the absolute (but not per capita) output of many major heavy industries in Communist China to levels comparable to those of industrial powers such as Britain and Japan.

According to official claims, between 1952 and 1957 the output of key heavy industries in Communist China rose as follows:

Steel	1.35 to 5.35 million (metric) tons
Pig Iron	1.9 to 5.94 million tons
Coal	63.53 to 130 million tons
Electric Power	7.26 to 19.3 billion KWH
Cement	2.86 to 6.86 million tons
Machine Tools	13.7 to 28 thousand sets

The process of industrialization encountered numerous problems, and even during the first plan period it was hectic and often confused. But the Chinese Communists showed a determination to push ahead regardless of costs, and that is exactly what they did.

The Peking regime very soon learned, however, that while the problems of industrialization might be great, the biggest question marks facing their economic development program were those posed by agriculture, which is, and will long remain, the foundation of the Chinese economy. The Chinese Communists faced a dilemma in their approach to agriculture. They needed to raise total agricultural output and a discontented peasantry would not be likely to spur production. But they also found it urgently necessary to ensure delivery to the state of the existing crop "surpluses," requiring control measures unpopular with the peasants.

During their struggle for power before 1949 the Communists had attracted positive support from large numbers of peasants, who were then the primary basis of Chinese Communist strength. Although the violent class warfare involved in "agrarian reform" between 1949 and 1953 was by no means universally popular, over 115 million acres of land were redistributed at that time to poorer peasants—certainly one of the largest real estate transfers in history—and this was obviously welcomed by millions who received land. But from 1953 on the Communists took a succession of steps—establishment of a state monopoly of grain, rationing, collectivization, and finally communization—which squeezed the peasants very hard, subjected them to rigid controls, and coerced them to give up control of the land which they only recently acquired. The regime, in short, came to depend increasingly upon coercion rather than attraction in its dealings with the peasantry.

Despite this emphasis on the need to control agriculture, the regime did take steps aimed at increasing overall production. Large-scale antipest campaigns were conducted and the use of insecticides fostered. Some increase in the use of fertilizers took place although supplies of chemical fertilizers remained very inadequate. Efforts were made in simple ways to alleviate the severe shortages of farm tools; mechanization remained, however, a hope for the future. State banks and cooperatives attacked the problem of farm credit. Efforts were made to introduce elementary training in improved farming techniques. In addition, using literally millions of drafted peasants as well as organized forced labor, the regime undertook thousands of small, and some very big, projects in flood control and irrigation.

Undoubtedly, however, one of the most important factors affecting agricultural output is the weather and this the economic planners have been unable to control. During the Chinese Communists' first Five Year Plan, natural disasters took place in 1953, 1954, 1956, and 1957. Both as a result of these disasters and the immediate effects of collectivization, agricultural production lagged far behind the output targets set by the planners. The shortage of grain and other agricultural products put a great strain on the economy.

According to official claims, grain output in Communist China increased from 154.4 million tons in 1952 to 185 million in 1957, giving an average annual rate of increase of 3.7 per cent. However, independent estimates based on both pre-Communist and Communist data indicate that Peking's figures for the earlier years are probably too low, while those for 1955-57 are doubtless too high; the average rate of increase in output of basic agricultural crops may, in fact, have been well under 3 per cent.

At the start of the first plan period, it should be noted, Communist China also conducted its first nationwide census. This 1953 count indicated that mainland China's total population was 583 million. Subsequently Peking officially estimated the rate of annual increase in Communist China's population to be over 2 per cent. The immediate impact of these basic facts and figures on Peking's leaders was clearly sobering and it led them to foster a birth control program for a brief period after 1953. In 1957-58, however, it was abandoned along with many other policies pursued up to that time.

THE "GREAT LEAP FORWARD" AND COMMUNIZATION

Although the Chinese Communists made some impressive economic gains during their first plan period, especially in industrial output, and, in fact, had achieved a number of their five-year goals by the end of 1956, during 1957 they began to encounter increasingly serious economic problems. It appeared as if their entire development program was beginning to lose its momentum as some of China's basic economic problems caught up with the regime. Problems resulting from collectivization, the lag in agricultural output, the constant growth in population, and increasingly serious food shortages, made 1957 a year of special austerity for the Chinese people. And the rapid decline in external economic aid from the Soviet Union forced Peking to rely almost wholly upon its own resources.

In retrospect it seems clear that a very important policy debate took place during 1957 among top Chinese Communist leaders—between groups that subsequently have been variously labelled by Western observers as the "moderates" or "planners," and the "leftists" or "radicals." The "moderates" apparently argued for a relatively careful, rational process of adapting economic policies to meet China's problems, and the initial version of Peking's second Five Year Plan seemed to reflect their views. The "radicals" apparently called, however, for bold and even reckless new policies based upon an intensification of revolutionary mobilization and fervor. By late 1957, the "radicals" had clearly won out. The essence of the new "leftist," "radical" policies was the idea of accelerating growth primarily by total mobilization of male and female labor (minimizing capital investment where possible), and increased efforts at ideological exhortation (minimizing reliance on material incentives).

In late 1957, Peking started on its new course by mobilizing a claimed 100 million peasants for intensive work on state-directed water conservation projects. Then, in early 1958, Chinese Communist leaders scrapped production targets that had previously been established, announced a "great leap forward" and a new "general line" for economic development, and began projecting rates of growth unprecedented in China or anywhere else. Virtually the entire population was mobilized to take part in a startling, new, decentralization program, in which medium-sized and small "factories" (including the much publicized backyard iron and steel furnaces) were built all over the country.

Then, in the second half of 1958, came the program for establishing communes. By the end of the year, after a hectic nationwide campaign, over 700,000 collective farms had been merged into slightly over 26,000 communes—huge multipurpose units designed to accomplish almost total economic mobilization of the population, to increase both local investment and central state control, to manage not only agriculture but also local industry, commerce, finance, education, and military affairs, and to promote communal living.

The atmosphere in Communist China during 1958 was one of frenetic mass activity, and toward the end of the year Peking's leaders announced fantastic claims of increased output, for example, that both steel and grain production had doubled in a single year, steel output allegedly rising from 5.35 million tons in 1957 to 11.08 million in 1958 and grain output from 185 million to 375 million tons in the same period. Apparently, the entire statistical mechanism in China went completely out of gear as local officials—feeling great pressure from above—made grossly exaggerated estimates of output. Later in 1959 recognizing that their initial estimates had been absurdly inflated, Peking's leaders themselves issued revised claims reducing the estimate for grain output in 1958 from 375 to 250 million tons. They also admitted that the backyard furnace campaign was a failure and that 3.08 million tons of the claimed steel output in 1958 was unusable for modern industry. (Independent Western estimates indicate that even after revision Peking's claims on grain output in 1958 were too high; actual output may have been closer to 210 than to 250 million tons.)

THE AFTERMATH OF THE "GREAT LEAP FORWARD"

Peking's attempt to forge "full steam ahead" continued into 1959, but it soon became apparent that the "great leap" was creating serious dislocations and other problems and that it could not be sustained. Imbalances of many sorts appeared, resulting from uneven development in various sectors of the economy; transportation, in particular, was badly overloaded and disorganized. The extraordinary pressure exerted on both urban and rural laborers could not be maintained. Moreover, in 1959, and then again in 1960 and 1961, mainland China continued to suffer natural disasters. Grain output, according to independent Western estimates, dropped to perhaps 190 million tons in 1959 and 180-190 million in 1960, while population growth continued unabated at 2 per cent or more per year.

In 1961, Peking began purchasing grain on a large scale from non-Communist sources such as Canada and Australia; by mid-1961, in fact, it had contracted for the purchase of over 10 million tons, 5 million or so for delivery in 1961. The Russians did not provide China with grain but they did agree in early 1961 to allow Peking several years to pay off trade deficits accumulated because of the Chinese inability to keep up the level of its agricultural exports to the U.S.S.R. Within China, while mass starvation was apparently being kept to a minimum, evidence of widespread malnutrition steadily increased during 1960 and 1961.

The Chinese Communists publicly blamed their food crisis during 1960-61 almost entirely upon natural disasters, but while such disasters did occur, they seemed insufficient to explain the situation fully. Moreover, Peking's leaders quietly began to modify many of the extreme policies of the "great leap" and communization, indicating that they themselves realized that natural disasters were not entirely to blame.

This process of taking a sizable step backward after the great leap forward was accelerated in early 1961. Peking began to emphasize the need for economic "regularization," and the communes were significantly modified by organizational decentralization and steps which gave more deference to the importance of material incentives for the peasants. Some experiments in small industries were modified or given up (the backyard furnaces were largely abandoned in 1959), although it was clear that medium and small-scale decentralized industry would continue to have an important role to play in Communist China. In general, the tremendous pressure from Peking was relaxed; the speed-up, in short, was slowed down.

Despite the slackening in the pace of Peking's development program immediately after the "great leap," the Chinese Communists' rate of growth was not unimpressive through 1959. According to independent Western estimates, in 1958 Communist Chinese GNP increased at the extraordinary rate of 17 or 18%, and then in 1959 the rate was perhaps 12%. In modern heavy industry, Communist China made remarkable progress in this period; steel production reportedly reached over 18 million tons in 1960. Subsequently, however, the rate of economic growth dropped to a much lower level. No overall production claims were published in Communist China during 1960-1961, but independent estimates place the rate of growth in 1960 at perhaps 4%, and in 1961 it probably dropped to a still lower level.

The biggest question marks regarding the economic future in Communist China are posed by the food shortage and the population explosion, both of which seemed to be further than ever from solution in mid-1961. The Peking regime's tight political control and firm determination to industrialize rapidly make it appear probable, however, that despite very serious economic problems the Chinese Communists might well be able to continue forging ahead toward their primary goal of building industrial power, even if this were only to be done by enforcing on the Chinese population continued austerity and even malnutrition or starvation.

Foreign Policy

China has vigorously entered the international world since the Communists came to power in 1949. It has fought a war in Korea, intervened indirectly in the war in Indo-China, re-established Chinese control over Tibet by military force, exerted pressure on several of its borders, and threatened military action against Taiwan (Formosa). It has extended the area of Chinese influence by political and diplomatic action, by economic aid and trade, and it has strongly pressed a claim to world power status.

Communist China has emerged as one of the two major powers in the Communist bloc and is now stronger in military might than any other nation in Asia. It is one of the most dynamic elements in contemporary world politics, a force in international relations which requires realistic evaluation.

Before examining the specific foreign policy and short-term diplomatic tactics of the Peking regime, it would be wise to attempt to define the long-term objectives and outlook of Communist China's leaders. This is necessarily a matter for speculation but it is nonetheless important.

There is little doubt that one of the basic long-term objectives of Chinese Communist leaders is the establishment of China as a recognized world power with a position of primacy in East Asia. This is not a uniquely Communist aim; it is one which has deep roots in traditional Chinese thinking, is reinforced by modern nationalism, and has been shared by recent Chinese leaders of every political coloration. Traditional Chinese attitudes of cultural and political superiority have led many Chinese to believe that their country deserves leadership in Asia and hegemony over surrounding areas. Chinese do not forget that if one views the last two millenia rather than the past century, China has been the strongest country in Asia over long periods and many Asian countries have at some time been tributary to China.

Throughout Chinese history, when a strong government has come to power it has attempted to re-establish a Chinese empire and extend Chinese influence; this process seems to be repeating itself. For several decades, furthermore, intense nationalism has developed in China and with it a desire to establish China as a strong modern state with a position of power and respect. The Chinese Communists have consciously appealed to nationalist sentiment, even though they also accept "Marxist internationalism," and in some respects the present Communist regime is a logical product of the nationalist movement. Both traditional and modern currents of Chinese thought therefore reinforce the drive to achieve world power status.

The Chinese Communists do not preclude the use of military force to achieve their basic objectives; they currently seem, in fact, to place more stress than the Russians on the revolutionary importance of military struggle and to be less concerned about the risks of war. The available evidence does not indicate, however, that they are overtly pursuing a program of general military expansionism or aggression. The principal use of Chinese Communist armies to date has been limited to areas which Peking's leaders have viewed as parts of China's empire and therefore Chinese territory in the past, or to areas bordering China which the Chinese Communists regard as regions of special interest both because of their strategic importance to China and because they are ruled by Communist regimes. Thus, although the Chinese Communists are clearly prepared to use military force when they believe China's vital interests, as they define them, are involved, Communist China, unlike Japan in the 1930's, does not seem to be pursuing a plan of Asian military conquest. Since late 1957, however, it has seemed to pay increased attention to the value of pressure on nearby areas, combined with diplomatic and political maneuver as well as with various kinds of persuasion and subversion.

Chinese Communist leaders seem able and willing to take a long view of history. They also appear to be genuinely confident that they are riding the wave of the future and that time is on their side. Consequently, they do not feel under compulsion at all times to force every issue to immediate conclusion; they seemingly do feel at present, however, that the Communist bloc has a strategic advantage which it should exploit in every way possible.

Several strategic concepts derived from their domestic revolutionary struggle are deeply embedded in their patterns of thinking and are undoubtedly relevant to their approach to international affairs today. One of these is the principle of tactical flexibility. The Chinese Communists push forward if chances of success appear to be good; they are willing to carry out tactical retreats and make temporary compromises without abandoning final aims if the risks of failure are great. Another tactical principle is summed up in the dictum: unite with the majority, attack the minority, divide the enemies, destroy the enemies one by one. This idea of expediency in making political marriages of convenience and dividing the opposition provides a guide to foreign relations as well as domestic revolution.

Peking views foreign policy in the broad context of a Marxist-Leninist image of a world engaged in an intense competition for world dominance. In this view the most important factor in the international situation is the long-term struggle between the Communist bloc led by the Soviet Union (and China) and the anti-Communist bloc headed by the United States.

The Chinese Communists' stress on "coexistence" is completely tactical. In this schematic conception of things, Peking believes that it has a special role in the competition for influence in the area of "colonial and semi-colonial countries," which lies between the two major blocs. When the Chinese Communists first came to power, feeling the flush of victory within China, their sense of international revolutionary mission was particularly apparent. During the period 1954-57 their backing of revolution throughout the "colonial and semicolonial" areas of the world was less blatant but their sense of special mission remained. And since 1957 they have shown a new militancy which has clashed at times with Moscow's tactics in this period.

SINO-SOVIET RELATIONS

Communist China's new posture toward the external world in 1949 began with the decision to align closely with the Soviet Union. The Sino-Soviet alliance of 1950 became the cornerstone of China's international relations. However, Sino-Soviet relations have gone through several significant stages of development since 1950, and in recent years the alliance has been subjected to tensions and strains on a number of issues.

Alliance between China and Russia is an entirely new phenomenon, unprecedented historically. It resulted from the ideological and organizational links between the Chinese Communist revolutionary movement and the Russians which had existed ever since the Chinese Communist Party was founded in 1921. During the first decade of the Chinese Communist Party's existence, Moscow exercised close, direct control over it. From the 1930's until 1949, the ties were much less close than in earlier years but connections were maintained. The Chinese continued to acknowledge Soviet leadership of world Communism and the Chinese Communist Party never adopted a position on any major international issue inconsistent with the Moscow line.

In late 1948 the Chinese Communists' orientation toward the Soviet Union was re-emphasized when a top Party leader, Liu Shao-chi, clearly rejected Titoism in an important document titled *On Nationalism and Internationalism*. Mao Tse-tung made the Chinese position even clearer in the summer of 1949; China, he stated, must "lean to one side" and wholly commit itself to the Soviet bloc; all other alternatives were rejected.

The Soviet Union immediately recognized the People's Republic of China after it was established and soon thereafter Mao Tse-tung went to Moscow, making his first trip out of China. During a nine-week period in Russia he laid the foundations for Sino-Soviet relations through direct negotiation with Stalin. The most important result of this trip was the Sino-Soviet Treaty of Friendship, Alliance, and Mutual Assistance, signed on February 14, 1950. This treaty, valid until 1980, binds China and Russia in a close military alliance. Both parties pledge to assist each other if either is involved in war with Japan "or any state allied with her"—an indirect but unmistakable reference to the United States.

Stalin insisted on certain Chinese Communist concessions, confirming at least temporarily the special Russian position in Manchuria which had been established at the end of World War II, on much the pattern of former Czarist rights. The Chinese Communists agreed to accept joint Sino-Soviet management of the Chinese Changchun Railway and joint use of the naval base at Port Arthur until signature of a peace treaty with Japan or until the end of 1952, whichever came earlier. They also acknowledged Outer Mongolia's "independence" and agreed to the establishment of Sino-Soviet joint stock companies in China.

THE KOREAN WAR

The Korean War broke out less than half a year after the cementing of the Sino-Soviet alliance and in the fall of 1950, as the North Koreans retreated, China intervened. No definitive account of the circumstances of China's entrance into the war will be possible until further information is available but several explanations are credible, and the Chinese Communists' decision may have been due to any or all of a number of factors. If there was a prior Sino-Soviet agreement on Chinese intervention, which is possible, it is not known. There are some indications that in early 1950 Chinese interest was primarily directed toward Formosa, Tibet, and problems of domestic consolidation. But, as the North Koreans retreated, the Chinese themselves probably concluded that the defeat of the North Korean regime would constitute a threat to China's security. The Russians may well have exerted strong pressure on Peking to step in to prevent complete defeat. When China intervened, the war was moving toward Manchuria and Peking may have feared invasion of this rich region on which its plans for industrialization depended. Moreover, the Chinese have long considered Korea an area of strategic importance to China and the Peking regime undoubtedly feared the consequences of control of the whole peninsula by unfriendly military forces.

The Korean War was a test of Sino-Soviet relations and the alliance stood up to the test at that time. Chinese troops did the fighting while the Soviet Union provided the equipment to fight with. The war placed a great strain on the Chinese economy but Soviet military advice and aid helped to build up the strength of Chinese armies, despite the tremendous casualties suffered in the war.

By late 1952, however, the Chinese Communists apparently decided that tactical compromise was necessary. The war in Korea conflicted with their desire to start industrialization in China; China needed more Soviet aid to begin its Five Year Plan; and the terminal date on the Port Arthur and Changchun Railway agreements was approaching. The Chinese, therefore, once more sent a major delegation under Premier Chou En-lai to negotiate with the Russians in the fall of 1952.

Negotiations between the Chinese and Russians continued until the middle of 1953. While the first agreement announced in September, 1952, returned the Changchun Railway to sole Chinese control, it also provided for continued joint use of Port Arthur, reputedly at China's request. No mention was made of the Korean War or Soviet economic aid to China at this time.

Although the course of those Sino-Soviet negotiations was veiled by secrecy, it is probably significant that it was not until after the death of Stalin in March, 1953, that agreement on Soviet economic aid to China was announced or that the Chinese Communists took the steps which made possible a Korean armistice agreement. It is very possible that Stalin was not enthusiastic about the Chinese desire to shift their own efforts and Soviet aid away from the war in Korea, where the fighting tied down a sizable proportion of the West's ground forces, to economic development in China, where industrialization would in time probably raise China's status within the Soviet bloc.

In the Stalin period, therefore, Sino-Soviet relations undoubtedly involved some hard bargaining and possibly even significant tensions. Khrushchev later accused Stalin of almost causing a rupture in Sino-Soviet relations. But despite frictions and tensions that existed under the surface, unity was successfully maintained and the Sino-Soviet alliance weathered a severe test in the Korean War.

THE POST-STALIN ERA

Subtle but definite changes took place in Sino-Soviet relations soon after the death of Stalin. The immediate although short-lived effect of these changes seemed to place the partnership on a stronger, firmer basis than ever before. Increased Soviet economic aid to China in this period has already been described. Political concessions were also made to the Chinese. The visit of Khrushchev and Bulganin to Peking in the fall of 1954 was the first visit by top Russian leaders to China, a fact significant in itself. In Peking they announced the restoration of Port Arthur to

China and dissolution of the joint Sino-Soviet stock companies. They also signed several important joint Sino-Soviet declarations on major Asian problems.

All in all, the 1954 agreements and joint statements constituted a major consolidation of the Sino-Soviet alliance. A new tone also began to characterize Soviet statements about China and Stalin's successors gave increasing deference to China. Communist China's status within the Sino-Soviet partnership steadily rose, even though the Soviet Union remained the senior partner.

In February 1956 the Soviet 20th Party Congress and Khrushchev's "deStalinization" policies ushered in a new turbulent period in Communist bloc affairs and a new phase of Sino-Soviet relations. The Chinese Communists reacted coolly to Khrushchev's extreme denunciation of Stalin, apparently fearing that it would have unsettling, disrupting effects upon the Communist bloc, as indeed it did have. When crises developed in late 1956 in Soviet relations with both Poland and Hungary, Peking became involved for the first time in East European affairs. In general, the Chinese Communists in 1956 and early 1957 seemed to play a mediating role in bloc affairs, trying to encourage a pattern of intra-bloc relations that would allow the satellites to have a substantial degree of autonomy in domestic affairs and yet would maintain bloc unity and solidarity.

PEKING'S MILITANT LINE

The latter part of 1957, however, marked a great change in Peking's general strategy regarding both foreign policy and intra-bloc relations, which coincided with the introduction of more radical policies at home within China. This change was first visible at the Moscow conference of Communist parties in November, 1957—soon after Russia had launched its first ICBM and sputniks—when Mao Tse-tung declared that in his view there had been "a new turning point" in the world situation as a result of which "the east wind prevails over the west wind; that is the strength of socialism exceeds the strength of imperialism." Mao argued, in short, that there had been a major shift in the world balance of power. On the basis of this assumption the Chinese began pressing for more militant policies toward the West and a tightening up within the bloc. The Soviet Union at this period, however, was still attempting to reach a rapprochement with Tito and was in favor of coexistence, disarmament, and detente with the West.

During 1958, 1959, and 1960, there were increasing signs of Sino-Soviet differences over a variety of problems and issues, resulting in some fairly serious frictions and strains in the alliance. In the spring of 1958, for example, Peking took a considerably more militant line than Moscow in attacking Tito and "revisionism." In mid-1958, when the Western powers intervened in the Middle East, the Chinese seem to have urged a stronger Soviet response. In late 1958, Peking precipitated the second offshore island crisis and, although it obtained some backing from Moscow, Russian support was probably less than hoped for. During 1958 and 1959, Peking applied new pressures of various sorts on several Asian countries, including Japan, Laos, Indonesia, and India. Moscow took a notably neutral stand on the Sino-Indian border dispute; Peking reciprocated by being definitely cool toward Khrushchev's visit to the United States and his build-up for the (abortive) summit meeting of 1960.

During this period a rather intense ideological dialogue developed between Moscow and Peking. The debate ranged over many issues: the nature of peaceful coexistence, the inevitability of war (especially local war), armed struggle versus peaceful tactics in Communist revolutionary struggles, the benefits and dangers of Communists allying with bourgeois nationalists, the feasibility of a detente with the West, the possibility of disarmament, and so on. On all of these issues the Chinese took the more militant, "harder," more revolutionary line.

In the background, moreover, there were doubtless other issues which were important, even though they were not explicitly or openly discussed. Most specifically, the Chinese Communists may well have felt that they were not obtaining sufficient backing from the Soviets on two prime Chinese aims: "liberation" of Taiwan and entrance into the "nuclear club."

In 1960 the Sino-Soviet frictions were intensified, reportedly as a result of a bitter exchange of letters between Moscow and Peking and heated debate over these letters at a gathering of Communist parties at Bucharest in June. In November-December, 1960, when another general meeting of Communist parties was held, one major aim apparently was to iron out existing differences and to reach some meeting of minds on the major issues which had been under debate. Whether the meeting in fact accomplished a meeting of minds is not clear. The declaration which emerged from it has been variously interpreted by Western observers; in general, it seemed to represent a compromise with Moscow coming out ahead on the crucial issues.

During 1961, elements of disagreement became even more apparent. When Russia became very critical of Albania, Communist China came to its support. When representatives of the Communist countries had gathered in Moscow, the Chinese representatives left well before the end of the meetings and even the ceremonials appeared to be more formal than friendly.

In all probability, some of the underlying problems will continue, as will competition for leadership and influence between the two major Communist parties. It seems equally probable, however, that despite tensions and frictions—which exist, after all, in every alliance—the overriding importance of common ideological assumptions, common goals, and common interests, will keep the two major partners from splitting and will impel them to continue working in close concert in their overall struggle against the West.

STRATEGY IN ASIAN FOREIGN POLICY

As suggested already, Peking's general strategy in its foreign policy has gone through several phases. In the years immediately following 1949, it is difficult to discern a rational pattern in its overall foreign policy other than force. Self-confident and arrogant, Peking's leaders seemed determined to establish what they conceived as their "rights" simply by demanding them, backing China's demands with military force, and intervening militarily in varying ways in situations relating to Tibet, Korea, Indo-China, and Taiwan. Bluster, threat, and pressure typified most of their action elsewhere. They exhibited undisguised hostility toward most of the non-Communist world. They refused to accept British recognition and their only performance at the United Nations was crude and inept. They openly approved of "liberation" wars based on China's "classic example" in Indo-China, Burma, Indonesia, Malaya, the Philippines, India, and Japan—all of which they classified as "colonial and semi-colonial countries."

During 1953 and 1954, however, an important change took place in China's approach to foreign relations. (As early as 1952 there were some indications of a general policy shift on the part of the Soviet bloc as a whole, including China, but Peking's flexibility was limited as long as the Korean War continued.) First came the Korean truce in 1953. Then in 1954 China played a major role in the Geneva Conference which brought fighting to a halt in Indo-China. Immediately thereafter the Chinese Communists began a freewheeling diplomatic campaign in South and Southeast Asia and extended their diplomatic activities elsewhere. They adopted a new posture of reasonableness and conciliation, designed to "reduce tensions." They began to go to great lengths to win friends and influence people. At the Bandung Conference of Asian and African nations in the spring of 1955, Communist China's representatives put on a remarkably skillful performance as sponsors of peace.

The 1953-54 shift by Communist China from a "hard" to a "soft" policy can be explained by a number of factors. Externally, the buildup of American-supported military strength around China, in Korea, Japan, Okinawa, Taiwan, and Indo-China had multiplied the risks to Communist China of military action and limited its ability to use threats and pressure successfully. Within China, the decision to push economic development seemed to put a brake on policies abroad which might place an additional strain on China's resources. The Chinese Communists apparently decided that their minimum immediate objectives could be attained in Korea and Indo-China by consolidation of Communist regimes in the northern halves of these countries. They also decided that there were considerable possibilities for diplomatic success throughout Asia if they adopted a new and more conciliatory approach.

The over-all strategy of Communist China's foreign policy which evolved during 1954-57 was therefore one in which the Chinese appealed to sentiment favoring Asia for the Asians, promoted the idea of peaceful coexistence, and tried to exploit neutralism and the desire for peace in order to prevent the development of any effective anti-Communist alliance in Asia. They also attempted to reduce fear of Communism and to build up an image of Communist China as a reasonable, peaceful country. As always, they did all they could to stimulate anti-Western feeling in Asia, portraying the United States as militant, belligerent, and imperialistic, and attempted to weaken the anti-Communist position in Asia by mobilizing Asian feeling against the West, particularly the United States.

Then, as suggested above, a major change of strategy and tactics occurred in late 1957, apparently as a result of Mao's assessment of a shift in the world balance of power, and Peking embarked on a new militant, "hard" policy that greatly changed the atmosphere throughout Asia. This new approach was marked by an economic embargo against Japan, a dispute with Indonesia regarding the Overseas Chinese, support for renewed insurrection in Laos, cutthroat trade competition in Southeast Asia, and a bitter border dispute with India.

In 1960-61 some of these policies were softened. Peking resolved its dispute with Indonesia, moderated its economic blockade of Japan, and signed important agreements with Burma, Nepal, and Afghanistan. But its basic strategy still appeared to be a militant, "hard" one. It continued a hostile attitude in the Indian border dispute and gave strong backing to the Pathet Lao who appeared to be close to winning control of Laos by a combination of insurrection and negotiations at the conference table in Geneva.

North Korea, North Vietnam, and Outer Mongolia are areas of special Chinese interest. In Chinese eyes they seem to be treated as buffer zones vital to Chinese security and Chinese influence in all these areas has steadily grown. Soviet influence is also important, especially in Outer Mongolia and Korea, and there currently seems to be a competition for influence between Peking and Moscow in both areas. (Russian influence obviously is still stronger than Chinese influence in Outer Mongolia and probably this is true in North Korea as well.)

One measure of the importance Peking places upon its relations with these neighbors is the fact that despite Communist China's own economic problems, it has granted substantial economic aid to all three areas. As of early 1961 Peking's grants and credits to North Vietnam totalled $457 million; to North Korea, $330 million; and to Outer Mongolia, $115 million. Peking also consistently throws its international support behind the North Korean and North Vietnamese regimes. The increased local militancy of both regimes from 1959 on had strong Chinese Communist backing.

TAIWAN

An area which the Chinese Communists regard as of primary importance to them is Taiwan, the Pescadores, and the Nationalist-held islands off the China coast. Peking insists that the future of Taiwan is a purely domestic issue, despite its international complications. In the Chinese Communists' view, Taiwan is Chinese territory and the "liberation" of Taiwan and defeat of the Nationalist regime are required to complete the unification of China. The Taiwan Strait is an area, therefore, where the Chinese Communists could well decide to use military force once again— if the risks were not excessive.

In 1949, the Chinese Communists regarded the invasion of Taiwan merely as a final mopping up operation in China's civil war and made active preparations to invade the island. The Korean War, neutralization of the Taiwan Strait by the U. S. Seventh Fleet, and subsequent American commitments to the Nationalist regime, fundamentally altered the situation, however, and blocked the Communist takeover. Peking continued to threaten "liberation" of Taiwan, but the Communists were unable to direct primary attention to it while they were committed in Korea.

In 1954-55 and 1958 the Chinese Communists again focussed their attention on the Taiwan area and turned the pressure on the offshore islands. In retrospect, it seems fairly clear that the Chinese Communists were not prepared in either instance to launch a full-scale attack on Taiwan or risk war with the United States, but that they were testing to see what they could gain in the Taiwan area by military threats and pressure. The situation during both of these crises was explosive, however, and contained the threat of major conflict between Communist China and the United States—possibly as a result of accident or miscalculation. After 1958 the Chinese Communists shifted again to psychological warfare against Taiwan and at various times attempted to entice defectors from the Nationalist side or offered to negotiate with the Nationalist Government itself on the "peaceful liberation" of Taiwan. It continued, however, to improve the Communist military position on the coast. In recent years, Peking has shown increasing concern that the U. S. would implement some sort of "two Chinas" policy that might obtain broader international acceptance of Taiwan's separation from mainland China.

It seems likely that the Chinese Communists wish to avoid major conflict with the United States and that they will try, therefore, to achieve control of Taiwan by political means. There is virtually no immediate possibility of Peking formally relinquishing its claim to Taiwan, however, and to date it has refused to renounce the use of force in that area.

There is a real possibility that the Communists may again decide to renew attacks against the offshore islands, which present fewer risks and greater possibilities for success than Taiwan itself.

JAPAN

Japan also looms large in Communist China's foreign policy. In power terms, Japan is the only Far Eastern country which can counterbalance or threaten China. Economically and politically, Japan is more "modern" and advanced than China; it constitutes therefore a real rival for influence throughout Asia. Few Chinese can forget the Sino-Japanese War and fear of a Japanese threat in the future is probably genuine in China. It was highly significant that Japan was pinpointed specifically as a potential threat in the Sino-Soviet alliance of 1950.

In the period immediately after 1949, the Chinese Communists were openly hostile toward the existing Japanese government and undoubtedly hoped that the Communist Party within Japan could gain power. As hopes for immediate Communist success within Japan receded, the Chinese Communists then decided to try to influence the policies of the existing Japanese government and to cultivate left-wing groups in Japan, such as the Socialists who have more influence than the Communists. Peking used trade possibilities as bait, returned many Japanese war prisoners in an attempt to influence Japanese public opinion, and directed propaganda in large quantities to Japanese groups of various sorts.

The immediate objectives of this approach were to weaken Japan's alignment with the United States, stall Japanese rearmament, neutralize Japan, and if possible sway the Japanese toward closer relations with the Soviet bloc. There is no doubt that Peking's energetic "people's diplomacy" did influence important groups in Japan. However, in 1958 Peking seemingly became impatient, adopting once more a "hard line" and embargoing trade with the Japanese. It was not until over two years later that it again began to put emphasis on the need to woo the Japanese.

SOUTH AND SOUTHEAST ASIA

Perhaps the regions in which the shifts in Communist China's foreign policy have had the greatest impact are South and Southeast Asia. In 1949 and immediately thereafter, Peking was openly militant and called for revolutions throughout much of South and Southeast Asia. Then it shifted to the more limited aim of neutralizing the region, minimizing Western influence, and opening the door to increased Chinese influence. From 1954 on, the main targets of Chinese Communist efforts in this region were the three leading neutralist countries: India, Burma, and Indonesia. Instead of denouncing non-Communist leaders in these countries as they had previously done, the Chinese Communists began praising them, playing on their anti-Western resentments, and attempting to obtain their political support for China. Communist China was not only tolerant of neutralism in this region; it became virtually a sponsor of it during 1954-57.

In many respects India, Burma, and Indonesia were favorably predisposed toward Communist China, viewing the revolution in China merely as part of the general Asian revolt against colonialism and poverty and minimizing any possibility of a threat to them from Communist China. The Chinese Communists consciously capitalized on these attitudes. Immediately after the Geneva Conference of 1954, Chou En-lai visited India and Burma. In both countries he signed a joint declaration supporting the so-called "five principles of co-existence." In the following spring he signed a similar joint declaration with the Indonesians.

Then, at the Bandung Conference in April, 1955, Communist China made a deep impression not only on the neutralists but on many other Asian and African leaders. China gained greatly in prestige as a result of the conference. In the period following Bandung, Communist China's diplomacy and propaganda clearly contributed to the growth of neutralism in South and Southeast Asia.

In 1958-59 there was another major shift, however, and Peking began to apply pressures in several South and Southeast Asian areas. The most dramatic event was the Sino-Indian dispute over Tibet and the Indian border. The net result of these trends was to change Peking's posture toward, and relations with, much of both these regions. During 1960, however, the Chinese again attempted to cultivate friendly relations with many nations in these regions, with the notable exception of India.

Although Communist China's greatest influence on international affairs has been in Asia, the Chinese have in recent years greatly expanded their contacts with the Middle East, Africa, and Latin America, demanding world recognition and a seat in the United Nations. They have also expanded their diplomatic and economic contacts in Europe and slowly but steadily have whittled away at the American-led opposition to full acceptance of the Chinese Communist regime in the Community of nations.

THE LURE OF TRADE AND AID

Conventional diplomacy and political maneuver are not the only means by which the Chinese Communists are attempting to expand their influence in Asia. The Communists operate in varied ways and on different levels, both overt and covert, to achieve their objectives.

Foreign trade, which in Communist China is completely state controlled and subordinate to politics, has become increasingly important as an instrument of Chinese foreign policy. Wherever hope for more trade exists, the Chinese Communists attempt to exploit it and use it as a vehicle for propaganda against United States policy and for the establishment of closer relations with China.

The lure of trade is particularly important in China's approach to Japan. In actual fact, there is little prospect of Sino-Japanese trade recovering to past levels even if restrictions are removed. Communist China is no longer importing sizable quantities of consumer goods such as textiles, which made up a large share of prewar Japanese exports to China and which constitute a major Japanese export problem now. At the same time, China's ability to export raw materials which Japan needs, such as coal, is now limited by her own growing demand for such materials. But there is much wishful thinking in Japan, and many Japanese businessmen blame the present low level of Sino-Japanese trade on political factors, which in turn they tend to blame on the United States. Even among those Japanese who are more realistic in assessing future trade possibilities, there is considerable feeling that any increase in trade with China is worth having.

Communist China's foreign trade is also important in its relations with Southeast Asian countries. China has signed trade pacts with almost all countries in this region with which diplomatic relations have been established, and politics has certainly influenced the pattern of this trade. In some cases China has bought major export products of Southeast Asian countries at high prices, such as rubber from Ceylon and rice from Burma. China's exports to these countries have dramatized the industrial development in China and thereby increased China's prestige. Peking has offered various types of machinery and high quality Chinese manufactured consumer goods for sale in Southeast Asia and has become a major competitor with Japan and the Western nations in such items. The appearance of these goods on Southeast Asian markets has been interpreted by many to mean that China under Communism has developed a surplus of manufactured goods, whereas in fact it merely indicates that a totalitarian regime can export what it wishes, regardless of domestic shortages.

In 1956 Communist China made its first grant of aid to a non-Communist Asian country; earlier it had given assistance to North Korea, North Vietnam, and Albania. By early 1961 it had promised $1.3 billion in foreign aid, of which $328 million was to non-Communist nations ($105 million in grants and $223 million in credits). It was in the aid business on a growing scale.

PROPAGANDA TECHNIQUES

Words are another important export and instrument of Communist China's foreign policy. A huge flow of written propaganda goes from China to all Asian countries which do not bar it, and Chinese publications in local languages receive a wide readership. The written word is supplemented by radio broadcasts. Much of Chinese propaganda is skillful, describing and exaggerating economic progress in China and building up the idea of Communist China as a model for Asia. Equally important are exchanges of cultural and other delegations. Peking has become a Mecca for fellow-travelling Asians and for many non-Communist Asians eager to see what is happening in China. People from all walks of life are invited for extensive tours of Communist China, all expenses paid; they are treated as honored guests and a significant percentage of them appear to be more impressed by the Chinese Communists' dynamic, constructive, purposeful activity than by the totalitarianism of the Peking regime. Many of these are effective propagandists for China when they return to their own countries.

The Chinese Communists have helped to establish many front organizations which serve as lobbying groups in other Asian countries. These include so-called friendship societies for furthering friendly relations with China; associations whose sole purpose is promotion of trade with China; and peace committees affiliated with the Peking regional headquarters of the Communists' world peace movement. The Asian and Australian Liaison Bureau of the Communists' World Federation of Trade Unions maintains links between Peking and Communist-dominated labor groups in Asia, while Chinese Communist women's and youth groups have similar ties throughout the region. The Chinese People's Institute of Foreign Affairs, Chinese People's Association for Cultural Relations with Foreign Countries, Chinese People's Committee for World Peace, and similar organizations maintain contacts with groups of many sorts in other countries. Through these various nongovernmental channels, the Chinese Communists are able to exert considerable influence in Africa and Latin America as well as Asia, in support of policies consistent with Peking's objectives.

In addition, of course, Communist parties in many countries exert an influence, varying in importance in different countries, which indirectly supports the policies of major Communist countries such as Russia and China. The Communists' ultimate hope is that these local Communist parties will be able to come to power by successful internal struggles and Communist China's moral support backs up the Communist movement everywhere. The Chinese Communists are once more, in fact, openly proclaiming support for revolutionary insurrections in many Asian, African, and Latin American countries.

THE OVERSEAS CHINESE

One further channel for Chinese Communist influence in Southeast Asia is provided by the existence of approximately ten million Overseas Chinese emigrants in the region who not only maintain many ties with their homeland but also dominate much of the small-scale trade in Southeast Asia. These Overseas Chinese are divided in their political allegiance; some are oriented toward the Nationalists. But Peking's influence has steadily grown and is now predominant. Many Overseas Chinese youth have been attracted by Communist ideology, while many of the older generation, most of whom are fundamentally nonpolitical businessmen, have cooperated with Peking for opportunistic reasons or have been put under effective pressure. Communist China has worked steadily to increase its ties with and influence over these Overseas Chinese (despite the fact that it has been willing to conclude a treaty with Indonesia by which it has relinquished citizenship claims affecting a part of the Overseas Chinese population in that country).

The danger of the Overseas Chinese being used as a local Fifth Column by Peking can be exaggerated, since in much of Southeast Asia the Chinese are small minorities who lack political power despite their strong economic position. But it is a safe prediction that the Chinese Communists will continue attempts to make use of the Overseas Chinese, and there are some areas where the local pro-Communist Chinese can present a serious political threat. In Singapore and Malaya together, the Chinese actually outnumber the Malays, and the Chinese are much more active in local politics there than elsewhere in Southeast Asia. In Singapore the strength of pro-Peking, pro-Communist Chinese labor, student, and political groups is disturbing. In Malaya, the government is anti-Communist but there is considerable Communist political infiltration and subversion and there is a serious problem of Malay-Chinese relations.

Through trade, propaganda, subversion, pressures upon Chinese minorities, and other means, the Chinese Communists are energetically attempting to exert an influence within other Asian countries (and, more recently, throughout Africa and Latin America), as well as attempting to influence the policies of existing governments. In most cases Peking probably does not expect dramatic immediate results from these efforts but they all contribute to what the Chinese Communists regard as a long-term struggle to expand the influence of Communism and of China.

Sino-American Relations

Direct relations between Communist China and the United States have been characterized since 1949 by intense mutual hostility, punctuated by open conflict as in Korea and by periodic crises as in the Formosa Strait. Intermitttent negotiations have taken place at Geneva and Warsaw, but relations have not been regularized and numerous issues are unresolved. As of mid-1961 the situation in the sense of any direct relationship appears to be "frozen." Nevertheless, the potential causes of renewed conflict remain, and the continuing state of tension between Washington and Peking affects the entire American position in Asia.

Before examining the more critical issues involved in Sino-American relations, perhaps it would be wise to re-emphasize certain basic assumptions about Communist China which are relevant to long-term United States policy.

First of all, the Peking regime, despite its many domestic problems, does have effective, in fact unprecedented, control over all of China, except for Taiwan and the other Nationalist-held islands off the China coast. The totalitarian methods by which the Chinese Communists have established this control are repugnant to the United States, but there is no more basis for disputing the *de facto* control of the Communist regime in China than there is for questioning the *de facto* control of the Communists in Russia. Successful internal revolt against Peking or successful reinvasion by the Nationalists of the mainland are both so improbable that they cannot be considered practical possibilities in considering American policy. Communist China is a reality, even though we do not like it.

Secondly, the strength of Communist China is growing. The present industrialization program will greatly increase China's independent basis for military power within a relatively few years. With Soviet assistance, Communist China's actual military power has already expanded to the point where China is clearly the strongest country in Asia. Peking's regular military forces, which total roughly two and one-half million troops, constitute the second largest standing army in the world. Since the start of the Korean War, reorganization, retraining, and re-equipping along Soviet lines have made them into a modern, although pre-atomic, force. Introduction of formal, nationwide conscription in 1955 provided a huge reservoir of manpower; China has possibly 30 million men in the important 20-24 military age group. A new officer corps has been trained. A sizable Chinese Communist air force has been built up, with about 2,500 planes of which 1,800 or more are jets. It is forecast that before very long Peking may explode a nuclear device. The possibility of military conflict with China is not one, therefore, which can be viewed lightly.

Actually, Chinese Communist military power is relatively immobile and cannot make itself directly felt outside a restricted area surrounding China. Lack of naval power limits the effective use of Peking's military power to adjacent mainland areas or islands near the coast. This is counterbalanced, however, by the fact that neither the United States nor any of its Asian allies possesses the kind of large land armies which would be required to make Western power felt effectively in China, especially if there were military demands upon them elsewhere. While atomic weapons might well be militarily effective although politically objectionable in some situations of limited conflict with China, their effectiveness in either a major conflict against huge land armies in China's vast spaces or in guerrilla warfare situations is open to question unless the war-making process were based primarily upon indiscriminate civilian and economic destruction.

Both China and the United States would have difficulty applying their power to the other in the event of major war. However, in the event of limited war in which the region of possible conflict might be the areas immediately adjacent to China, Chinese land forces would be difficult to block with American air and naval power alone. "Indirect aggression" or "military subversion," such as in Laos and Vietnam, seems in any case to be the greatest immediate danger. Unfortunately, the United States has neglected developing adequate capacities both for limited conventional war and for local guerrilla war—although new efforts to remedy these deficiencies were started in 1961.

Thirdly, although it would be unwise to ignore the tensions and strains between China and the Soviet Union or to fail to exploit them in any way possible, American policy must be based on the expectation that Peking and Moscow will not split, and that despite differences they will, in fact, act in concert on key issues in international affairs in the struggle with the West. It is certainly desirable to attempt to capitalize in any way possible on Sino-Soviet differences and, perhaps, to encourage Moscow to restrain Peking. However, a policy aimed at causing an open split or dependent upon one has little meaning under present conditions.

Finally, Communist China certainly cannot be disregarded. It presents serious problems for the United States not only in the areas of tension immediately surrounding China but throughout Asia and, in fact, the entire underdeveloped world. Peking is conducting an active foreign policy which is affecting the political atmosphere and situation in all of Asia and in many other areas. The problem of dealing with the Chinese Communists is not restricted, therefore, to the critical areas of possible military conflict adjacent to China. It is a problem of competing with Communist China for influence throughout the broad area of the uncommitted countries and even in those countries which are now American allies. This is not primarily a military problem; it is one involving political, economic, and, perhaps most important of all, psychological factors. Not only Chinese pressures and threats but propaganda appeals to Asian feelings about colonialism and racialism are directly aimed at the United States. The goal is to cause the United States to become more and more isolated.

In the competition for influence throughout Asia, Peking's prestige has steadily risen. The Korean War, Geneva Conference on Indo-China, Bandung Conference, and Geneva Conference on Laos, have been important milestones in this process. Asian leaders are still divided between those who admire and those who fear Communist China, but there are few who are not strongly affected by China's influence. Although, therefore, there are issues of fairly critical short-run importance between the United States and Communist China, influence throughout Asia is of paramount long-run importance. Problems of our China policy must be considered in this context as well as in relation to more specific current problems such as those affecting Taiwan, the offshore islands, Americans imprisoned in China, and restrictions on China trade.

THE PROBLEM OF RECOGNITION

Viewing present American policy toward China in the light of these assumptions, several observations can be made. One of these is the fact that American policy is based upon a central fiction. The United States refuses officially to recognize the existence of the Peking regime as either the *de facto* or *de jure* government of China, and it continues to support the claims of the Nationalist regime to be the government of all of China.

It would be possible for the United States to acknowledge and accept the realities of a new *status quo,* without necessarily deciding to accord *de jure* recognition to the Peking regime until such a move seemed more desirable and feasible than at present and without deciding to abandon defensive support of the Nationalists as the regime which possesses *de facto* control over Taiwan. In actual fact, the United States has had to negotiate with representatives of Communist China at Panmunjom, Geneva, and Warsaw, at least implying thereby realization that the Communists control the mainland of China, but it has never officially extended either *de facto* or *de jure* recognition.

General American policy with respect to the recognition of governments has varied from time to time and is certainly not clear today. Many different requirements for recognition have been suggested, ranging from objective tests such as the determination of *de facto* control to the test of political or moral approval. The arguments for objective, nonpolitical tests are strong, however, and the United States in the past has recognized a number of Communist or dictator-controlled states of which it certainly did not approve either politically or morally.

Partly because of the United States policy on nonrecognition, the world is now divided in its relations with "China." As of mid-1961, 52 nations still recognized the Chinese Nationalist regime; 39 recognized the Chinese Communists; and 19 recognized neither. Peking has steadily widened its diplomatic relations, however, and a rapid shift in the present pattern could take place if it were seated in the United Nations.

There are many arguments that have been advanced both for and against United States recognition of the Chinese Communist regime. In addition to "moral" arguments, many opponents of recognition assert that such a move would have a very adverse political impact throughout Asia. On the other hand, most advocates of recognition argue that political and power realities will be a much more important and decisive influence on the situation than legalistic forms. They maintain it would be highly desirable to have more regularized channels of continuous diplomatic contact with Peking, if for no other reason than to probe constantly the Chinese Communists' intentions and to ensure that they are fully aware of existing American policies and commitments.

Actually, there seems to be little real prospect of *de jure* recognition being feasible even if the United States government were to decide it is desirable. Peking has declared that it will not consider establishing diplomatic relations with the United States as long as the American government supports the Nationalist regime on Taiwan, while the United States has made amply clear that it has every intention of living up to the commitments it has made to defend Taiwan. Whether Peking will adamantly maintain its present stance for the indefinite future remains to be seen, but as of the present time there is little doubt that if the United States were to attempt to establish diplomatic relations with Communist China, it would be rebuffed. Since this would clearly be undesirable, *de jure* recognition does not for the moment seem to be a practical possibility deserving of serious consideration. *De facto* recognition would, however, seem to be both feasible and desirable, if the United States decides to evolve a policy that is more fitted to the realities of the situation.

CHINA'S SEAT IN THE UNITED NATIONS

A much more immediate issue concerns the seating of Chinese Communist representatives in China's seat in the United Nations, presently occupied by representatives of Nationalist China. The United States has steadfastly opposed such an action and has taken the lead in mobilizing the necessary votes to prevent it. The problem is not one of admitting a new member, in which case the members of the Security Council would have a veto according to the Charter, but rather is one of deciding whose credentials to accept for occupancy of an already existing seat.

The number of countries recognizing Peking and willing to vote for its acceptance into the United Nations has steadily grown and is now approaching the point where the United States is in danger of being outvoted within the United Nations. In 1960, for the first time, the annual United States-backed resolution to defer discussion of the China issue in the General Assembly failed to obtain an absolute majority— even though it did pass by a vote of 42 for, 34 against, and 22 abstaining.

Many factors help to account for the steady weakening of the opposition to seating Communist China, but among the most important have been the great increase in the number of new states in the United Nations. There has been a growing feeling, especially among Asian, and African, and some Latin American nations that Communist China should be seated.

By early 1961, it was widely believed that the "moratorium" on discussing the issue of seating Communist China in the General Assembly might be defeated as early as September, 1961, and that thereafter there would be only a brief period of time before it would be seated. Senators

George D. Aiken and Wayne Morse reported to the Senate Foreign Relations Committee: "It seems reasonable to conclude that future United States policy must be based on the assumption that Red China could be seated in the United Nations as early as the 16th General Assembly Session [September, 1961], whether we agree or not." They then went on to ask: "Does the United States have sufficient bargaining power left to ensure representation for Formosa? If so, should we attempt to negotiate an arrangement whereby 'two Chinas' might be represented or would it be better to continue present policy, come what may?"

The problem did reach the floor of the 1961 General Assembly. The United States was successful in obtaining the approval of a procedural interpretation that the issue was won which would require a two-thirds vote. When the matter did come to a vote, the seating of Communist China once again failed to obtain even a simple majority.

There are those who would have the United States declare that if Communist China were admitted to the United Nations, it would withdraw. They believe that such an ultimatum would hold the line and would be willing to pay the price of destroying the United Nations if it failed. This seems to be a rather drastic step for such a limited objective. To those who feel that the present United States position cannot be defended indefinitely, the realistic alternatives actually appeared to be either the seating of Communist China in place of the Nationalist regime, which would be a major defeat for the United States, or the working out of some sort of "two Chinas" formula, within the context of a changed American approach to China policy.

Several alternative "two Chinas" policies in the United Nations seem to be at least theoretically possible. One might be a formula linking the seating of the Peking regime in China's present seat in the Security Council and General Assembly with the admission, or readmission, of the Nationalist regime into the General Assembly as a new state. The Soviet Union would doubtless veto the latter, however, so the immediate result of such an approach would at best be a stalemate with no Chinese representation in the United Nations.

Another possible alternative, which was privately discussed during early 1961 both within and outside of the United Nations, is based on the concept of "successor states." It might be possible, in the view of some observers, for the General Assembly to declare that in its view there are now two "successor states" to the Republic of China which was a charter member in 1945. Therefore both of these states should now have representation—Communist China to take over China's permanent seat in the Security Council as well as the Assembly, and Nationalist China to have a seat in the Assembly. If such a declaration were to be made, the Security Council would then have to act on the credentials of the Chinese representative in that body, but it presumably would then proceed to seat Communist China.

Assuming that some "two Chinas" position of this sort were to be adopted, it seems likely that the immediate reaction of both Peking and Taipei might be to boycott their designated seats, since they are both on record as strongly opposing any "two Chinas" formula. In time, however, the pressures of international opinion might make both Communist and Nationalist China somewhat more tractable on this issue.

At present the obstacles to achieving any "two Chinas" solution appear to be formidable. Within the United States, strong Congressional opinion reinforced by organized groups such as the Committee of One Million argues for no change in United States policy. Within the United Nations, the danger is that a majority of members, while perhaps sympathetic to the idea of seating "two Chinas," might shy away from the complexities and complications of trying to implement such a program and might, therefore, vote for what appears to be the simplest solution —i.e., the seating of Communist China in place of Nationalist China. If this happens, there is the possibility that some groups within the United States which basically oppose the United Nations in any event might attempt to use this issue to urge American withdrawal—a step which would greatly and adversely affect the United States' entire international position.

THE OFFSHORE ISLANDS

Another important problem involved in the United States' China policy is created by the continued possibility of military conflict between the United States and Communist China in the Taiwan region, where a small spark might start a major conflagration. The present lull has not changed the basic situation there, and the offshore islands continue to be an area of possible conflict. The definite and publicly declared American defense commitments to Taiwan and the Pescadores, plus the difficulty of long amphibious invasions and the improved defensive capabilities of the Nationalist regime, probably bar a Communist attack on Taiwan itself for the present at least. The offshore islands, however, are close to the coast and are much more vulnerable.

The United States has been purposely vague about any commitments to defend these offshore islands, and this uncertainty may have helped to restrain the Communists so far. The danger, however, lies in the possibility that Peking may decide to act on the assumption that it can take the islands without full scale American intervention or even despite intervention. If this happens, the United States, once attack began, might decide that intervention was necessary since Communist success could be interpreted as calling an American bluff. This constitutes an explosive situation, despite the present inaction in the area.

The offshore islands are psychologically and to some extent militarily useful to the Nationalists, but they are not essential to the defense of

Taiwan. The Communists' claim to them is accepted as legitimate by the majority of world opinion. This is a situation in which the United States might find itself involved in fighting which would have almost no international support. Under these circumstances, it would appear that the offshore islands region is one in which a tactical withdrawal would minimize the risks of major conflict. The Nationalists adamantly oppose withdrawal, but in this instance their interests do not coincide with those of the United States. Understandably, in view of their desire to return to the mainland, the Nationalists would welcome a major conflict between the United States and Communist China, but certainly United States policy is to reduce the likelihood of military action in that region, if possible. The United States should take effective action, therefore, to persuade the Nationalists to evacuate the offshore islands. And it should clearly disassociate the United States from their defense.

THE TAIWAN PROBLEM

Taiwan and the Pescadores present a different problem. It is a problem for which no "solution" acceptable to all parties is now possible. Neither Communist China nor the Nationalist regime wants, or is likely to be willing in any formal sense to accept, stabilization on the basis of the present *status quo*. The area will probably be one of tension for a long time to come. But the possibilities of military conflict between the United States and Communist China over these main islands are not so great. The United States has made firm commitments to support defensively the present regime on Taiwan, and it can and should continue to guarantee the defense of Taiwan and the nearby Pescadores.

The population of Taiwan, not only the Nationalist refugees on the island but also the local Taiwanese, who make up most of the population of well over ten million, clearly do not want Communist control and would suffer from it. In addition, Taiwan has a real strategic importance; failure to deny it to the Communists could create serious dangers for nearby areas such as Okinawa and the Philippines. Complete abandonment of Taiwan would probably have an extremely adverse political effect on the American position throughout Asia. It would not necessarily improve United States relations even with those countries most critical of American policy, since it would be interpreted as proof of perfidy and undependability, and it would demoralize the United States' allies.

The best hope for reducing tension in the Taiwan area and at the same time preventing Communist takeover is the transformation of the Nationalist regime from a claimant seeking to rule over all China, which is unattainable and unacceptable to most of the world, to a stable local regime ruling Taiwan and the Pescadores. It might then slowly obtain longterm international acceptance and support. In time even the Communists might be forced tacitly to accept it as a fact, however vehemently they might continue to press their claims. The obstacles to such a "solution" are formidable, not the least of them being complete Nationalist as well as Communist opposition to the idea, but possible alternatives are blocked by even greater obstacles to long-run success.

It is only realistic, therefore, to accept the proposition that in the China-coast area, the most that the United States can hope and work for is stabilization of a new *status quo*, with Taiwan and the Pescadores maintaining their independence under an internationally acceptable local regime. At worst, the existing situation, especially if one includes the offshore islands, could deteriorate from the present stalemate to open conflict between the United States and Communist China, a conflict which would involve many strategic and logistical problems and in which the United States might find itself internationally isolated.

OUR RELATIONS WITH ASIA GENERALLY

Since the United States cannot at present significantly influence the situation within Communist China or hope for an immediate split between China and Russia, it makes sense to concentrate American attention on the problem of effectively offsetting Chinese Communist influence elsewhere in Asia. In short, China policy should be a corollary of broader policy toward Asia rather than vice versa. Just as Russian policy forced us into a closer relationship with Western Europe, China policy should focus our attention on the rest of Asia.

The United States must make a much larger commitment than it has to date to the task of assisting all the non-Communist states in Asia to build strong and viable political systems, economies, and social structures. The soundest approach to the defense against the expansion of Chinese Communist influence in Asia is to focus on helping to solve the real problems of all of the nations in the region, whether they are formally allied with the United States or militarily nonaligned.

Militarily, there are several problems. There is an immediate military problem of improving defense against possible military aggression in the areas adjacent to China; the United States has made sound progress toward this end, but there is a great and urgent need for the United States to improve its capacity to help Asian nations combat revolutionary guerrilla warfare. There is an immediate need to improve the capacity of the non-Communist nations to fight limited, conventional warfare, and the long-run military requirement of creating a counterbalance in Asia to Communist China's power. An effective Southeast Asia Treaty Organization and strong regimes in Japan and India committed to the containment of Communism could provide this. In the meantime, the power balance to China must be maintained to a large degree by United States commitments and forces in Asia, a situation which, in some respects while politically vulnerable, is nevertheless essential and unavoidable.

In addition to the military problems, there are the equally if not more important problems of how to contribute to the economic and political development of stable, healthy, non-Communist regimes throughout Asia and offsetting the affects of Communist-bloc influence and leadership. This will require more effective programs of economic and political assistance. The ability of the United States to exercise leadership will depend to a considerable extent upon how Asians view the general American posture toward Asian affairs and the confidence which they have in American motives and goals.

The United States must assume a posture which convinces Asians that it not only will resist any Communist military aggression, but also will do everything possible to help Asian nations solve their urgent existing problems. The United States must also attempt to find broader ground for common action and cooperation in meeting the many problems posed by Communist China; it should, in short, attempt to move from a unilateral to a multilateral policy toward China.

4.

The United States and Taiwan

♦ ALLEN S. WHITING AND
ROBERT A. SCALAPINO

Perhaps there is no better way to introduce the complex problem of United States-Taiwan relations than to juxtapose without comment six recent quotations from various parties to the issue:

. . . there is only one China in the world, namely, the People's Republic of China. Taiwan is an inalienable part of Chinese territory. The Chinese people are determined to liberate Taiwan. They are resolutely opposed to the plot to create "two Chinas" under any form by the United States or by any other country.
—Peking NCNA English-language broadcast, August 7, 1961.

. . . the so-called "two China" concept is, to put it bluntly, only wishful thinking entertained by neutralists who, being ignorant and irresponsible and

For the 1956 edition, the chapter on Taiwan was written by Allen S. Whiting, then at Michigan State University. In 1953-55, Professor Whiting traveled in the Far East on a Ford Foundation fellowship. He has written *Soviet Policies in China, 1917-24*, and, with E. B. Haas, *Dynamics of International Relations*. He has lectured widely and written many articles on the Far East and Russia.

The chapter has been brought up to date by Professor Robert A. Scalapino, author of Chapter 1 above.

disregarding moral considerations, hope to achieve peace without paying any price for it.

—Chiang Kai-shek, interview published June 12, 1961.

. . . the facts of international life require that (Communist) China be seated in the United Nations

—Lord Hume, British Foreign Minister, February, 1961.

. . . I suggest we explore a broad settlement of issues [with Khrushchev]—including Formosa—by negotiation, not force.

On the Communist side, the concessions would include the extension to China of any system of international inspection of disarmament, ending the threat of force against Formosa and subversion in Indochina, a peaceful frontier settlement with India, free elections under United Nations supervision in Korea, and acceptance of the right of the inhabitants of Formosa to determine their own destiny by plebiscite supervised by the United Nations. On our side, concessions would presumably include an end to the American embargo on China's admission to the United Nations (not to be confused with diplomatic recognition), the evacuation of Quemoy and Matsu and the inclusion of Korea and Japan in the atom-free zone and area of controlled disarmament.

—Adlai E. Stevenson, *Foreign Affairs*, January, 1960.

. . . Formosa's political status is founded on a myth that Chiang Kai-shek, who was driven from the mainland 11 years ago, remains the ruler of 650,000,000 Chinese. This myth—rejected by most Asians, by our NATO allies, by our closest friends the Canadians, and by a large number of Americans—is supported only by three or four Asian governments under heavy pressure from Washington, by our Department of State and by some members of Congress. Perpetuation of the myth will increasingly isolate Formosa at a time when its leaders should be striving in every way to identify their future with the mainstream of thought and action in free, non-Communist Asia.

—Chester Bowles, *Foreign Affairs*, April, 1960.

The President reiterated firm United States support for continued representation of the Republic of China in the United Nations, of which she is a founding member. . . .

The President confirmed the intention of the United States Government to continue its military aid program in the Republic of China and to provide substantial assistance to the Republic of China in support of its economic development program designed to achieve accelerated social and economic progress for the welfare of the people of Free China.

—Joint communique issued by President Kennedy and Premier Chen Cheng, Washington, August 2, 1961.

Historical Background

For more than a decade, United States aircraft and ships patrolling the 100-mile wide strip of water separating Communist China and the Nationalist refuge of Taiwan (Formosa) have prevented Peking from making good its threat to "liberate" the island. In recent years, we have sought to commit both the Communists and the Nationalists to a settlement of the Taiwan issue through peaceful means, albeit with scant success. Meanwhile, a military build-up on both sides has taken place. The Communists have added substantially to their military strength in the area immediately opposite the Formosa Straits. Nationalist forces have been greatly aided by a constant flow of American funds, equipment, and training. In periods of crisis, the Seventh Fleet has been augmented, and with the advent of certain new weapons and weapons-carriers, the American striking power in the Western Pacific has been enlarged. Meanwhile, statements from Peking, Taipei, and Washington continue to be irreconcilable and offer little hope for any immediate compromise. Will the gradual acceptance of a *de facto* situation ultimately "solve" or reduce this problem? Will some dramatic event occur to change the status-quo without major conflict? Or is Taiwan a time bomb which will eventually set off general war in Asia?

Historically, Taiwan has been both a part of and separate from mainland China. In the modern period, it came under Japanese control. After the Sino-Japanese War of 1894-95, both Taiwan and the neighboring Pescadores Islands were ceded to Japan. With defeat in World War II, Japan lost her rice-rich tropical colony. The United States, the United Kingdom, and China pledged at the Cairo Conference in 1943 that "Formosa and the Pescadores shall be restored to the Republic of China." This pledge was restated in the surrender terms drawn up by the three powers as the Potsdam Declaration of July 26, 1945, later adhered to by the Soviet Union. Although neither statement constituted a legal transfer of title, General MacArthur's General Order Number 1 of August 15, 1945, gave Generalissimo Chiang Kai-shek *de facto* control of the islands by granting his representatives power to accept surrender of Japanese forces there.

In the absence of a Japanese peace treaty, Nationalist authorities administered the island as an army of occupation. A deep wedge was driven between "the local people" and the mainlanders in this early period, a wedge that continues to plague the Kuomintang government. Meanwhile, the swift rush of events in 1949-50 catapulted Taiwan into world attention as Chiang Kai-shek's regime retreated in defeat from the Chinese mainland. Six months later, the United States abandoned its "let the dust settle" policy with respect to the unfinished civil war. Reacting to North Korean aggression, President Harry S. Truman on June 27, 1950, ordered the Seventh Fleet to neutralize the Formosa Strait. Before the year ended, massive Chinese Communist intervention in Korea had forced the United States to reconsider its position on the Chinese problem. In the midst of bitter political charges and countercharges, the Truman administration moved to give political and economic support to the battered Nationalists on Taiwan, and to continue recognition of the Nationalists government as the "Republic of China."

The legal status of Taiwan, however, remains unsettled. The Japanese Peace Treaty, effective April 28, 1952, stripped Japan of "all right, title and claim to Formosa and the Pescadores." It did not, however, establish present or future legal rights in connection with these islands. Both the Communists and the Nationalists are well aware of this fact, however much they may insist that the area is indisputably a part of China. The United States, while continuing to recognize the Republic of China, has increasingly used the term "Taiwan" to designate this government in recent years. President Kennedy especially has alarmed Nationalist leaders by repeatedly referring to "the defense of Taiwan" and our commitments to "the government and people of Taiwan." The term "Republic of China" has been confined in usage mainly to official documents and communiques. In this, American leaders have merely given voice to the *de facto* situation.

Thus in international law and in the eyes of a majority of nations of the world, these contested islands remain on the agenda of unfinished business of World War II. Only the victorious allies of the war, working in concert or through the United Nations, can legally resolve the status of this territory. Neither a legal nor a political solution appears likely in the near future, however, and the threat of crisis or war is always present. But in the meantime, the Nationalists exercise *de facto* control over the Taiwan-Pescadores area, and over the offshore islands of Quemoy and Matsu. The Communists hold *de facto* power on the mainland. Two governments exist, and both governments, while claiming to be the only legitimate government of China, are constrained from reopening any full-scale civil war by a number of factors. And as time passes, the *de facto* situation acquires increasing recognition.

Taiwan is a rich tropical island, slightly larger than Massachusetts and Connecticut combined. Its 250 miles of length are ridged by steep mountains, and its 60 to 90 miles of width include flat arable land only along the west coast. Its eleven million inhabitants are 98 per cent Chinese with the remaining 2 per cent Indonesian-speaking aborigines who live mostly in the mountains. Of the Chinese, approximately four-fifths are descendants of South China emigrants who settled the island from the seventeenth to the late nineteenth century. After Japan took Taiwan, migration virtually ceased until nearly two million mainland refugees sought a haven in the period 1946-49. Thus substantial cultural differences have existed between "the local people" and the mainlanders, despite the fact that both are of the Chinese race. To be sure, the Taiwanese themselves are not a unified group, but they—at least the older generation—shared a set of experiences vastly different from the mainlanders who came after World War II. These cultural differences, reenforced by occupational and political disparities, have presented a problem on Taiwan, albeit one not openly discussed.

Some sources would argue that substantial progress is being made in knitting the two groups together. A common education and through it a common language are being cultivated. The younger generation is also serving together in the armed forces, and an increasing amount of intermarriage is taking place. Over time, no doubt, if Taiwan is not united with the mainland, the process of "Taiwanization" will continue. Gradually, the nine million Taiwanese will absorb the two million mainland refugees, and a new, syncretic culture will result. At present, however, the gap between these two groups is still very real, and it has substantial political implications.

Conditions on Taiwan

MILITARY DEVELOPMENTS

When Nationalist troops straggled in chaos and confusion to their island retreat in 1949, few observers gave this defeated, demoralized army any chance for survival. Today, the Nationalist military force, while small, is perhaps the best equipped and some would argue, the best trained in the Far East. Many millions of American dollars have been expended on it over the past decade. The composition of the force has also changed. It has been necessary to retire many older elements, replacing them with young conscriptees, mainly Taiwanese. At present, over 50 per cent of the enlisted ranks, and approximately one-third of the officers of the Nationalist army are Taiwanese. Inevitably, some questions exist about the morale and the commitment of Nationalist troops, especially of the Taiwanese components. Kuomintang leaders were heartened by the sturdy defense of Quemoy-Matsu during the sustained Communist shellings of 1958. However, their new forces have never really been put to a full-fledged test. There is reason to believe that these troops would fight effectively to defend Taiwan. It is much more dubious as to whether they would fight to "return" to the mainland, a place where many of them have never been.

Problems of political factionalism within the army also exist. These are not new. The Nationalist army has been deeply involved in politics since its origins, nearly forty years ago. Chiang Kai-shek himself rose to power in the Kuomintang via his control of Whampoa Military Academy and the army. Today, the two chief rivals to succeed Chiang, Premier Chen Cheng and Chiang's son, Chiang Ching-kuo, both have extensive military backgrounds and connections. Any basic political change, including the succession to the Generalissimo, will involve the army. Hence it is both cultivated and watched by men ambitious for power.

With a population base one-sixtieth that of their opponents, the Nationalist army can neither conquer the mainland nor, in the long run, defend itself without outside assistance. The present Nationalist military force numbers about 600,000 men, of whom approximately one-half can be considered combat effectives. This must be compared with the much larger force in the Communist army, not to mention the so-called People's Militia. The Communists, moreover, have now built a network of air bases, rail lines, and military installations, with special attention to the mainland area opposite Taiwan. They also are seeking to convert a peasant army, backward in equipment and technique, into a professional, modern fighting force, one which will ultimately be armed with both conventional and nuclear weapons no doubt.

Under these circumstances, it is understandable why the Nationalists continuously scan the horizon, hoping to see signs of revolt on the mainland. Their only chance of a return to power in China lies in a massive popular revolution—or in global war. Despite the fact that the Nationalist forces can never be truly competitive with Communist military power, however, the Taiwan government currently spends a huge proportion of its budget on military expenditures. Such costs constituted 80 per cent or more of the total budget in 1961, notwithstanding extensive American aid. Some American officials have been openly critical of this heavy military spending, citing the dangers of inflation and the obstacles presented to more rapid industrial development. In Taiwan at present, approximately one million people are either a part of the armed forces or civilian employees of these forces. Although military pay is extremely small, it represents an enormous burden upon the people of Taiwan, who number in total only eleven million men, women, and children.

Thus the military picture is clouded by various concerns: morale, manpower, and maintenance. For the moment at least, moral is probably dependent upon the uses to which the Taiwan forces are put. As long as a certain estrangement exists between the Taiwanese and the mainlanders, however, and political intrigue involving the army remains high, morale will be an uncertain matter. There is little that can be done to increase the size of the military forces on Taiwan. Under present conditions, these forces are not sufficient to be a significant offensive threat, but they are more than sufficient to defend the island, given the American commitment to assist in such defense. The current military establishment is certainly larger than the island can legitimately support. It represents a major drain on the national economy. However, the Nationalist government can be expected to resist vigorously any proposal for a reduction in military spending, because that government does not think of its military forces as mere defense units. A military force of maximum size symbolizes the dream of returning to the mainland.

ECONOMIC DEVELOPMENT

Taiwan had made substantial economic progress under Japan in the period before 1945. Its people had acquired many industrial and agrarian skills and had attained a standard of living second only to Japan in the Far East. Wartime damage and the chaos of the immediate postwar era made deep, if temporary inroads into the economy. By 1952, industrial production in Taiwan had returned to top prewar levels. Since that time, both industrial and agrarian gains have been substantial. In very considerable part, of course, this has been a result of massive American aid. The huge sums provided in the last decade have helped to produce substantial improvements in the Taiwan economy as in its military defenses.

Between 1950 and 1960 real national income doubled. The per capita increase, when this figure is adjusted for the 3.4 per cent annual rate of population increase, is 4.6 per cent annually. One index of the prosperity is electric power consumption which increased nearly 400 per cent in the course of that decade. At the end of 1960, the volume of industrial production in Taiwan was more than double that of ten years earlier. Industrial exports also had reached a figure of U. S. $170,000,000, or double the value of 1952. The private sector of the economy had increased in importance, representing about 60 per cent of the total industrial production, and a campaign had been launched to attract more private foreign capital. Such capital investments totalled about U. S. $60,-000,000 at the end of 1960. A new foreign investment law, enacted in December, 1959, permits full remittance of profits earned by foreign concerns, with a capital repatriation of 15 per cent annually. Other incentives now include a five-year tax holiday for new enterprises, a corporate income tax cut from 32.5 per cent to 18 per cent, and tax exemption on reinvested earnings. In 16 months after the passage of the law, foreign investment amounted to $10 million, as compared with $1 million attracted during the previous 8 years. There also appears to be some increase in domestic savings and investment.

The Taiwanese farmer has generally shared in the good times. Socio-economic conditions in the rural areas have greatly improved, aided by the 1953 land reform program and the excellent work of the Sino-American Joint Commission on Rural Reconstruction. Taiwan and Japan are notable examples of what can be accomplished by land reform in non-Communist Asia. Nearly 75 per cent of the Taiwanese rural families were affected by land redistribution or rental reduction. Tenant-cultivated land was reduced from 41 to 16 per cent of the total land under cultivation. At present, approximately 80 per cent of the rural families own all or part of their land, while 20 per cent are tenants or hired hands. The Joint Commission has supplemented this basic change through an effective program of technical assistance and social services in rural areas.

As noted earlier, agrarian production was reasonably high in the era of Japanese control, but it has been substantially increased since 1945. Better seeds, more effective irrigation, extensive use of fertilizers, and new cultivation methods have all contributed to this end. Some rural mechanization has now taken place. And despite industrial gains, agriculture still accounts for nearly two-thirds of the national product. Taiwan continues to be predominately an agrarian society. Agricultural production not only feeds the rapidly expanding population but provides the major portion of Taiwan's exports.

There can be little doubt, however, that the industrialization process on this island will be accelerated in the years ahead. Taiwan hopes to increase her national income at the rate of 8 per cent annually in the period between 1961 and 1964, with per capita income rising 5 per cent per annum, and 300,000 new jobs being provided each year. This will require a high degree of concentration upon industrial development, since added increments to agricultural output will become increasingly difficult to obtain. Naturally, those industries will be encouraged which have export possibilities and make maximum use of indigenous resources. In the past, the processing industries and textiles have received special attention. Present priorities are being given pulp and paper, lumber, textiles, electrical products and appliances, chemicals, sugar, cement, glass, plastics, fertilizers, and pharmaceuticals.

While economic conditions for the common man have generally improved both in the city and in rural areas, the Taiwanese economy presently faces certain serious problems. The very high rate of population increase threatens per capita gains. As noted earlier, the population has already surpassed eleven million, and has been increasing at a rate of 3.4 per cent per year. This is one of the highest increase rates in Asia, and the figure shot up to 3.9 per cent in 1960. In the past, for both cultural and political reasons, the government has been unwilling to support any intensive program of birth control, and thus the problem has grown ever more critical. Economic development, and particularly industrial development, must move at a higher rate than population or underemployment and unemployment will result. Already, a special problem exists with respect to the intellectual elite. High school and college graduates find it extremely difficult to discover outlets for their training and talents. A dissatisfied, displaced young intellectual class is developing.

The burden on the economy of a relatively huge army has already been stressed. In addition, the Nationalist Government maintains a sizable bureaucracy, partly in order to take care of mainland refugees. Most of the two million refugees in Taiwan must be supported directly or indirectly by the government. The heads of family are either attached to the civil government, to the military services, or to such occupations as university teaching. Some hold straight sinecures or pensions. This constitutes a grave problem. On the one hand, most refugees are very unhappy with their present economic lot. Government salaries and wages in all of the above fields are extremely low. Indeed, Taiwan has witnessed a certain leveling process whereby the common man, particularly the farmer, has risen in terms of economic standards, while most of the elite, transplanted from the mainland, are below the levels to which they were accustomed. Bitter complaints from the latter group are often heard, that they have lost everything and that most of the wealth around them belongs to the Taiwanese. This has affected morale, efficiency, and honesty in government circles. On the other hand, the Taiwanese often feel that they are required to support a large number of "unproductive" people, while at the same time they are denied access to official positions and thus to the social and political status some of them desire.

Under these conditions of the supply of goods and the distribution of incomes, inflation is a serious problem. Recently the government issued new 100 yuan notes, whereas previously 10 yuan notes had been the highest denomination. This is indicative of the trends. Despite gains in production wholesale prices are recorded as having doubled in the last eight years. The struggle to prevent rampant inflation is a constant battle. As long as military expenditures are out of all proportion to the island's economic capacities, this threat will continue. In sum, Taiwan would have a bright economic future if it did not face a population explosion on the one hand and unrealistic military-political ambitions on the other. If the population problem were tackled seriously, and if the military forces could be reduced to dimensions fitting the defense needs of Taiwan, there could be optimism concerning the economic prospects on this island. It is not only a fertile land, but one whose people have acquired many skills in both industry and agriculture. Further progress could be made as these skills are put to fuller and more productive use.

AMERICAN AID

Since 1951, the United States has contributed more than one billion dollars in military and economic aid to Taiwan. On a per capita basis, this island has probably received more assistance from us than any other area in the world. American aid to Taiwan has fallen into two major categories. The first and larger program has been exclusively military aid, comprising equipment or "hardware" for Nationalist forces. No specific figures or breakdown of this program is released, but authoritative sources place its current level at between U. S. $200 and $300 million yearly.

The second program is termed economic assistance, although much of it has been geared to defense requirements. Direct Forces Support has covered items of direct use to the Chinese military effort but not furnished under the Mutual Defense Assistance Program. These include raw cotton for uniforms, construction materials for barracks, airfields, medical supplies, and the like—all items which conceivably might serve later civilian as well as present military needs. The second category, Defense Support, indirectly benefits the military and directly benefits the civilian economy through construction of roads, bridges, and dams, increased facilities for production and distribution of electric power, and exploitation of natural resources. However, imports of salable commodities have comprised from one-half to two-thirds of this category. These are commodities not locally available or procurable by means of Taiwan's own foreign exchange earnings, such as wheat, soya beans, raw cotton, and machine tools. Local currency obtained from these sales constitutes the bulk of the counterpart funds which in turn support a large portion of the military costs and finance part of local budget deficits. The third category, Technical Cooperation, provides teaching and training on the spot as well as some funds for travel and education in the United States.

Despite repeated all-island surveys by teams of competent American experts and endless conferences among high Nationalist officials, the fact remains that this is an Alice-in-Wonderland economy. It is made unreal by Nationalist ambivalence as to whether Taiwan should be developed as an independent unit or integrated into a reconquered mainland. As the hope of rewinning China fades, this becomes less important, but no corresponding cut in military investment results.

The unreality is perpetuated by a general assumption that whatever the deficit, American assistance will meet the difference. Domestic politics in the United States is beyond the scope of this study, but in discussing Taiwan-American relations, one cannot ignore the fact that a very important third dimension of these relations exists in the form of loosely-knit but powerful groups in the United States that operate constantly on behalf of Nationalist interests. These pressure groups include some important members of the U. S. Congress. It is interesting to note that no foreign government in the world keeps such careful tabs on political trends and the voting records of individual Congressmen as the National- ists, nor does any foreign government take such pains in entertaining prominent American visitors, including many members of Congress and ranking Pentagon officials. As Peking conducts its intensive "cultural relations" diplomacy, bringing countless foreign delegations to the main- land, so Taipei expends considerable sums on similar operations. The journey to Taiwan, and even to Quemoy-Matsu, has become a common- place venture for the American politician. In the case of both Peking and Taipei, such expenditures appear to pay off. Taiwan is one of the few areas where the aid funds have actually been increased by Congress over those requested by the administration. Nationalist confidence that politics will prevail where economics fails lowers the incentive for them to utilize their resources most effectively.

Compared with the incompetent, corrupt regime which ruled a China devastated by decades of civil war and foreign aggression, Taiwan presents an impressive picture, even granting the foundations laid by Japanese rule. There have been some recent, worrisome evidences of corruption among government officials. This problem appears to be minimal in scale, however, if compared with the prewar era. The modern network of roads and the expanding electrical grid which ring the island, the implementation of land reform, and the introduction of certain new, progressive economic practices on the whole speak well for the investment of Chinese manpower and American money over the past ten years. In spite of the huge sums spent on the military, Taiwan is an example of effectiveness of American economic aid. The question of long-range economic viability, however, hinges as much on military and political as on economic decisions.

POLITICAL DEVELOPMENT

Internal political conditions on Taiwan are of direct pertinence to American policy and Taiwan-American relations. At present, these con- ditions do not give great cause for optimism. In the first place, the Nationalist government has done little to achieve mass support, or attain a mass base. Despite some reform efforts that government remains basically a personal autocracy administered along authoritarian lines. When he chooses, Chiang Kai-shek *is* the government. Nothing or no one can prevail against him. The Kuomintang, moreover, remains a highly elitist party with limited public appeal and with serious factional problems. After its mainland defeat, the Kuomintang conducted its own "self-criticism" and "rectification" campaigns. Grave shortcomings were admitted and a call to Spartanism was issued. The experience of total defeat was not without some benefits. The party was able to rid itself of a number of opportunists and unsavory elements. Many of the remaining men are dedicated, sincere, and able.

At the same time, however, the Kuomintang falls between two stools. It does not allow the range of political freedom and competition associated with political democracy on the one hand, and it does not possess the ruthlessness, dyanimism, and efficiency of Communist totalitarianism on the other. The Lei Chen case is an excellent example of the problem. Lei Chen was the publisher of *Free China,* a fortnightly magazine that represented one of the few truly independent journals on Taiwan. In the fall of 1960, he was suddenly arrested and after an eight-hour trial by military court, sentenced to ten years' imprisonment. The charges against him ranged from defeatism to subversion, but his real crime was very simple: he sought to form a true opposition party to the Kuomintang. Lei was arrested because he and others were on the verge of launching a new party, the China Democratic Party, which intended to support a vigorously anti-Communist program. It also intended to be predominantly a Taiwanese party. Lei was the only mainland refugee on its seven-man presidium. Despite the protests of men like Hu Shin and Carsun Chang, the petitions of scores of intellectuals on Taiwan, Lei Chen remains in prison. It is not surprising that few of the neutrals or our allies will accept the label "Free China" as presently applied to Taiwan. There is much less freedom on the mainland, to be sure, but that does not automatically confer a favorable image on Taiwan.

The Kuomintang operates a one-party state now as in the past. Perhaps is would be more accurate to call it a one and one-half party state, since it allows a few house-pet parties, as indeed do the Communists in Peking. Neither group, however, will tolerate any real opposition. There is also a similarity in the basic structure of these two parties. The Kuomintang continues to follow the Communist organizational model which it acquired in 1924. It has made some progress in establishing cell organizations throughout the island, and channeling political action through them. There is little indication, however, that the party has really appealed to the Taiwanese, or that it has genuine mass support. Meanwhile, factionalism within the party continues to be very strong. In recent years, the struggle for the right to succeed the Generalissimo has grown in intensity as "the old man" advances in years. On the one hand, there is the so-called moderate faction, headed by Premier Chen Cheng. On the other hand, there is Chiang Ching-kuo, the Generalissimo's son, and his followers. Chiang Ching-kuo has his base of power in the secret police and the military; he is probably more hated and feared than any man on the island. Despite this fact, many observers believe he has recently gained ground, as a result of his political-military connections and his father's blessing. Others feel that Chen Cheng can garner the necessary strength to succeed Chiang Kai-shek when the time comes. Some believe that both Chen and Chiang Ching-kuo have lost strength, and some other man may come forward as successor to the Generalissimo.

It is doubtful that Chiang Kai-shek will relinquish power as long as he lives. At seventy-three, he has withdrawn somewhat from active, day-by-day control over all matters, but as noted earlier, he is still the supreme, unchallengeable ruler whose word is law when he chooses to exercise authority. Probably factionalism within the Kuomintang can be contained as long as he lives. His death is likely to provoke a crisis of major proportions. The Communists also are well aware of this fact. They have long made a strong bid for a bloodless, political victory on Taiwan. "Come home and all will be forgiven," is their plea. They have promised positions to all repentant Nationalists, and insisted that if the Nationalists continue to stay on Taiwan, ultimately the Americans will succeed in the "two China plot" and sell them out to the Taiwanese.

As yet, Communist blandishments appear to have had little influence. It is well known, however, that some negotiations have taken place in Hong Kong among various intermediaries. Conceivably, the United States might be confronted with a challenge under certain circumstances, wherein a portion of the Nationalist elite would seek to deliver Taiwan to the Communist government. It seems more likely, however, that the internal Kuomintang struggle for power will ultimately involve greater utilization of the Taiwanese. Even the use of the army internally, or the use of such groups as the Youth Corps would represent a trend in that direction. But there could also be an appeal issued in broader political terms, a turning outward on the part of some party elements to the public, in the hope of getting the support necessary to sustain their position. Thus increasing democratization could occur under the Kuomintang, but if it does, it is likely to produce new political crises.

STIRRINGS FROM BELOW

Internal political conditions cannot be discussed without some additional reference to Taiwanese-mainlander relations. As suggested earlier, although most of Taiwan's population came originally from mainland China, five decades of Japanese administration weakened spiritual and cultural ties with the motherland. Under Japanese imperialism, the Taiwanese were denied self-rule, and many resented Japanese control. On the other hand, the Japanese provided law and order and economic development. No real Taiwanese nationalist movement emerged, as in Korea, nor any strong desire to be united with a weak and divided China. Thus the islander regarded the Nationalist take-over with mixed feelings, translated into growing animosity against corrupt carpet-bagging practices under early postwar military commanders. Accumulated pressures on both sides caused a major anti-Nationalist outbreak in February, 1947, which was followed by heavy Nationalist repression. The thousands subsequently imprisoned or executed included many of Taiwan's leading professional citizens. Others fled to Hong Kong or Japan.

Personal relations between the Taiwanese and the mainland refugees have probably improved in recent years. After the arrival of Chiang on the island in 1949, political reforms and economic rehabilitation were undertaken. In more recent years, the younger generation has been brought closer together by learning in a common language, serving in the armed forces together, and in some cases, intermarrying, as noted earlier. However, strong elements of difference and distrust still exist. Perhaps the greatest gap between the two groups can be summed up in one word: commitment. The Taiwanese are committed to Taiwan; the great majority of the refugees are still committed to returning home, or this failing, to emigrating elsewhere. There are also the substantial socioeconomic differences suggested earlier. The mainlanders serve mainly in government, in teaching and the professions, and in the armed forces. The Taiwanese are the farmers, workers, merchants, and industrialists. As time passes, of course, this division is breaking down, but it remains important. The Taiwanese have no real role in the Kuomintang or the national government. Politics is dominated by the mainlanders, although some trusted Taiwanese are allowed to occupy Kuomintang posts and a few independent or opposition elements win local elections. On the other hand, the mainland refugees play a surprisingly small role in commerce and industry, and many of them exist on a meager standard of living in comparison with prewar days.

Thus in the last fifteen years, Taiwanese-mainlander relations have been characterized by both revolution and evolution. Which will prevail in the future? Today, Taiwanese revolutionary activities are mainly centered abroad, in Tokyo, Peking, and the United States. On September 1, 1955, various representatives from Taiwan met in Tokyo, and established the "Provisional Government of the Republic of Formosa," electing Dr. Thomas W. I. Liao as President. Liao, who did graduate work at the University of Michigan and Ohio State University, claims to have substantial underground support in Taiwan. The Peking operation is naturally Communist and seems to have little, if any, support. In the United States, a number of Taiwanese students are affiliated with the United Formosans for Independence. Like the Chinese nationalist movement of sixty years ago, these movements are manned mainly by students and intellectuals.

In all probability, most Taiwanese would regard "independence" in some form as their ideal. Pro-Communist sentiment at present is negligible; Nationalist support fairly limited; and nostalgia for the Japanese era, while rather widespread, is strongest among the older groups. The chances are fairly good that this general problem will be solved by evolution. As long as economic conditions continue to be reasonably good, the Nationalist military force remains disciplined, and some social mobility is possible, mass revolt is unlikely. Meanwhile, a dual process of acculturation and assimilation is taking place. A modernized Chinese culture is being implanted, with liberal borrowings both from Japan and the West. And the dominant Taiwanese population is starting to absorb the refugee minority.

United States Interests

American policy toward Taiwan during the past ten years has developed out of various military, political, and moral considerations, defined in terms of our national interest. The intervention of the Seventh Fleet stemmed from military considerations coincident with North Korean aggression. In the face of Communist military activity in Korea, the Philippines, Indo-China, and Malaya, the American government acted to protect its flank and prevent the Communist absorption of an island close to our major defenses.

The strategic significance of Taiwan has been a debatable issue. At one point, it was argued that this island had little military value. With the decision to throw the American mantle of protection around it, however, the strategic importance of Taiwan was defended in many quarters. During World War II, Taiwan had served as a valuable supply base for the Japanese. In hostile hands, it could threaten the new American "perimeter defense" line that extended from the Aleutians through Japan down to Clark Field. It could threaten the Philippines, so it was argued, and serve as a springboard for submarine and air control over communications lines between the United States and Southeast Asia. The difficult question perhaps is the extent to which these considerations have become obsolete because of technological developments in the field of guided missiles and thermo-nuclear warfare. In short, how important is Taiwan militarily in the age of intercontinental ballistic missiles? Or should we assume that for Asia this is still the age of limited and conventional warfare?

In any case, under the Mutual Defense Treaty of 1954, the United States is clearly pledged to render assistance in the event of an attack upon Taiwan and the Pescadores. In return, Article VII of the Treaty grants the United States the right to establish land, air, and sea forces in these areas. A new and major commitment has thus been undertaken in the Western Pacific area.

Politically and morally, the American interest has been somewhat ambiguous. Taiwan has been included as a part of the "free world," and many fine sounding speeches about democracy and liberty for the Chinese people have been made. It has been suggested that a Free China can stand as a beacon of hope for the oppressed masses on the mainland, and eventually gain their loyalties. Yet here as in other parts of non-

Communist Asia, the pathway of democracy has indeed been a thorny one. As we have noted, Taiwan is in fact a one-party state, an authoritarian regime, albeit one relatively mild in comparison with the totalitarian state that now exists on the mainland. Perhaps eventually, the principle of self-determination for the people of this area will be established. Until that time, the freedom issue is somewhat beclouded, although few noncommunists would take exception to our belief that the eleven million people of this island should not be turned over to Communism unless that is their will.

In recent years, there has been a certain deterioration of American-Nationalist relations, climaxed by the anxieties of 1960-61. Nationalist China has long been a major issue in American politics. It will be remembered that one of the slogans of the original Eisenhower campaign was the "unleashing" of Chiang Kai-shek, as a part of a general roll-back campaign against Communism. Needless to say, the real issue was not whether Chiang would be allowed to attack the mainland, but rather whether we would continue to act as a shield against Communist assault. In the course of the Eisenhower era, however, our ties with Taiwan became more binding and intimate. Despite the fact that John Foster Dulles had earlier stated the case for admission of Communist China into the United Nations, the Korean War and other events had led to total hostility between the United States and the mainland regime, and in men like Walter Robertson, Assistant Secretary of State for the Far East, and William Knowland, Republican leader in the Senate, the Chiang Kai-shek government had completely devoted friends. In unprecedented amounts, American military and economic aid flowed into the island. Even in this period, however, there remained a certain difference in objectives: the Nationalists were committed solely to a return to the mainland; the United States was interested in building up a stable, non-Communist Taiwan.

As the years passed, various irritations developed because of this difference in commitment. Basically, the Nationalists were opposed to any signs of American accommodation to or coexistence with the Communist bloc. Of necessity, they favored a position of complete militancy. Events in the 1960-61 period moved toward a climax. The Nationalists were very hopeful of a Republican victory in the 1960 elections. They feared that Kennedy would favor a "two-China" policy, withdrawal from the offshore islands, and a general accommodation to existing realities, including that of Communist China. In the first months of the Kennedy administration, a "crisis in confidence" developed on Taiwan. President Kennedy and his top diplomatic advisers were openly criticized for a "soft" policy toward Communist China, advocacy of a "two China" policy, and an indicated willingness to recognize the government of Outer Mongolia.

The visits of Vice-President Johnson to Taiwan and Premier Chen Cheng to Washington in the spring of 1961 allayed Nationalist fears to some extent. The Kennedy Administration pledged that it would continue to support the Republic of China and oppose Communist China, both in and out of the United Nations. It also dropped plans for the recognition of the People's Republic of Outer Mongolia, at least temporarily. Suspicion continues to exist on Taiwan, however, that the present administration in Washington regards a "two China" policy as inevitable, and has been secretly negotiating with its major allies and the neutrals in an effort to establish a common China position. On the other side, suspicion exists in Washington that the Nationalists, despite their pledges, have not given up the dream of engaging in military action against the mainland and might seek to involve us in such a conflict. It is also felt that this is a government still reluctant to accept either economic realities or the essential requirements of political democracy. Yet the Nationalists continue to have powerful support in the United States and Congress passes in ritualistic fashion a yearly resolution pledging full support to our present policies.

IMPACT ON OTHER COUNTRIES

From our declared allies, the Taiwan issue brings mixed response. Asian countries dependent upon American military protection, such as South Korea, South Viet-Nam, and the Philippines, welcome a strong American position on behalf of the Nationalists. Our NATO allies, however, are far less enthusiastic about American commitments to this regime. They have serious doubts about both the political and the military wisdom of our China policy. The fact that the United Kingdom, Norway, The Netherlands, and Denmark have all recognized Communist China further complicates the political problem. The United Kingdom, Canada, and France also have made it clear that they could not support any action in defense of the offshore islands, Quemoy and Matsu, presently held by Nationalist forces. Although Washington has intentionally remained vague about its plans with respect to these islands, an attack upon them could spark a chain of incidents which would increasingly involve American units and bring the explicit Taiwan commitment into effect.

It is with the neutrals of the Afro-Asian world, however, that American policy runs into its greatest difficulties. The roster of those who recognize Peking includes the United Arab Republic, Yemen, Afghanistan, India, Burma, Ceylon, Nepal, Indonesia, and many of the newly independent African states. There can be no doubt that in Asia, suspicions of Communist China have grown in the past few years. Tibet, border issues, and other problems have emerged, and any romantic notion of Asian brotherhood has been greatly dissipated. At the same time, however, most of the countries that border China believe that realities must be faced. The Chinese Communists have *de facto* control over 675,000,000 people and are involved in every issue that affects Asia. The nationalists on Taiwan have *de facto* control over only 11,000,000 people and cannot be called China. Thus present American policy is considered too negative, defensive, and unrealistic by most of the Afro-Asian bloc, and it has little support.

United States Policy Alternatives

There has been a growing recognition in the United States of a need for reexamining our policies toward Communist China and Taiwan, despite the difficulties—both domestic and foreign—in effecting any change. It is an elemental fact that past policies have become increasingly difficult to sustain in the light of world developments. Perhaps there are compelling reasons nonetheless for a continuance of these policies. Perhaps some changes should be made. In any case, a reappraisal of policy alternatives would seem in order, indeed, would seem imperative. It is entirely possible that there is no "good" China policy for the United States at present. Each possibility seems to carry extraordinarily grave risks and represent serious problems. We must choose between various alternatives, however, and each should be considered.

A policy position which is based on the maintenance of the status quo would involve continued recognition of the Taiwan government as the Republic of China, and continued support for that government as the representative of China in the Security Council of the United Nations. Thus it involves continued opposition to Communist China at every level. It also involves full military and economic commitment to the Nationalist government, including some commitment to Quemoy-Matsu, with the question of whether to participate in their defense left to the discretion of the President, depending upon whether he determines that an attack upon them is a part of an attack upon Taiwan-Pescadores.

The arguments in favor of this policy may be summarized as follows:

1. Communist China is a declared, implacable opponent of the United States, dedicated to the removal of American influence in Asia and the eventual subversion of all non-communist societies. It is imperative, therefore, to maintain maximum opposition to the Communist regime, and to recognize only the Nationalists as the legitimate representatives of the Chinese people.

2. Massive popular unrest on the mainland may lead to the overthrow of the Communist government. In any case, it is fictional to assert that this government "represents" the people of China. Any recognition given it lessens the possibilities of eventual freedom for the 675,000,000 Chinese now awaiting liberation.

3. A policy of complete support for the Republic of China will reassure such Asian allies as South Korea, South Viet-Nam, the Philippines,

and Japan of our determination to hold to our commitments, irrespective of the difficulties involved, whereas any retreat will undermine Nationalist confidence in the American will to resist Communism and in American pledges of support. Continued support for the Republic of China may even increase our prestige, at least privately, with some of the "neutral" nations, by demonstrating that our support can deter aggression in case they should wish to call upon our protection.

4. Perpetuation of the Republic of China presents the 13,000,000 overseas Chinese in Southeast Asia with an alternative, a Chinese society that is anti-communist with which they can have cultural ties. Thus it will help to maintain an anti-communist position within this group, as well as keep alive the resistance of Chinese on the mainland itself.

5. Support for the Republic of China is the only moral policy for the United States, since it places us in total opposition to the ruthless totalitarianism of the Communist regime.

What are the arguments against the status-quo policy? Perhaps the major ones can be summarized as follows:

1. The present policy is unrealistic, and consequently, an increasing source of weakness to the United States rather than strength. The fiction that the Taiwan regime is China cannot be maintained much longer, especially in the United Nations. Only a policy that faces the facts of life in Asia, and has the support of our allies and the major neutrals has any chance of long-range success. Admittedly, Communist China is extremely hostile to the United States, but the containment of Communist China depends upon a policy which can be based on collective action.

2. Any thesis that the mainland regime is likely to be overthrown or that the people of the mainland are yearning for the return of Chiang Kai-shek must be relegated to the category of wishful thinking. It would be foolish to base American policy upon such improbable concepts.

3. While some of our minor allies in Asia would be disturbed about a shift in American policy toward Taiwan, all of the major non-Communist states in the Far East—India, Japan, Indonesia, and Pakistan—favor a more flexible, realistic policy. Indeed, it is our present separation from these states on China policy that constitutes the greatest weakness at present. We are trying to "go it alone" in company with a few small allies. Even these allies, moreover, could adjust to a policy shift, if reassurances were given them and the timing were proper.

4. The overseas Chinese will accommodate themselves to reality, irrespective of American policy. Moreover, circumstances in the country where they reside together with trends in mainland China will be the critical factors in determining their allegiance. In the final analysis, they will either be assimilated into their society as citizens, or they will look to Peking as the source of power and the capitol of their ancestral home. Taiwan can never fulfill these needs.

5. The moral arguments for the status-quo policy are largely spurious.

It is true that Communism represents a ruthless suppression of human rights, but until the people of Taiwan have the right of self-determination, the right to participate freely in their own government, and until men like Lei Chen are free, it is deceitful to talk of "Free China," and our stand on behalf of freedom.

ACCEPTANCE OF THE COMMUNIST POSITION

A quite different alternative would envisage American acceptance of the major Communist demands in connection with Taiwan. This would involve our complete withdrawal from the island and our acquiescence in its incorporation into the mainland, politically, economically, and militarily. Probably the advantages and the disadvantages of this policy are sufficiently clear to require little elaboration. On its behalf, it can be argued:

1. To accept Taiwan as a part of mainland China would reduce tension in the Far East and the threat of eventual war. As in the case of any emerging national power, Communist China will insist upon defining and defending her boundaries. Historically, Taiwan was a part of China. The Chinese—including the Nationalists—will never be reconciled to its separation. Hence, at some point, union will take place, either through political or military action. Just as we insisted upon the withdrawal of European power from the Western Hemisphere and the enforcement of the Monroe Doctrine, so China will insist upon our withdrawal from the Formosa Straits area and the unification of her territory. Unless and until we accept this elemental nationalist position, there can be no peace in Asia and no agreement upon other issues.

2. If we permitted—or insisted upon—negotiations leading to a union of China and Taiwan, the Nationalist elements would be able to strike a bargain, since the Communists are anxious to obtain this territory peacefully and have already offered Nationalist leaders positions and security if they will come home. We could also offer to accept in the West any persons who did not choose to live under Communism, thereby giving the people on Taiwan an alternative.

3. In the final anaylsis, the removal of the Taiwan problem would strengthen our relations with non-communist Asia, because it would permit us to concentrate upon basic economic and social problems in this area and reduce the military emphasis which has hitherto prevailed.

Against these arguments the following points may be advanced:

1. To capitulate to the Chinese Communists on the issue of Taiwan would not reduce tension or the threat of war because the Communists would then be emboldened to demand other concessions amounting to control of Asia. The balance of power in the Far East would be disrupted, our allies would become completely disillusioned, and even the neutrals would be intimidated. Moreover, the thesis that Taiwan is a part of

China can be challenged. Historically, Taiwan has been autonomous or independent from China on numerous occasions.

2. To turn Taiwan over to the Communists would be militarily foolish, politically disastrous, and morally wrong. A Communist Taiwan would jeopardize Japan to the north and the Philippines to the south. Indeed, all of southern Asia would be threatened by such a symbol of Communist victory.

A "TWO-CHINA" OR "ONE-CHINA ONE-TAIWAN" POLICY

Perhaps the third broad alternative confronting the United States today can be labelled a "two China" or "one-China one-Taiwan" policy. Such a policy might take a variety of forms, but basically it envisages an acceptance of the fact that mainland China and Taiwan will remain separate political entities for the indefinite future, with two governments having *de facto* control over their respective territories and people. Therefore, the mainland government should be recognized as the government of China, with control over 675,000,000 people. It should be involved in international affairs, brought into the world of international law and order to the extent possible, and caused to make commitments on the range of issues affecting Asia and the world. The government on Taiwan should be recognized as the government of Taiwan, and similarly involved in international affairs and commitments on this basis. The arguments in favor of such a policy can be set forth as follows:

1. A "one-China one-Taiwan" policy is the only policy that accords with reality, and that can garner maximum support from the non-Communist world. And in the final analysis, the policy with respect to the China issue that is most likely to work is one having the support of the great majority of states, especially those that surround Communist China. Present American policy is too negative, unilateral, and defensive to acquire such support.

2. This policy has both politics and morality on its side. If the United States were to insist that ultimately the people of Taiwan should have the right to determine their own future, whether through a United Nations plebiscite or some other means, this would be in accord with historic American principles, and would be respected throughout the democratic world.

3. This policy, as it developed, would help to infuse new life into Taiwan's political and economic development. Once again, the United States might take the lead in providing alternatives to those mainland refugees who did not wish to remain on the island if it were to be independent, thereby reducing political tensions. To adjust Taiwan to reality, however, would aid in overcoming the present unhealthy psychology of day-dreaming about a return to the mainland and excessive pre-

occupation with military affairs to the detriment of the economy and civil liberties.

4. Admittedly, a "one-China one-Taiwan" policy is not acceptable at present to either the Communists or the Nationalists. While this is an obstacle, however, it is not as insuperable as some critics maintain. In fact, China and Taiwan do exist, and exist separately. A process of increasing adjustment to this fact is taking place in many parts of the world. It is also true that neither Chinese government fully supports our present policy. The Communists of course do not support it at all. The Nationalists resent any negotiations we have with the Communist bloc, want our full support for a "return to the mainland" program, resist the idea of developing a self-sufficient Taiwan, and in many other ways, take exception to certain aspects of American policy. The fundamental question is not whether a "one-China one-Taiwan" policy is acceptable to the Communists or Nationalists, but rather whether it is acceptable to the great bulk of the non-Communist world, and thereby whether it offers some hope for a strong, collective policy on which we can unite with our allies and the neutrals. We live with many policies today that are fully acceptable to no one, but nonetheless, they continue and gradually gain acceptance.

5. If we do not fashion some realistic policy in the near future, we face a humiliating defeat both in the United Nations and in world diplomatic circles. With the neutrals and our allies deserting us rapidly on the China issue, we cannot afford to "let the dust settle" any longer.

On the other side, the following points are made:

1. As long as the Communists and Nationalists both adamantly oppose the "two-China plot," this policy cannot be successfully effectuated.

2. To push for such a policy will exacerbate political tensions within Taiwan, and may risk an upheaval that could only be of advantage to the Communists. Even if "two Chinas" do in fact exist, it is better to stand firm on our present policy for the moment, allowing more time to pass, so that further adjustments on Taiwan can take place.

3. In no case should the United States take the initiative with respect to a "one-China one-Taiwan" policy, since this would be understood as weakening our stand against Communism and deserting an ally. Even if we have to acquiesce in the eventual admission of Communist China to United Nations, others should take the positive action.

4. We can afford to wait. Political and economic conditions on the mainland are sufficiently serious to indicate that the future of Communist China remains in some doubt. It is premature to abandon the concept of the Taiwan government as the Republic of China, even if for the moment it does represent a political fiction.

THE OFFSHORE ISLANDS

In brief form, the three choices given above represent the three major policy alternatives confronting the United States and the basic arguments for and against each alternative. There is, however, one special problem that should perhaps be treated separately, namely, the issue of Quemoy-Matsu, the offshore islands. This issue, which figured in the 1960 U. S. Presidential campaign, has been a thorny one for some years. It represents a potential danger to our entire Asian policy and a problem with simple answers which have complicated implications.

The Quemoy-Matsu islands, at their nearest points, lie from three to six miles off the coast of China, near the great harbor of Amoy. While we persuaded the Nationalists to give up the offshore Tachen islands in February, 1955, we did not insist upon evacuation of this group. Moreover, in the later period of the Eisenhower Administration, the United States Congress passed a resolution declaring that we would defend this area if, in the opinion of the President, an attack upon these islands constituted a part of an attack upon Taiwan-Pescadores. A heavy bombardment did take place against the island of Quemoy in 1958, and since that time, a routine, every-other-day shelling has been maintained from time to time by the Communists in order to keep the Quemoy-Matsu issue alive.

Ironically, it is in the interests of both the Nationalists and the Communists to have these islands in Nationalist hands at the moment. The reason why the Nationalists have insisted that they will never evacuate the islands, and at one point, stationed approximately one-third of their total troops there, was political and psychological, not military. Quemoy-Matsu are not vital to the defense of Taiwan. Nationalist occupation of these islands, however, does symbolize the Nationalist commitment to return to the mainland and does keep the civil war alive.

For this latter reason, the Communists also have an interest in temporary Nationalist retention of the islands, and this may well be the reason why no major assault has been launched, although such an assault would be very costly in lives. If the Communists held these offshore islands, it would be extremely difficult to continue the civil war on a token basis, and a *de facto* "two Chinas" would then exist in an even more conspicuous sense. It is very doubtful whether the Communists want this to occur. To keep Taiwan, the Pescadores, and the offshore islands as one package is in their interests as it is in the interests of the Nationalists.

Whether it is in the interests of the United States is a very different matter. An overwhelming majority of world opinion, including that from the non-Communist world, accepts these islands as a part of the mainland. If war were to break out over them, we or the Nationalists would have little if any support. Quemoy-Matsu do not have the political and moral significance of Berlin. Their status is not the product of any international agreement. Their civilian population of 50,000 could easily be evacuated. Their symbolic significance is primarily that they keep the Chinese civil war alive. In truth, it would appear that we have been trapped in connection with these islands. The Nationalists have informed us publicly and privately that irrespective of our attitude, they will remain on the islands because of the political and psychological issues involved. The Communists will certainly not help us extricate ourselves, because the present situation is to their advantage also. Hence the dilemma as to what we can or should do. A number of Americans feel that we should make it emphatically clear to the Nationalists that our commitment to defend Taiwan and the Pescadores does not extend to the offshore islands, and that we should accompany this statement with an insistence upon withdrawal. We could give the Nationalists time to make such a withdrawal, after which we would make our policy clear to the world, and place our military units, including the Seventh Fleet, in new defensive positions to take account of the new policy.

Regardless of our policy, however, it is essential that this country remain clear in its own mind about the offshore islands, lest erroneous concepts of responsibility impel us to hasty action or involve us in post-mortems of guilt assessment. Defense of those islands involves no moral obligation on the part of the United States, no strategic implications, and little legal concern. They remain an unsettled issue, the resolution of which may well involve bloodshed. American participation in that bloodshed would be difficult to justify.

Conclusion

For the foreseeable future, we shall be engaged in a continuous reappraisal of our China policy. It may be that this reappraisal will leave us with the same policy as before, replete with its assets and liabilities. Clearly, there is no easy solution to the China problem for the United States, no bright and shining path toward the future. It seems more likely, however, that we are reaching the end of an era, and that the success or failure of our Asian policy will be heavily dependent upon how well we can adjust to the pressing realities of the new era, and whether the timing of that adjustment is such as to maximize our bargaining power. On this latter point, there are reasons for deep anxiety. Already the hour is perilously late.

In some fashion, we shall have to adjust to the fact that Communist China exists, is rapidly becoming a major world power, and is involved in every issue concerning Asia and the globe. The process of adjustment has already begun, of course. We are engaged in both bilateral and multilateral negotiations with the Chinese Communists. At the same time, we shall continue to recognize the government of Taiwan as having control over the eleven million people on this island, and having the right to be recognized as the *de facto* government of this area. Such recognition would be bolstered in the eyes of our allies and the neutrals if the true wishes of the people on this island could be ascertained and supported. In the meantime, however, we shall continue to pay legal homage to the Taiwan government as the Republic of China, while recognizing that in fact it is only the government of Taiwan, and seeking to develop world support for it, as such.

Conclusion:

The broader perspective

THE TENTH AMERICAN ASSEMBLY

♦ WILLARD L. THORP

The problems which have been outlined in the previous chapters were the subject of intensive discussion in November, 1956 at the Tenth American Assembly at Arden House, Harriman, New York. About sixty participants focused their attention on questions regarding American attitudes and policies toward China, Japan, Korea, and Taiwan. After several periods of exceedingly active discussion in smaller groups, a report was prepared which was approved as representing the general agreement of the participants.

The specific findings and recommendations in summary form and omitting some qualifications were as follows (the time was November, 1956):

1. The United States must continue to pro-

183

vide substantial military assistance for a prolonged period to the Republic of Korea and Taiwan and for the time being to Japan.

2. Japanese trade should be encouraged with countries other than the United States. The United States should recognize the vital importance of trade to Japan and try to strike a proper balance between local domestic strains and the efforts of Japan to be self-supporting. This can be aided if Japanese trade is developed on the basis of diversification and gradual expansion.

3. Measures should be explored looking toward a liberalization of such trade with Communist China as would not impair the security position of the non-communist countries.

4. Emphasis should be placed on assisting the economic development of the Republic of Korea and Taiwan. This implies generous economic support, which would be more effective if it could be based on long-run planning. Greater reliance should be placed on aid through international agencies where appropriate.

5. Emphasis should be placed on cultural communications through educational exchange, informational programs, and other means of gaining improved understanding of each other.

6. The flow of information to the United States concerning Communist China should be permitted and facilitated, particularly through the relaxing of restrictions in the travel of newspapermen and scholars and the importation of publications.

7. Vigorous action should be taken within the United Nations to achieve the unification of Korea.

8. Japan should be admitted to the United Nations.

9. The United States should oppose the seating of Communist China in the United Nations. However, this issue should not be given such importance as to be allowed to affect the future relationship of the United States to the United Nations.

10. In the light of the record of various unprincipled and arrogant actions by Communist China, the United States should not recognize it. However, the policy of nonrecognition must be continuously reappraised. This may be one of many matters which must be considered in any exploration of the possibility of resolving many of the outstanding issues by negotiation.

11. Far Eastern problems should be the subject of persistent intergovernmental consultation.

12. Wide public discussion of Far Eastern problems should be encouraged.

THE REGIONAL ASSEMBLIES

After the Arden House meetings, six regional assemblies were held

Midwest Assembly at St. Louis, Mo.	March, 1957
Cleveland Assembly at Cleveland, O.	April, 1957
Duke Assembly at Durham, N. C.	June 5-8, 1957
Western Assembly at Lake Arrowhead, Cal.	June, 1957
Southeastern Assembly at Pine Mountain, Ga.	April,1958
Dallas Assembly at Mineral Wells, Tex.	November, 1958

As might be expected, the findings and recommendations of these various groups were not identical, although the differences were more a matter of emphasis than of principle. Some were more concerned than others with continuing the American embargo on Chinese trade. In some cases, the opposition to seating Communist China in the United Nations was much less strong, although it was always assumed that this would be done in such a way as not to prejudice the position of Taiwan.

Two additional points should be noted. First, it was recommended that the legal status of Taiwan should be clarified by international agreement or reference to the United Nations. Second, that the security treaty with Japan should be converted into a mutual defense treaty, including a provision for periodic renegotiation of its leased base provisions.

In addition, two Assemblies were held for high school students, one in Minneapolis, Minnesota, on March 27-29, 1958 and one at Normal, Illinois, March 22-24, 1959. They also drew up conclusions and recommendations. While not reporting on all their conclusions, most of which did not differ from those already noted, they did urge active steps to expand Japanese trade, the limitation of Japanese rearmament to defense, and encouragement of closer relations among Asian non-Communist countries. Among these younger groups there appeared to be stronger sentiment for the recognition of Communist China if American prisoners were released and the status of Taiwan were satisfactorily assured. They recognized that this implies seating Communist China in the United Nations.

Although the world seems to be in a state of constant change, it is interesting to note how few of these issues have disappeared during the last five years. To be sure, Japan is now in the United Nations. American aid can be planned on a somewhat longer-term basis. And the United States did remove its restrictions on the visits of newspapermen to Communist China. On the other hand, the issue of the seating of Communist China in the United Nations has grown steadily more disturbing, and the demands by American manufacturers for protection against Japanese imports are mounting. In fact, history clearly supports the conclusion of all the Assemblies, that, while our objectives must be firm, our policies of action must be flexible.

*   *   *   *   *

There is something a little unrealistic and unfinished about reviewing foreign policy country by country or even in considering four countries together. National boundary lines are not absolute, and each of the previous chapters has pointed out problems which must be considered in the light of their implications or even their direct significance to countries other than themselves or the United States. Nevertheless, the greater part of foreign policy operation is bilateral in character. Even though the purpose may be much broader in its scope, the implementation of a broad objective often requires a careful construction country by country.

In a very real sense, foreign policy must start with our attitude toward the country concerned. Our policy can be negative and obstructive; or we can refuse to become involved; or we can seek out forms of cooperative endeavor toward constructive ends. As to one of the countries discussed in the background papers, there is very little of substance that we do with respect to Communist China, though our policy clearly falls in the first category. Our contacts are very slight, and, in fact, we do not formally recognize its existence as a nation.

But with respect to the other three countries, Korea, Japan, and Taiwan, the problem is rather one of how much we wish to become involved. In each of these cases, there are many possibilities for cooperative constructive action. Each of them is faced with economic problems which are difficult, if not impossible of solution from within their own borders. Each is experimenting with new quasi-democratic political forms which need sympathetic encouragement. Each is endangered by its overt opposition to Communism. And each is uncertain and dissatisfied with its present position among the sovereign nations of the world. All of these basic problems provide us with an opportunity to give constructive aid.

As to the provision of aid, we cannot be too confident about what can be achieved through outside assistance. We can build up a military structure but we cannot assure its proper use at the right time in the right way. We can contribute to economic development by providing essential goods and services, but we cannot count on establishing conditions where growth will be self-sustaining. Assistance for both these military and economic objectives takes form which are covered in existing aid programs. However, the objectives of economic and political stability are much less easily anticipated. These stem from the presence or absence of internal political, social, and economic equilibria. Instability may appear in various forms, including inflation and political disturbances. Each nation has its own special features and complications. And the best intentions in the world and the most generous legislative authorizations must ultimately be expressed in actions which are adapted to the conditions and structure of the country involved.

But the case for separate country consideration begins to break down even if we look only at the four, for they are interlocked in many ways. Their economies have traditionally relied upon each other, but trade is not flowing freely along the prewar channels. The relationship between Korea and Taiwan and their former ruler, Japan, is beset by tensions. And Communist China represents a danger and an attracting force which must enter into many of their considerations.

The separate chapters have also emphasized an even broader dimension in the evaluation of our policies—the relationship between United States policy toward these four countries and our overall position in Asia. Most of the world is polarized toward Communism or the free world, but much of Asia stands in what is called a neutralist position. While their great concern is their own internal development, they cannot escape from the necessity of international relations. Having struggled so recently to achieve their independence, they are very sensitive as to any foreign involvements. They view the capitalistic West with considerable skepticism; they likewise are not convinced by the glowing Communist picture of the future. Because of the activity and specificity of American policy toward the Far East, our performance there becomes important in its demonstration effect on other Asian countries as an expression of our attitudes and motivation in our foreign relations.

Nor are the implications of our policies limited to the other Asian nations. Many other countries, particularly those in Western Europe, have an equally great concern with our behavior in the Far East. We have already witnessed differences over the recognition of Communist China and over the treatment of the offshore islands on the Chinese coast opposite Taiwan. We have had divergences with many of our allies over East-West trade and over the admission of Japan to the GATT. There are bound to be areas of honest disagreement due to different national interests in particular situations, but controversy and friction do make cooperation more difficult. Our relations with the other countries in the free world are of tremendous importance, and so our relationship with them must enter into our calculations with respect to Far Eastern policy.

Finally, we must consider Far Eastern policy in terms of our own broad objectives in the world today. For some years, the central core of our policy has been to set up defenses in the free world against Communist aggression. To this end, we took the lead in a great cooperative effort to build an adequate military defense as speedily as possible. This policy was extremely urgent at its inception, and its success undoubtedly explains in large part the present reduction in the fear of external aggression in most countries.

This great effort has provided a shield even for the neutralist countries which did not participate. They might not be independent today if this defensive force had not been brought into being. The Communists, however, have seized this opportunity to describe the United States as a militaristic nation. On the contrary, the essential purpose of this costly undertaking was not to make war, but rather to make it possible for independent nations, including the United States, to develop in their own way free from the threat of attacks from outside.

Essentially, the search for military security is a costly and negative enterprise, and American foreign policy must also make clear its constructive elements. During all the period of extraordinary military buildup and expenditure, there was no letdown in American foreign aid either for relief purposes or for economic development. But poverty and discontent are still omnipresent in the Far East. We may have succeeded in limiting Communism as a military threat but the Communist ideology still has its appeal. The internal dangers of takeover by the extreme left or the extreme right are still present. It is to the problem of how to help these countries to progress toward independence as free democratic societies that American foreign policy in the Far East must basically address itself.